Getting Started with Entity Event-Driven Embedded Systems

Vol 1. GPIO and Asynchronous Programming with Microdot: Raspberry Pi Pico W and Pico 2W

Getting Started with Entity Event-Driven Embedded Systems
Vol 1. GPIO and Asynchronous Programming with Microdot: Raspberry Pi Pico W and Pico 2W
by Byron Mattingly
ISBN: 979-8-2955-5027-0

Publisher: Cassandra STEAM Press, www.CassandraSTEAMPress.com
September 2025: First Edition

for Lisa
sine qua non

About the author

Byron Mattingly has been an embedded systems software engineer and hands-on technical manager for over 20 years in regulated development in the medical devices, pharmaceutical, and avionics industries. Currently his work is focused on designing and integrating complex IT systems and training and deploying AI/ML models interacting with embedded systems. An early adopter of the Raspberry Pi platform, he is an open source contributor and avid proponent of STEAM education.

Table of Contents

Preface vii

Entity Event-Driven Embedded Pico Systems 1
Learn how you can transform your Pico into an Entity Event-Driven Embedded System

1. Programming the Raspberry Pi Pico in MicroPython 21
Start writing MicroPython for your Pico using Thonny (or your favorite IDE)

2. Hello, world! (from the astronauts and JSON) 55
Become familiar with your Pico's computational and machine-to-machine (M2M) capabilities using JSON

3. Hello, blinky! Physical computing with the Pico 105
Learn how to start connecting and controlling the physical world with your Pico's pins

4. Web API hosting with Sockets 129
Discover how to transform your wireless-enabled Pico into an Entity Event-Driven Embedded System with socket programming

5. Web API Hosting with Microdot 177
Transform your Pico into an Entity Event-Driven Embedded System using Microdot

6. Pelican Crossing using asyncio and Microdot 239
Implement concurrency on your Entity Event-Driven Embedded Pico Systems using asyncio's and Microdot's cooperative multitasking approach, improving responsiveness and efficient resource usage

APPENDICES

A. Raspberry Pi Pico W pinout guide 297

B. Raspberry Pi Pico W Features 299

C. Raspberry Pi Pico 2W pinout guide 301

D. Raspberry Pi Pico 2W Features 303

E. Raspberry Pi fixes Erratum E9 bug affecting the Pico 2W 305

F. Attributions and License Information 307

Preface

The Raspberry Pi Pico is fast, versatile, and energy-efficient.

This book is a streamlined but gentle introduction to the complex world of Entity Event-Driven Embedded Systems. Remarkably, the heart of such systems can be a Raspberry Pi Pico, a microcontroller board that debuted in 2022 for $4 USD and which, at the time of this writing, now costs around $7 to $8 USD in its latest versions. There's a reason that the educational, maker, and hobbyist communities as well as industry have already purchased millions of these systems.

Importantly, the Pico is communications-savvy. It can communicate through its GPIO pins, built-in hardware buses (like SPI and I2C), and its onboard WiFi and Bluetooth modules, not to mention its Programmable I/O (PIO) hardware—a feature that functions as a set of small, independent state machines that can be programmed for customizing low-level interfaces.

This book builds knowledge from the ground up, offering a step-by-step approach from "Hello, world!" to highly responsive (~a few ms) interrupt driven concurrent systems using MicroPython's asyncio library. It gets you started with using the Pico's GPIO pins and WiFi by way of a few LEDs and asynchronous programming with Microdot, a remarkably small *ultra-lightweight* web server framework that's even lighter(!) than Python Flask.

To begin, you'll need a Raspberry Pi Pico W or Pico 2W, a few inexpensive electronic components (like a breadboard, some LEDs, a button switch, etc.) and to know a little Python ahead of time. Fortunately, there's a tremendous amount of comprehensive, free educational resources to help out in this last regard. The Raspberry Pi foundation (https://www.raspberrypi.org/), to name just one.

The introductory chapter addresses the question *Why Entity Event-Driven Embedded Pico Systems?* It sets up the theory behind the later chapters. (It's repeated in some of my other books because it forms the basis for them, too.) Feel free to skip it and come back to it later once you've started building some Entity Event-Driven Embedded Pico Systems of your own. Then we start experimenting with and learning about your Pico W or Pico 2W, writing and explaining each MicroPython program along the way so that by the time you work through all of the examples and reach the end of the book, you'll have a very good idea of what it means to start creating your own *Entity Event-Driven Embedded Pico Systems.*

Example Code

The code examples used in this book can be downloaded from GitHub:

https://github.com/cassandrasteampress/event-driven-pico-code-vol1

To download all the files as a ZIP archive, click on the *Code* button and then *Download ZIP*. After the download has completed, you can extract the contents to a convenient location on your computer.

Electronics Hardware

Information for the electronics used in this book can be found at:

https://github.com/cassandrasteampress/event-driven-pico-kits

Acknowledgements

I used Fritzing (fritzing.org) for the breadboard layouts and component diagrams, Inkscape (inkscape.org) and GIMP (https://www.gimp.org/) for the other illustrations.

Introduction

1. What is an Event-Driven Architecture?

2. Why Entity Event-Driven Embedded Systems?
    a. What are Entity Event-Driven Embedded Systems?
    b. What are Entity Event-Driven Embedded Pico Systems?

3. Developing Entity Event-Driven Embedded Pico Systems
    a. Host / Target Setup
    b. A System of Systems

4. Defining Embedded Systems
    a. What is an Embedded System?
    b. Intended Use and User Requirements
    c. Working with Constrained Resources
    d. When Less is More

5. Defining Embedded System Entity Events
    a. What are Entity Events?
    b. Benefits of Entity Events

6. Setting Context Boundaries
    a. Communication Interfaces
    b. Bounded Context of a Domain Model
    c. Modelling Bounded Contexts
    d. A Simpler Notation: Hexagons with interfaces

7. Some Notes before Proceeding
    a. Avoiding Technical Jargon, Definitions and Generalizations

8. Chapter Summary
    a. What is the purpose of your Entity Event-Driven Embedded Pico System?

9. References and Further Exploration

Entity Event-Driven Embedded Pico Systems

Learn how you can transform your Pico into an Entity Event-Driven Embedded System

Since the late 1980s and early 1990s, *Data-Driven Architectures* have become widely adopted for data-driven approaches to complex decision-making. This architectural paradigm focuses on integrating data across various layers of an organization, data processing and analysis, and leveraging data analytics and insights as core elements that shape informed decision-making and system functionality. Data-Driven Architectures are particularly effective in environments like data warehouses which prioritize efficiently storing, processing, and analyzing data to facilitate better decision-making.

In the late 1990s and early 2000s, as systems became more distributed and required real-time processing, *Event-Driven Architectures* have gained prominence, fueled by the need for a more flexible and responsive architecture. Due to their ability to respond to events with low latency and handle high volumes of data, this pattern emerged for creating high-performance and scalable designs.

Event-Driven Architectures are ideal for real-time, reactive systems that require rapid processing and immediate responses to events as they occur. These designs are usually made up of strongly decoupled applications such as microservices that asynchronously receive and process events produced by other applications—financial trading systems, real-time monitoring systems, and embedded systems, for example. They are designed to be highly adaptable, robust, and efficient.

This book is on how to start transforming your Pico W or Pico 2W into an *Entity Event-Driven Embedded System* that can actively participate in Event-Driven Architectures.

Why Entity Event-Driven Embedded Systems?

The event-based model differs from a request-based model which reacts to requests from a customer web page—for instance—to retrieve an order history. Such requests can be data-driven and deterministic, bounded by a specific context. An event-based model, on the other hand, responds asynchronously to particular situations the system must react to and not to a specific request, *per se*.

Events are records of occurrences over time. Not only have modern Event-Driven Architectures enabled the real-time consumption of such events in very large datasets, these events can persist at scale and be made available to any service interested in them as often as needed.

While the need for producing events is not new, the need for systems that communicate events that contain sufficient information for applications like microservices and multiple data consumers to process those events according to their specific use cases *is* definitely new. In particular, embedded systems must now interface with microservices and other data consumers in a variety of different contexts. Providing these applications with a stream of quality data in the form of uniquely identifiable Events and in a format that can be readily understood is ultimately the goal of Entity Event-Driven Embedded Systems.

Recently, AI agents are starting to go beyond "request-and-respond" frameworks and are transitioning to autonomous systems capable of reasoning, planning, and orchestrating complex dataflows and workflows based on high-level goals. AI agents in real-time Event-Driven Architectures continually process inputs, sifting through and making sense of Entity Events that can originate from endpoints like embedded systems. AI agents not only consume data, they can play an active role in determining Events in Event-Driven Architectures. For example, AI agents coordinating a city's traffic light system could dynamically re-route traffic patterns by adjusting light sequences on individual traffic lights based on sensory input (e.g. radar, lidar, and button presses at pedestrian crossings) gathered at traffic intersections.

What are Entity Event-Driven Embedded Systems?

An *Entity Event* is something of interest to an application in an Event-Driven Architecture that took place which is directly associated with a specific entity. Entities can be a system component, an object or a user which generally have attributes describing their current state. An Entity Event provides sufficient contextual information for a microservice or other data consumer / AI agent to understand what happened and what or who was involved. An Entity Event is always linked to a single, distinct entity in an Event-Driven Architecture.

Entity Event-Driven Embedded Systems produce events of interest to microservices and other data consumers / AI agents. Building Entity Event-Driven systems is about creating systems that asynchronously *generate* events in real-time in Event-Driven Architectures.

In physical computing, we define an Entity Event for an embedded system as something significant and uniquely identifiable (e.g. with a UUID, system ID and universal timestamp) that occurs to which its application responds, either by taking a measurement of the physical world (e.g. a sensor reading like temperature) or taking an action in it (e.g. controlling a component like a motor). The system reacts to a *situation* as a kind of stimulus and is able to communicate what happened and its response.

What are Entity Event-Driven Embedded Pico Systems?

Entity Event-Driven Embedded Pico Systems are small and purpose-built. Their internal applications connect to electronic components that interact with the physical world, sensing and controlling it. These applications also produce output event streams. They communicate data in machine-to-machine (M2M) exchange formats (like JSON) to event brokers through their APIs.

For the examples in this book, you'll include just enough data in an Entity Event relevant to acting on the event. This includes a unique Entity Event identifier (a UUID tag) and information that addresses the questions *Who* (which Pico system)? *What* (the data payload)? and *When* (a universal timestamp)?

Entity Event-Driven Embedded Pico Systems that provide this minimal information through their network interfaces can thereby provide output event streams for microservices and other data consumers / AI agents whose needs and goals for brokering and orchestrating events in modern Event-Driven Architectures may range from simple to complex.

Entity Event data payloads capture structured information. *What* to include in the data payload, however, depends entirely on the applications that utilize that information. The "thicker" the Event, the more extensive the payload, the more time it takes to generate and to process the Event. Overly thick events can slow the overall responsiveness of an Event Driven Architecture. A balance must always be found between not enough and too much information. An Entity Event must only contain the essential details about an event; nothing extra. Microservices and other data consumers / AI agents should be able to process the Entity Event directly without relying on other systems for core event information.

Developing Entity Event-Driven Embedded Pico Systems

Host / Target Setup

Your computer (the host)

We'll use a Windows 11 PC and / or Raspberry Pi OS on a Raspberry Pi 4 / 400 host computer for developing and writing MicroPython code that runs on the Pico W or Pico 2W as the target system. The example projects work equally well under both—you may use either Pico variant. Since a new generation macOS computer (e.g. running macOS Sequoia (15.x) or macOS Tahoe (26.x)) behaves similarly to the Raspberry Pi OS computer (their underlying operating systems are both Unix-like), you can use it instead as the host system, if you prefer.

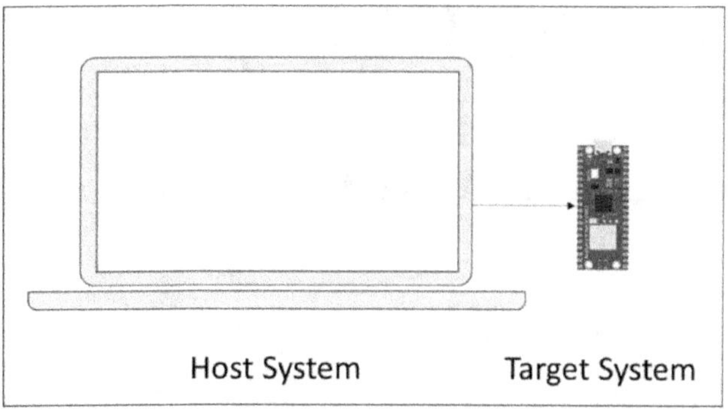

Fig 0-x Host System to Target Pico

Your Raspberry Pi Pico (the target)

In 2020, as a way of promoting learning about embedded systems programming in schools and the maker / hobbyist community, the Raspberry Pi Foundation introduced the Pico for $4 USD, a microcontroller board about the size of a stick of chewing gum that incorporates an RP2040 microcontroller.

Fig 0-x. Pico W and Playing Cards

In 2022, the Raspberry Pi Foundation introduced the Pico W for $6 USD which adds an Infineon CYW43439 single-chip combo device to the original Pico. This addition enables Wi-Fi 4 (802.11n) and BLE 5.2 (Bluetooth Low Energy) connectivity.

According to Raspberry Pi CEO Eben Upton, as of February 29, 2024, approximately 4 million Picos had been sold up to that point:

- https://www.tomshardware.com/raspberry-pi/raspberry-pi-celebrates-12-years-as-sales-break-61-million-units

In November of 2024, the Raspberry Pi Foundation introduced an upgraded version of the Pico W as the Pico 2W for $7 USD.

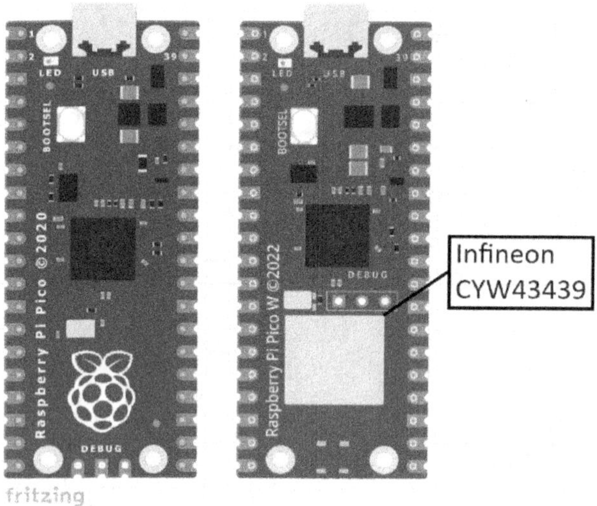

Fig 0-x. The Raspberry Pi Pico (left) and Pico W (right)

At the time of this writing, both the Pico W and Pico 2W sell for about $7 USD to $8 USD apiece, respectively, making it easy and convenient for students, makers and hobbyists to connect electronic components to it using a solderless breadboard.

For the projects in this book, you can use either the Raspberry Pi Pico W or the Pico 2W. They work equally well with the code examples. We'll refer to both variants simply as the "Pico".

Fig 0-x. Pico WH (Pico W with Headers)

A system of systems

Many different kinds of external electronic components (e.g. LEDs, displays, sensors, and motors) can be connected to a Pico. In general, these physical components are considered separate subsystems (self-contained systems within a larger system). They are components that talk to the Pico microcontroller board (itself a system) through a communications interface which, depending on the component, can be as simple as a holding the voltage on a GPIO pin on the board high or low or as complicated as a wireless exchange using HTTP or BLE protocols.

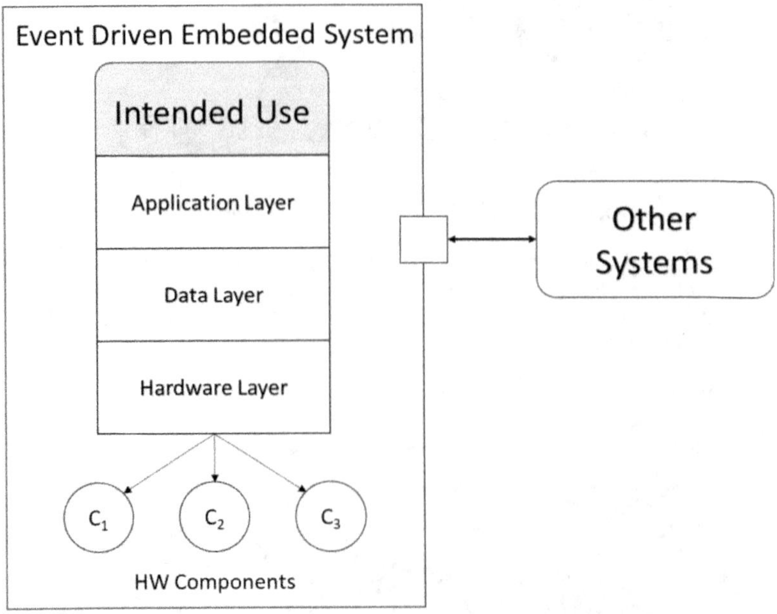

Fig 0-x. Entity Event-Driven Embedded System of (sub)systems

The Pico and its connected subsystems is a "system of systems" with the programs you write in MicroPython communicating with its various subsystems (components) and thereby sensing and controlling the physical world. Although an embedded system like the Pico can operate autonomously, an embedded system often communicates and interacts with other embedded systems and computer systems. It depends entirely on its intended use and its context of use.

Defining Embedded Systems

What is an embedded system?

Unlike a general-purpose computer, an embedded system is a computerized system designed for a specific purpose, to do one thing and to do that thing and well.

Intended Use and User Requirements

For the examples presented throughout this book on embedded Pico systems, the *purpose* of an embedded system can be defined in terms of its intended use and the user requirements that support the intended use in its context of use. Quite simply, the *purpose* of an embedded system answers the two questions, *What is this application supposed to do* (the intended use)? and *How does this application achieve that* (the user requirements)?

To illustrate the difference between intended use and user requirements: the purpose of a two-car residential garage may be to store vehicles, bicycles, and some outdoor lawn and garden equipment and to protect these from the elements. *How* it achieves that purpose might be with a covered roof, insulated walls, garage doors, a cement floor, etc.

Understanding the specific purpose of an embedded systems application is essential in keeping it simple and robust. Complex designs that are supposed to do many different things with lots of interconnected different parts are inherently costly to design, build and operate. Moreover, they tend to be complicated, break easily, and are expensive to repair or replace.

Working with Constrained Resources

Embedded systems are quite often based on microcontrollers (such as the RP2040 or RP2350) mounted on a PCB board designed by electrical engineers (like the Pico W which is a microcontroller board for the RP2040 or the Pico 2 W which is a microcontroller board for the RP2350). But microcontrollers are by their very nature resource constrained. Programming them can be a challenge because they are limited by:

- Processor speed
- Code space (ROM or flash)
- Memory (RAM)
- Processor peripherals
- Power consumption

To avoid unnecessary complexity and complication, the best approach to designing microcontroller-based embedded systems is to make them as simple as possible (but, to paraphrase Einstein, no simpler!) for their specific application—make them *do the right thing* and *do that thing right* but minimize the system's dependencies on other systems. Put differently, the simpler you can make such an embedded system that still does what it is supposed to do and do it correctly while keeping it loosely coupled to other systems, the better.

How do you simplify complex designs? Modularize the individual subsystems (self-contained systems that are part of a larger system) that comprise them and, at the same time, make sure that their subsystems integrate well with each other and the other systems to which they might interface.

Less is More. Simpler is better.

Whether you are a hobbyist / maker or a technical professional, there is an upside to tailoring an embedded system according to its resource constraints. They are more eco-friendly. Such systems are less wasteful of materials, of power consumption, and are easier to design and less costly to build and maintain than systems that try to do lots of different things with lots of different parts. The simpler you can make an embedded system that still does what it is supposed to do and do it correctly, the better.

In fact, one of the greatest challenges in designing and developing large complex systems on any project is that their subsystems don't always work well together. Integration testing done too late in a project's lifecycle frequently reveal incompatibilities that kill a project outright because of budget. Simpler systems are easier to understand, to try out firsthand, and to debug. Their development lifecycles are shorter.

A commercial aircraft, for example, can have millions of parts, all of which that must integrate flawlessly as planned. If they don't, costly rework or schedule overruns might result during development or after the aircraft goes into production. Worse, as a result of integration errors, an aircraft may experience a catastrophic failure. But even for small learner and small hobbyist / maker projects based on the Pico, it can be frustrating to redo and rebuild parts of an embedded system over and over again. It's a huge waste of time. No one wants that.

Defining Embedded System Entity Events

What are Entity Events?

Entity Events record data acquired from sensing or controlling the embedded system itself and / or the physical world around it. They provide *metadata* along with that data which provide sufficient contextual information required to identify and accurately describe that data. They record what happened to an entity and the actions it might have taken.

Entity Events are most often represented in a key / value format. The key uniquely identifies the event, while the values store the details of the event. We will structure Entity Events that uniquely identify the properties and state of our Pico-based embedded systems at a specific point in time such that the resulting event streams emitted by these systems can be constructed or reconstructed if necessary. Example:

Key	Value
event_id	3e93b24c-6345-4009-af70-a1ac3548e2fb
time_unix	2147483647
machine_unique_id	314159265358979323846zza

Fig 0-x. An embedded systems Entity Event is keyed on the unique event ID

In the examples in this book, your Pico will uniquely identify Events that are associated with entities (e.g. systems, objects, humans) and communicate those events asynchronously in the form of JSON objects (think Python dictionaries and lists) for machine-to-human and machine-to-machine communications. In so doing, your Entity Event-Driven Embedded Pico Systems will be able to participate in multiple domain contexts as a "source of truth" in Event-Driven Architectures.

Since Entity Events are uniquely identified by their event IDs, a microservice that receives Entity Events from one of your embedded Pico systems can both broker a queue of such events and simultaneously preserve the *data integrity* of that queue because it has all the information for doing so. If necessary, it can tell if something's changed in the queue.

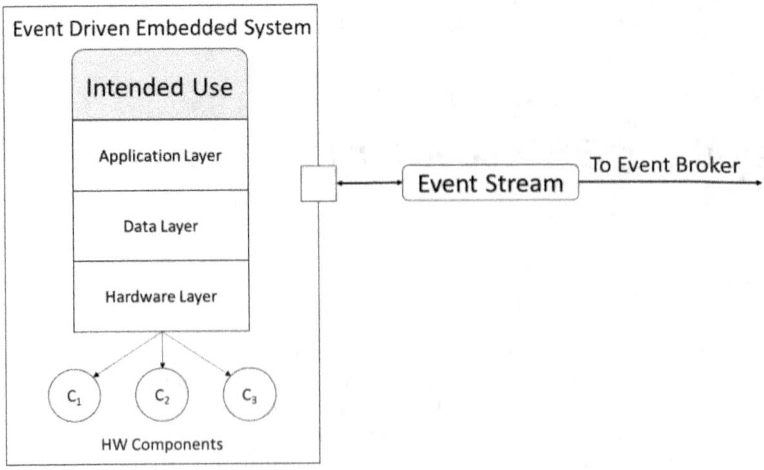

Fig 0-x. Entity Event-Driven Embedded System as an event stream source

The same type of interaction likewise holds true for a data consumer / AI agent consuming Entity Events from an embedded Pico system. These data consumers both can both broker a queue of such events and simultaneously preserve the *data integrity* of that queue because they have all the information for doing so, and, if necessary, determine whether something has changed in the queue.

Benefits of Entity Events

There is a significant benefit to constructing embedded systems with Entity Events as a key element of their designs. The Agile principle of "testing early and testing often" especially applies to communication interfaces. Agile testing can trace back to original sources if events are uniquely identified as they are with Entity Events.

To illustrate: the "babbling sensor" problem in avionics where a sensor on a flap or aileron fails to measure the force a pilot supplies to the flight control surface but nevertheless floods the onboard network with nonsensical readings. Since a flight control computer for a fly-by-wire (FBW) system must determine how to manipulate the control surfaces of a jet aircraft while it is airborne, it becomes critical to identify and isolate the defective sensor from the other sensors on the network.

Entity Events make this diagnostic task much easier because the readings from each sensor are uniquely identified. You know the point of origin for the event. It's easier to test for and to debug.

Fig 0-x. Babbling sensor on a flight control surface

Because of their uniqueness, Entity Events make it simpler to design and build testable interfaces during a project lifecycle. As a project progresses, integration tasks are made easier when the data associated with events are uniquely and unambiguously identified. Even better: the sooner you can test an interface for your system and the sooner you can progressively and iteratively integrate that system with other systems, the sooner you can see how well it works in its context of use. That's a win for any development task.

When developing safety critical systems for regulated industries such as avionics, identifying and controlling risks of all kinds (security risks and risks to people, to other systems, to the environment, to business needs, etc.) is the first and foremost consideration. The earlier a design focuses on the interface requirements between systems and subsystems, the better. Identifying these requirements and associated messaging along the communication boundaries is essential to analyzing and managing the risks of a particular system. These requirements not only define what a system does but provide a means to test it. Do the system and its subsystems meet their interface requirements? Is the integrated system under test *doing the right thing* (its purpose) and is it *doing it right* (working correctly)?

Setting Context Boundaries

Communication interfaces set context boundaries

The guiding principle of this book is to focus on the communication interfaces between systems and subsystems right away and to stay focused on and keep testing these interfaces until your project is done—maybe even longer(!). While it is impossible to anticipate every possible scenario under which your Entity Event-Driven Embedded Pico System will have to communicate, it is definitely possible to design communication interfaces that are simple and easy to use right from the start.

Importantly, these interfaces can help explicitly define the context boundaries of your embedded system which can then make it easy for you and for others to use and later *re-use* them in different projects and different architectures involving other systems. This beginning book on the Pico attempts to show you how to do so by defining the messages that are sent and received across a communications interface as an Entity Event.

Bounded context of a domain model

Complex systems are inherently collections of multiple domain models defined by the range of their applicability according to their bounded contexts. Although communication interfaces are by no means the only way to define a bounded context, it is often a very straightforward way to do so—testing of a given context amounts to communicating with the boundary that contains its subdomain.

Typically, a communications interface encloses just one embedded system. Communications between this system and other systems are via network calls which enforces decoupling. Bounded contexts help minimize a system's interdependence on other systems and domains so that changes made to it minimally impact its neighboring contexts.

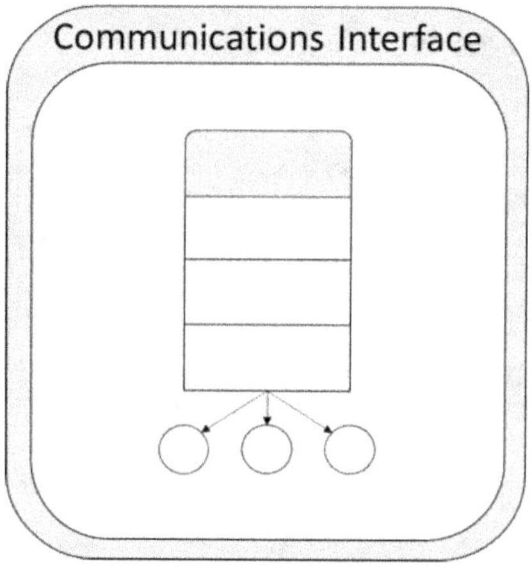

Fig 0-x. Bounded context of a single system defined by its communications interface

Designed with the communications interface in mind, the embedded system is readily available for other systems to interact with as required, provided those systems adhere to its interface requirements. Different microservices and data consumers / AI agents, for instance, might broker different event queues with multiple embedded Pico systems.

Modelling bounded contexts

For large complex projects in regulated industries, a formalized interface requirements document like an ICD (Interface Control Document) may be required to describe the different configurations for exchanging events over a bounded context with an Event Broker. For example, here's how a Systems Engineer might use SysML notation to model this particular use case between a Pico embedded system and a microservice Event Broker:

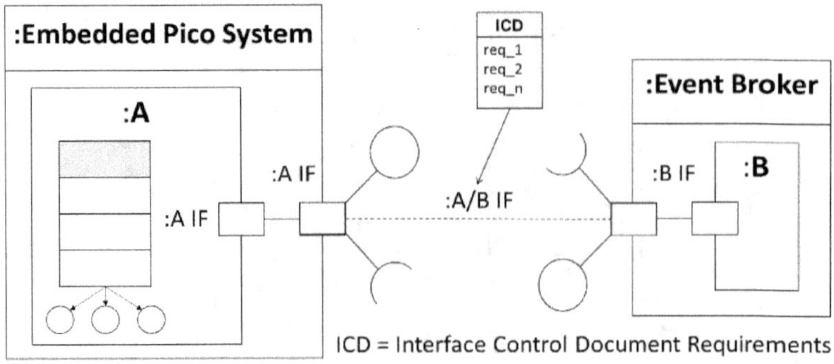

Fig 0-x. SysML Systems Engineering Model of a communications interface defining a bounded context

A systems engineer modelling the bounded context of an embedded system might view the system as having multiple communications interfaces even though the internal workings of that particular system remain the same, just like an application might offer multiple APIs. This book won't begin to cover all these possibilities but only caution against the temptation to create so many interfaces that they can become unwieldy to manage as well as introduce other difficulties (such as documenting them).

A Simpler Notation: hexagons with interfaces

We do not need to elaborate on the application, data and hardware architectural layers working inside an Entity Event-Driven Pico Embedded System. Our hobbyist / maker embedded systems are simple MicroPython applications running on the Pico often with just a few dozen lines of code. The application implements one or more interfaces that communicate Entity Events to external systems.

For us, the most important information about an Entity Event-Driven Pico Embedded System is the intended use of that system and what is required by the interface that its application provides. Put differently, what's the purpose of the Pico system and how should other systems interact with it?

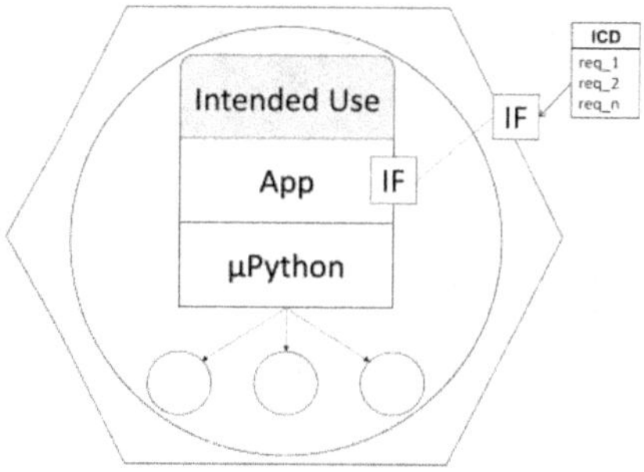

Fig 0-x. Pico embedded system using hexagonal notation

To the extent possible, our aim is to reduce embedded systems based on the Pico to the point that they are no longer considered complex. This is the (IEEE / INCOSE / SERC) systems engineering definition of a "component" (https://sebokwiki.org/wiki/Component_(glossary)). Simple embedded systems, when designed well, are both coherent (logically self-consistent) and cohesive. They are easier to understand, design and control throughout their lifecycle than complex systems of systems. Systems of systems made up of redundant components are robust—certainly more robust than systems of systems that are redundant at the system level.

As a component, an Entity Event-Driven Embedded Pico System is a basic modular building block that can be used and re-used in multiple configurations depending on its interfaces. Starting with very simple applications, we will stay focused in this book on each system doing one thing well and on communicating Entity Events with its interface(s).

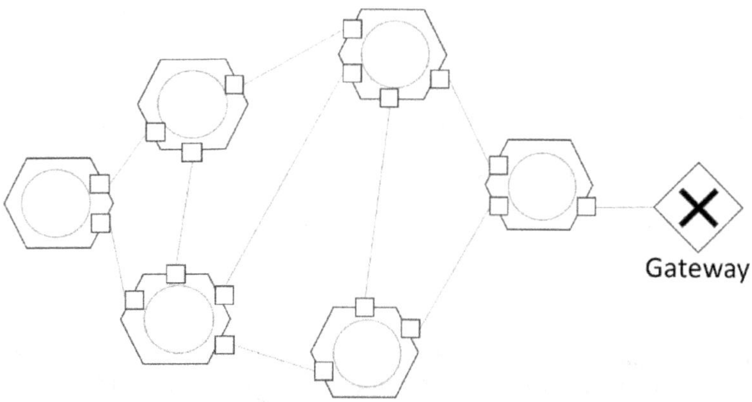

Fig 0-x. Example of Pico embedded systems in a mesh network connected to an exclusive gateway

Some Notes before Proceeding

Avoiding Technical Jargon, Definitions and Generalizations

You'll notice that throughout this chapter I have tried to avoid technical jargon, definitions and generalizations. In a rapidly changing technology like embedded systems, these evolve frequently, whereas the core design principles underlying the technology change more slowly. In the long run, understanding basic concepts is what matters, such as the importance of designing simple systems that do one thing well but that also emit Entity Events. By progressively working through the examples in this book, I'm hoping you'll find that a very good way of keeping embedded systems as simple as possible is through bounded contexts defined by their communication interfaces.

Of course, different disciplines have different point of views on how best to do this: an electrical engineer, for example, may look at an embedded system quite differently than a systems engineer would, or a software engineer might. These subject matter experts are like the proverbial blind men describing an elephant's various parts in terms of their individual perspectives.

For this reason, I have tried to avoid hard and fast rules. Invariably, there are numerous exceptions and corner cases when applying definitions and generalizations to the simplest of embedded systems. It can't be helped. Use cases vary by context. Contexts change over time. Definitions change as generalizations evolve to account for new types of situations. Everything changes as the technology elephant keeps plodding forward, inexorably.

For example, an electronic communications interface defined by a few GPIO pins on the Pico is quite different than a wireless communications interface using the Pico's WiFi or BLE subsystems. When to use which type of interface depends entirely on the use case. What system or subsystem does the Pico need to interface to? What assumptions can be made about the context of use?

Whether internal or external, interfaces have to be understood on their own terms, their pros and cons. For the purposes of learning how to transform your Pico into an Entity Event-Driven Embedded System, I gloss over some of these differences with all due respect to the subject matter experts who would prefer a catalog of distinctions and nuances. *—I understand.* My rationale: I don't want to assume that a beginning learner has the benefit of specialty technical knowledge in any particular field. Learning basic concepts and the tools that go with them requires an incremental bootstrap approach.

Chapter Summary

Does your embedded Pico system do the right thing and do the thing right?

With respect to learning how the Pico fits into your Entity Event-Driven Embedded Systems projects, I believe that the questions inevitably come down to: does your Pico do what it's supposed to do, and does it do it correctly and simply as possible for the given use case? In other words, does it *do the right thing* and *do the thing right*?

Let's see how to answer these questions with MicroPython and your Pico!

References and Further Exploration

- *SEBoK Component (glossary)* https://sebokwiki.org/wiki/Component_(glossary)
- *Fundamentals of Software Architecture*, 1st edition by Mark Richards and Neal Ford (O'Reilly, 2020, ISBN-13: 978-1492043454,)
- *Software Architecture: The Hard Parts*, 1st Edition by Neal Ford and Mark Richards et al, (O'Reilly, 2021, ISBN-10: 1492086894)
- *Building Event Driven Microservices* by Adam Bellemare (O'Reilly, 2020, ISBN-13: 978-1492057895)
- *Domain-Driven Design: Tackling Complexity in the Heart of Software* by Eric Evans (Addison-Wesley, 2003, ISBN-10: 0321125215)
- *Making Embedded Systems*, 2nd edition by Elecia White (O'Reilly, 2024, ISBN-10: 1098151542)

Chapter 1

1. Background

2. The Thonny IDE
    a. What is the Thonny IDE?
    b. Installing and Launching Thonny
        i. Raspberry Pi
        ii. Windows
        iii. MacOS
        iv. Linux
    c. Introducing Thonny

3. Introducing MicroPython
    a. What is MicroPython?
    b. Installing MicroPython

4. Connecting Thonny and your Pico
    a. Connecting your Pico to your host computer
    b. Connecting Thonny to your Pico
    c. Hello from your Pico!

5. Chapter Summary

6. References and Further Exploration

Programming the Raspberry Pi Pico in MicroPython

Start writing MicroPython for your Pico using Thonny (or your favorite IDE)

Python is a widely used, highly expressive, yet very powerful scripting language that is relatively easy to learn. As a post-doc at Cambridge University, the Australian physicist Damien George (https://dpgeorge.net/) created *MicroPython* at the end of 2013 in a Kickstarter campaign (Project: 214379695).

MicroPython is an implementation of Python 3 for microcontrollers and embedded systems that is optimized to run on hardware constrained by limited resources, such as memory and processing power. It combines the simplicity and readability of Python with modules that interact directly with hardware peripherals and components.

In January 2021, MicroPython was ported to the RP2040—the microcontroller on the original Raspberry Pi Pico and Pico W. On November 1, 2024, the v1.24 release of MicroPython officially added support for the RP2350-the microcontroller on the Raspberry Pi Pico 2 and 2W.

Thonny (https://thonny.org/) can be installed on a host computer and MicroPython on a Pico W or Pico 2W. All of the examples in this book can run on both Pico variants. We'll simply refer to the Pico W or Pico 2W as just "Pico" and note if there are differences between the two variants to consider along the way.

There are many popular IDEs (Integrated Development Environments) available that can be employed for writing and running MicroPython programs on your Pico. Some of these IDEs are very rich in features and can handle lots of different programming languages at the same time. If you have a favorite IDE, it will likely work for most, if not all, of this book's examples without any issues.

Thonny is a beginner-friendly IDE, however, that focuses on a single language—Python. With its built-in tools support for MicroPython (since v3.2), it is particularly well-suited for MicroPython development on the Pico. Its clean, uncluttered design and integrated features make it straightforward to navigate and understand for those new to developing and debugging MicroPython code. Thonny is freely available for multiple platforms and is officially supported by the Raspberry Pi Foundation. It is included by default in the Raspberry Pi OS. We'll use Thonny for presenting the code examples throughout this book.

The Thonny IDE

Using Thonny, you can run Python code on your host computer and MicroPython code on your target Pico. As previously mentioned, Thonny is an IDE for programming Python and MicroPython that currently comes pre-installed with the Rasberry Pi OS. It also readily installs on host platforms like a Windows PC or an Apple Mac. Thonny has a straightforward and intuitive GUI (graphical user interface) that is relatively easy to use.

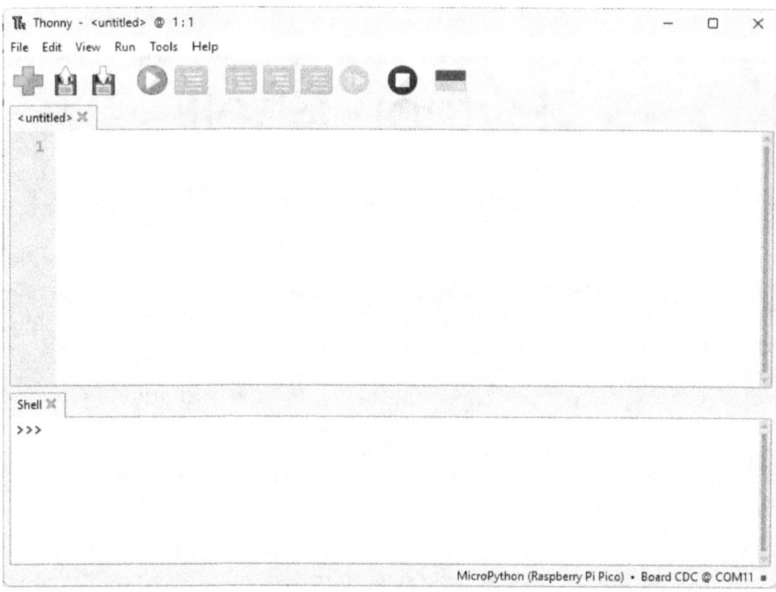

Fig 1-x. The Thonny IDE in regular mode

The Thonny IDE collects all the tools you need to write and develop MicroPython code for the Pico into a single user interface. Thonny even allows you to run code interactively in its Python Shell which makes it easy to debug code line by line.

Thonny's user interface consists of a menu toolbar along the top, an editor window where you write and debug programs and scripts, and a Python Shell where you run individual Python commands and view output in interactive REPL (Read, Evaluate, Print, and Loop) sessions.

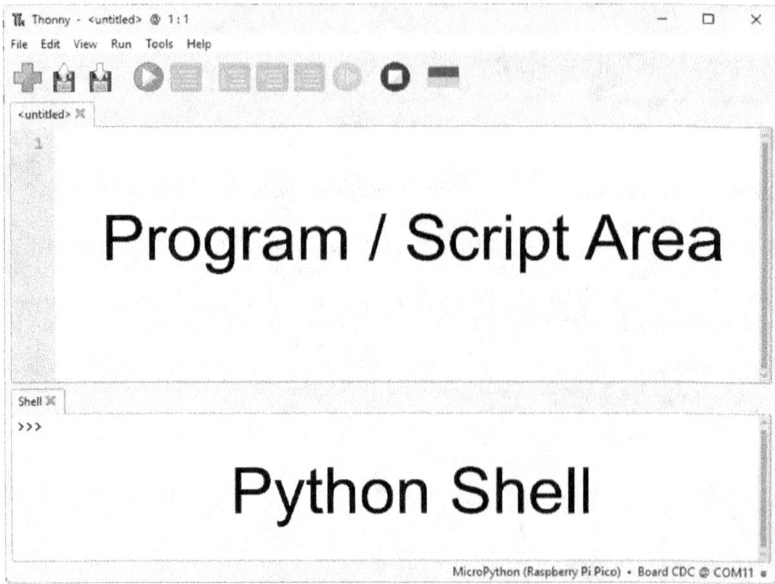

Fig 1-x. The Thonny IDE layout

The drop-down menus in the toolbar running along the top edge of Thonny's IDE allow you to create new programs, save them, load them, and run them. The Program / Script Area directly underneath the toolbar is where you write and edit your programs. The Python Shell below the Program / Script Area allows you to type individual Python commands and run them one at a time by pressing the Enter key after each line. The Python Shell is a great way to try things out without having to run a whole program. It also provides information about a running program.

With Thonny, you are able to select which Python interpreter to run your code—Thonny's Local Python 3 interpreter on your host computer or the MicroPython one installed on your target Pico. Moreover, your programs and scripts can be stored as Python modules (text files) either on your host system, or on your Pico, or both. Thonny executes the lines of code in a Python module from top to bottom in the same folder that it finds the module, just as if you typed those lines at a prompt in the Python shell.

Thonny has two main modes, a *Simple Mode* and a *Regular Mode*. The Simple Mode interface uses friendly icons that are labelled but the Regular Mode is almost as friendly and a little easier to navigate most of the examples in this book because it also includes a menu bar. Thonny also has an Advanced Mode which can be especially useful for debugging large, complicated programs. But for our purposes, we'll stick with Regular Mode since it has everything we need for this book.

If you find yourself in Simple Mode, you can easily change to Thonny's Regular Mode by clicking on "Switch to regular mode" link in the upper right hand corner of the IDE and relaunch Thonny.

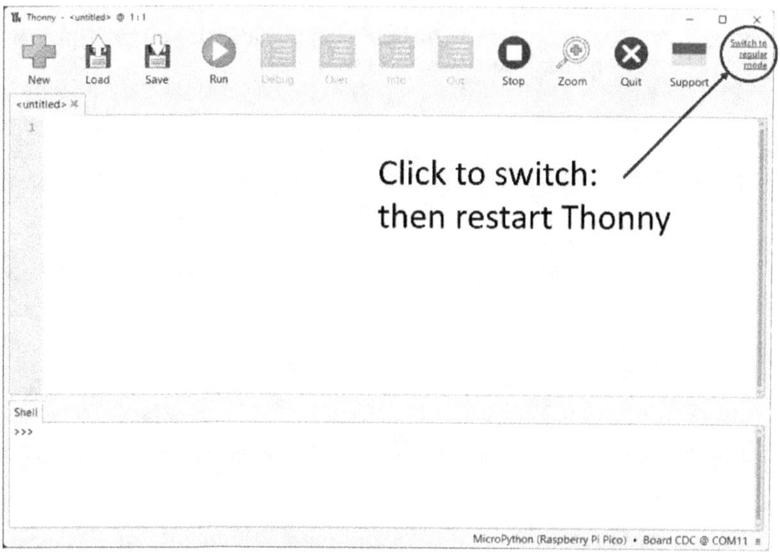

Fig 1-x. The Thonny IDE in simple mode

Installing and Launching Thonny

Thonny can be downloaded and installed on a recent Windows PC, Apple Mac, or Linux computer; Thonny already comes pre-installed on the Raspberry Pi OS!

From the Thonny homepage, download the most recent version of Thonny and run the appropriate installer for your host computer, following the installation wizard.

Raspberry Pi OS

Thonny comes pre-installed with the Raspberry Pi OS. It is typically found in the Programming section of the Application Launch Bar on the desktop Panel. (Look for the panel with the Raspberry Pi icon.) To launch Thonny, select "Thonny Python IDE" from the Programming submenu.

Windows

If you hover a mouse on "Windows" in the "Download version" box on the Thonny homepage (https://thonny.org), various ways to install Thonny on a Windows computer should appear.

Download and open one of the installers and follow the instructions to set up Thonny on your Windows computer. Example:

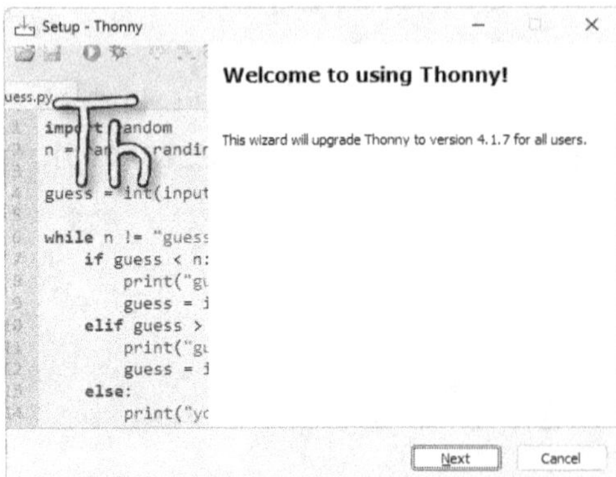

Fig 1-x. The Thonny Setup for Windows

Continue clicking "Next", "Allow", "Continue", "Agree", etc. and select a destination on your computer for the installation until setup is complete.

Click the Thonny "Th" icon to launch the IDE or launch Thonny from the Windows Start Menu.

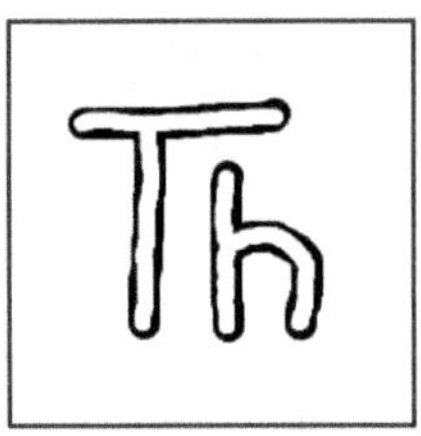

Fig 1-x. The Thonny logo on Windows

macOS

If you hover a mouse on "Mac" in the "Download version" box on the the Thonny homepage (https://thonny.org/, an installer should appear along with a "pip install thonny" command (for advanced users who would prefer to reuse an existing Python installation on their MacOS computer instead).

Download and open the package installer)or use the pip command if you already have Python installed) and follow the instructions to set up Thonny on your Apple Mac, clicking "Allow", "Continue", "Agree", etc. and a Destination on your computer as appropriate for the installation until setup is complete. Select the Thonny "Th" icon (or use The Dock, Spotlight search, or the Finder application as appropriate):

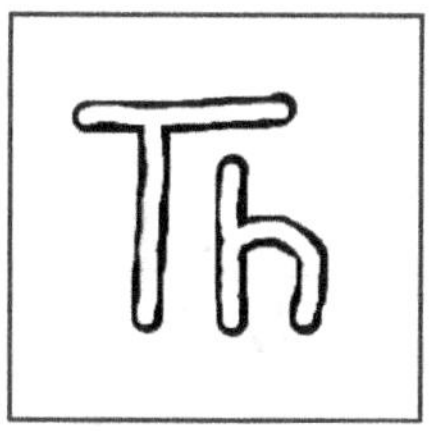

Fig 1-x. The Thonny logo on the macOS

Then click "Let's go!" to launch the IDE:

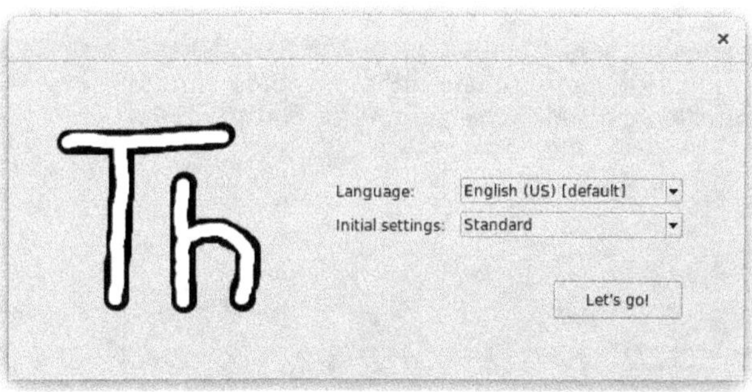

Fig 1-x. Starting Thonny in the macOS

Linux

If you hover a mouse on "Linux" in the "Download version" box on the Thonny homepage (https://thonny.org/, an installer should appear along with a "pip3 install thonny" command (for advanced users who would prefer to reuse an existing Python installation on their Linux computer instead).

Open a terminal window and at a command prompt, enter:

```
$ bash <(wget -O - https://thonny.org/installer-for-linux)
```

and follow the instructions to set up Thonny on your Linux system, clicking "Allow", "Continue", "Agree", etc. and a Destination on your computer as appropriate for the installation until setup is complete.

Select the Thonny "Th" icon if it is present on the Linux desktop:

Fig 1-x. The Thonny logo on Linux

(If the icon is not present, you may be able to use the desktop environment's application menu or launcher, or typing "thonny" or "python3 -m thonny" in a terminal to launch the Thonny IDE.)

Then click "Let's go!" to launch the IDE:

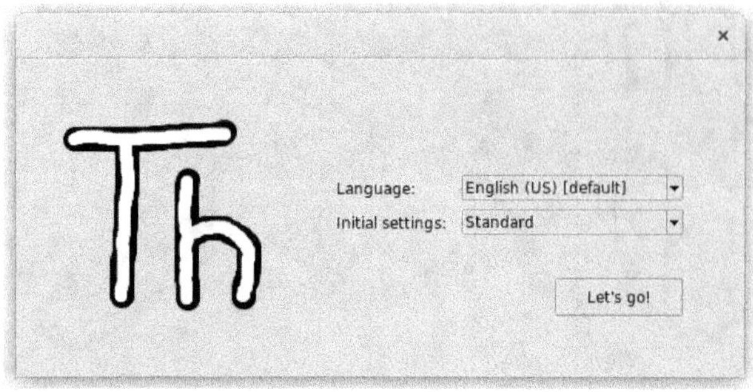

Fig 1-x. Starting Thonny in Linux

Introducing Thonny

Thonny includes a Python interpreter when it is installed on your host system which means that you can write and run Python programs independently from the MicroPython interpreter on your target Pico. This can be very useful for debugging the logic of a program even before you try it out on the Pico. You can also save these programs on your host system for later use.

In the Python Shell area, type 'print("Hello, world!")' and hit Enter:

Fig 1-x. Displaying "Hello, world!" in the Thonny Python Shell

Now copy your program from the Shell to the Program / Script area:

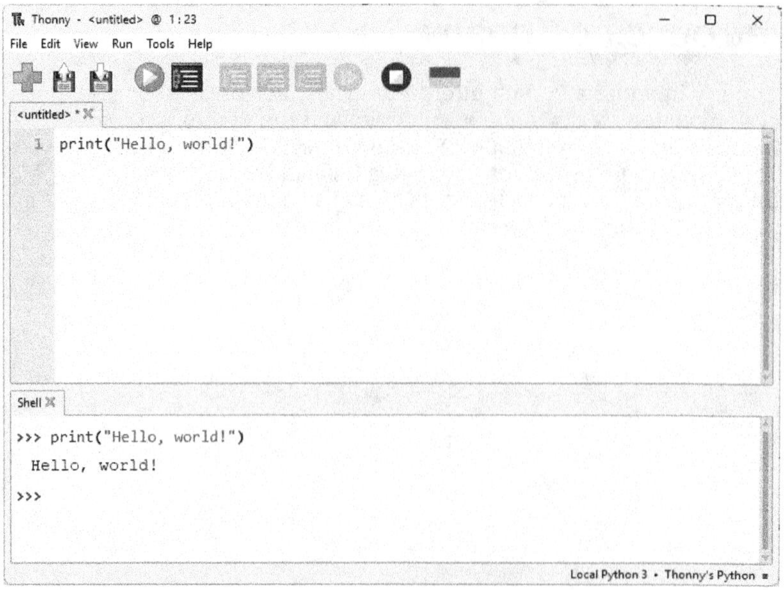

Fig 1-x. "Hello, world!" in the Thonny Program / Script Area

and run it from the Program / Script area by clicking the green Play button or “Run current script” in the Run menu.

You should see:

Fig 1-x. Running a program in Thonny

Congratulations—you've run your first Python program in Thonny!

You can save your program to your host system using the "File Save as..." menu option or by clicking the disk icon with the down arrow on it. Give your program a name like "hello_world.py".

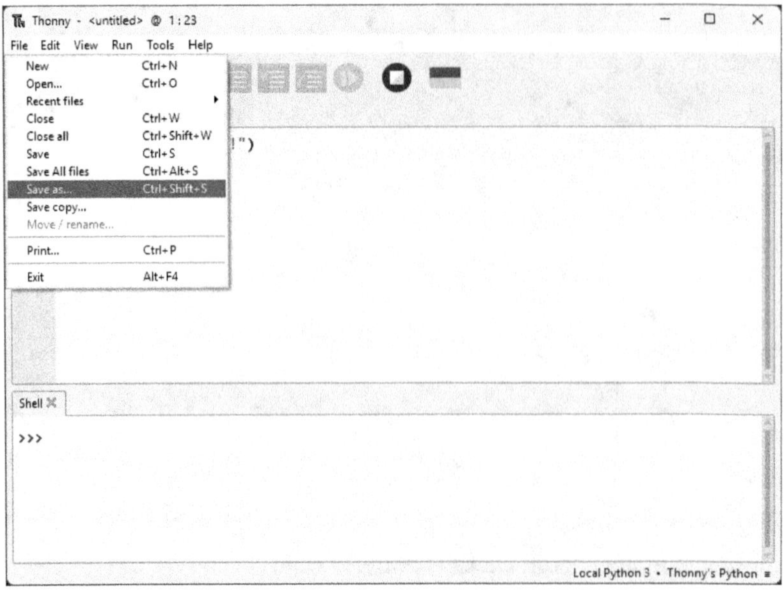

Fig 1-x. Saving a file in Thonny

Notice that if you close Thonny and restart it, Thonny will open hello_world.py back up again. (If for some reason Thonny doesn't reopen hello_world.py, you can open it from the File menu.)

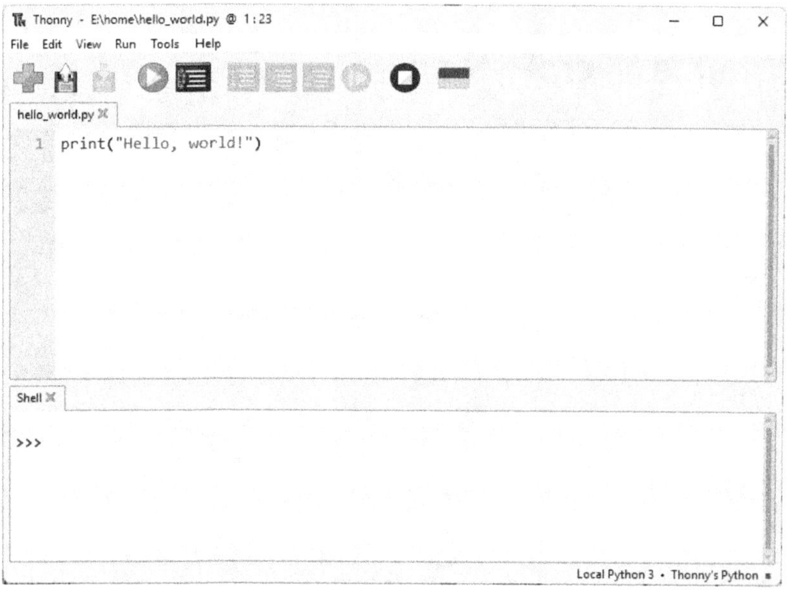

Fig 1-x. hello_world.py opened in Thonny

Introducing MicroPython

What is MicroPython?

MicroPython runs directly on "bare-metal" hardware without an underlying OS. It includes a subset of the Python standard library that makes it compatible with "normal" Python depending on the hardware constraints. While it is "compact enough to fit and run within just 256k of code space and 16k of RAM", it is "packed full of advanced features such as an interactive prompt, arbitrary precision integers, closures, list comprehension, generators, exception handling and more" (https://micropython.org/). This allows you to develop code on a desktop host system and easily transfer it to a target microcontroller or embedded system.

Installing MicroPython

MicroPython is distributed in the form of a UF2 (USB Flashing Format) file that must be flashed to the Pico's flash drive. You can do this using Thonny or you can download the latest version of MicroPython as a UF2 file onto your host and manually copy it onto your Pico.

If you want to update to the latest version MicroPython, note that reflashing the Pico can erase and overwrite any programs or files that are currently stored on it. So save any of them that you want to keep to your host computer first! (You should do so throughout this book because it's always a good idea to save your work.)

How to put a Pico into bootloader mode

Regardless of which method you choose to flash your Pico, it should first be put it into bootloader mode by plugging it into a host computer with a micro USB cord while *simultaneously* holding down the BootSel button near the USB port.

Fig 1-x. Bootsel Button on Pico

The Pico should then show up as a USB drive on the host computer. It's now in bootloader mode.

Flashing a Pico with Thonny

Thonny, it can flash a Pico for you.

Select "Options..." from the Tools menu and choose "Install or update MicroPython" in the lower right hand corner of the Interpreter tab:

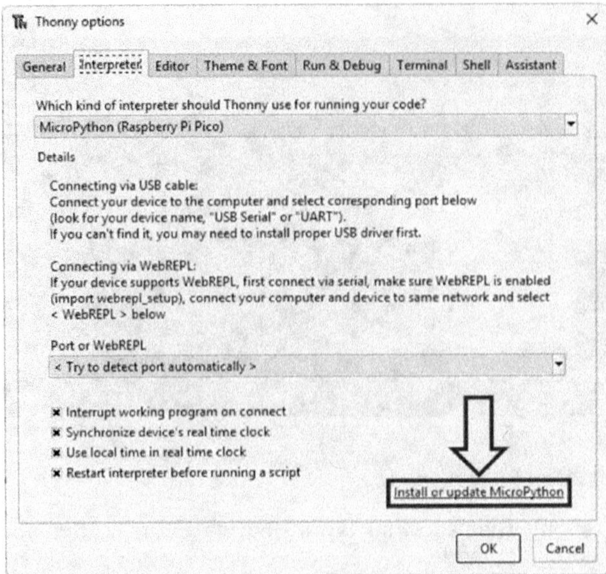

Fig 1-x. Installing MicroPython with Thonny

A window titled "Install or update MicroPython (UF2)" should appear that shows your Pico as the Target volume. It displays the steps necessary to flash the Pico.

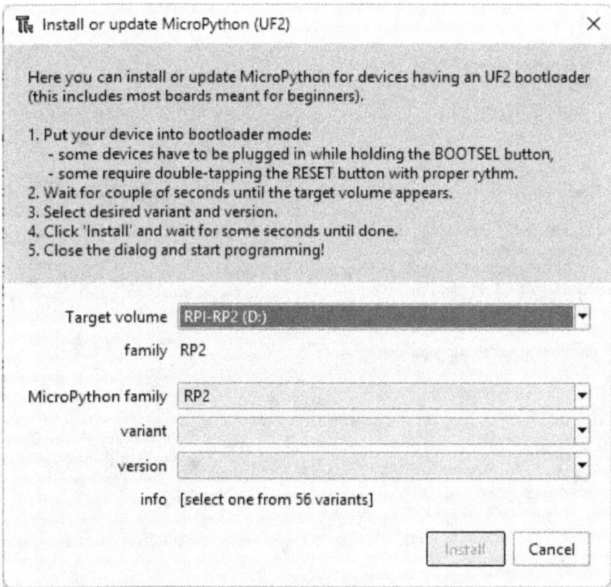

Fig 1-x. Installing MicroPython on a Pico W or Pico 2W

From the variant dropdown list, choose which Pico you have.

Raspberry Pi Pico W

Install the latest version of MicroPython for the "Raspberry Pi Pico W / Pico WH" if you're installing MicroPython on a Pico W or Pico WH:

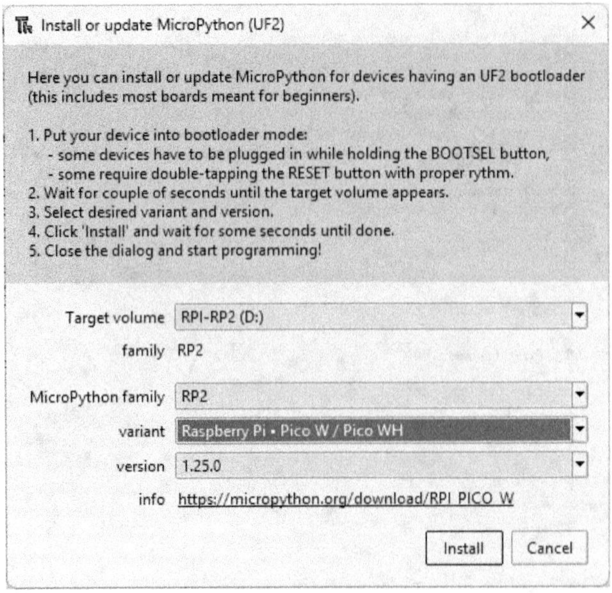

Fig 1-x. Installing MicroPython on a Pico W or Pico WH

Close the dialog window when the installation says it's Done!

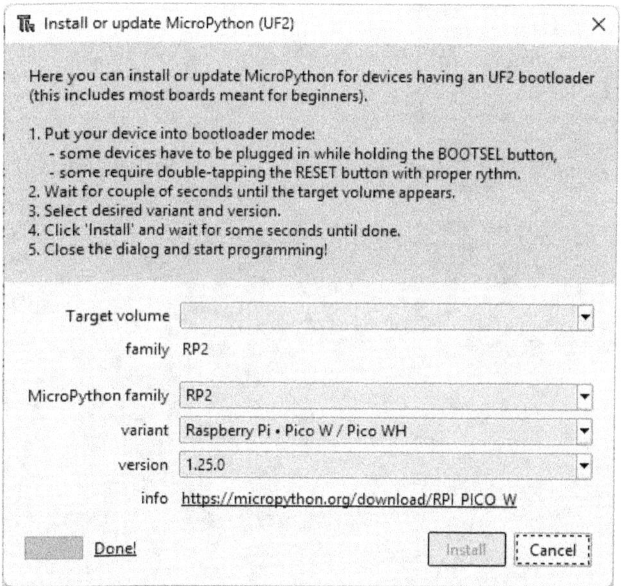

Fig 1-x. Installing MicroPython on a Pico W or Pico WH

That's all there is to it! MicroPython is now installed on the Pico W or Pico WH!

Raspberry Pi Pico 2W

Install the latest version of MicroPython for the "Raspberry Pi Pico 2 W" if you're installing MicroPython on a Pico 2W:

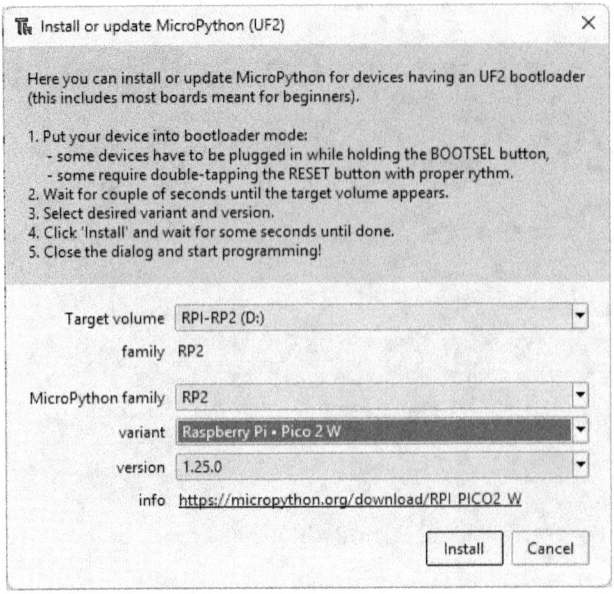

Fig 1-x. Installing MicroPython on a Pico 2 W

Close the dialog when the installation says it's Done!

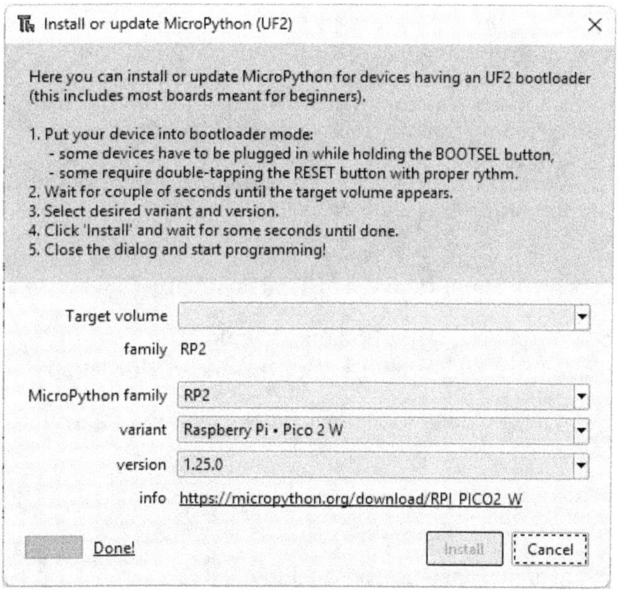

Fig 1-x. Installing MicroPython on a Pico 2W or Pico 2WH

That's all there is to it! MicroPython is now installed on the Pico 2W or Pico 2WH!

Copying the MicroPython UF2 file onto a Pico

Alternatively, the MicroPython UF2 file can be manually copied onto a Pico by first downloading the UF2 file onto the Pico.

Detailed instructions accompanied by animated graphics for flashing a Pico can be found on the official Raspberry Pi website at:

- https://www.raspberrypi.com/documentation/microcontrollers/micropython.html#drag-and-drop-micropython

At the time of this writing, the latest version for the Pico W or the Pico 2W can be downloaded from the official Raspberry Pi website at:

- **Pico W**: https://micropython.org/download/RPI_PICO_W/
- **Pico 2W**: https://micropython.org/download/RPI_PICO2_W/

(Make sure that you download the correct version of MicroPython for your Pico.)

After putting a Pico into bootloader mode, the MicroPython UF2 file can be dragged and dropped onto it.

MicroPython is now installed on the Pico!

Connecting Thonny and your Pico

Connecting your Pico to a host computer

If you haven't already, connect the host computer to the Pico with a microUSB cable. Most microUSB cables work with the Pico. The ones that don't are usually power-only cables that lack data wires, but these are becoming increasingly rare as most people expect to use their microUSB cables for both power and data (such as charging their smartphones or copying pictures from their phone to a laptop computer).

Fig 1-x. Pico W connected to host PC

Connecting Thonny to a Pico

If Thonny is installed on a Windows PC, the words "Local Python 3" may appear in the lower right hand corner of Thonny before the Pico is connected to the host:

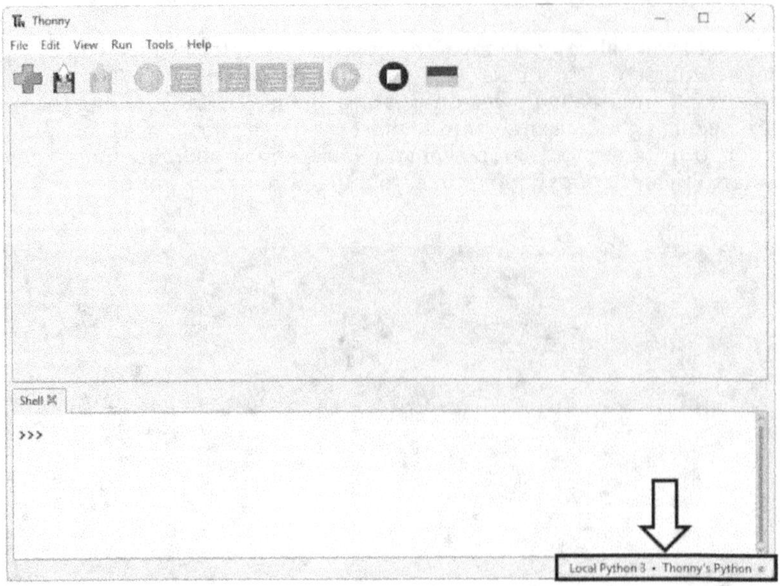

Fig 1-x. Thonny's Local Python 3 interpreter

This means that Thonny is using the Python interpreter on the host computer.

If you hover or right click over the lower right hand corner with your mouse in Windows, for example, you may see something like:

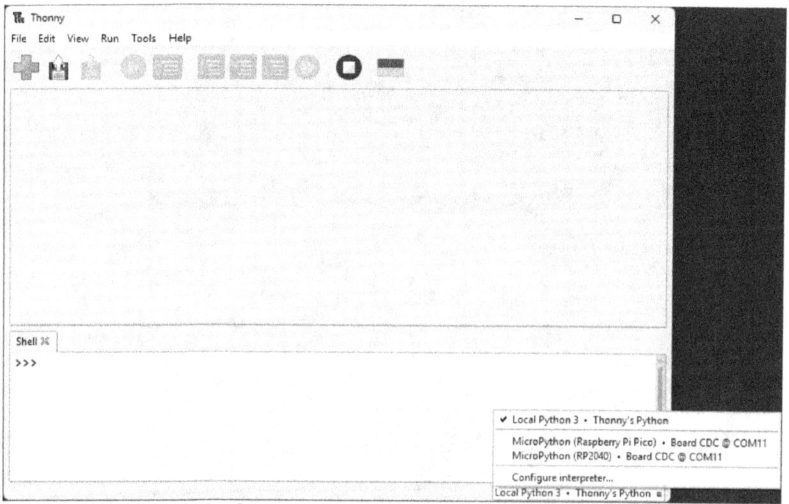

Fig 1-x. Thonny's Python Interpreter Options

To use the *MicroPython* interpreter that is installed on the Pico, select Thonny Options from the Tools Menu bar:

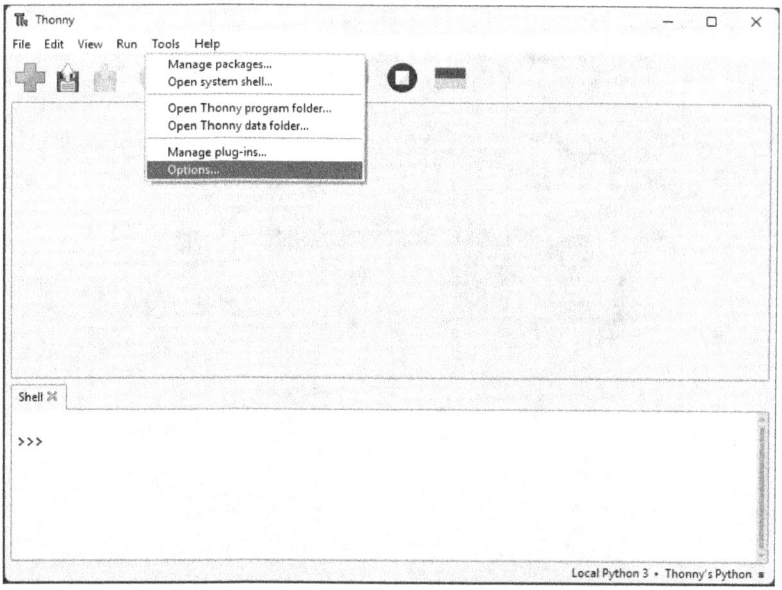

Fig 1-x. Thonny Options Menu

and choose "MicroPython (Raspberry Pi Pico) from the Interpreter tab:

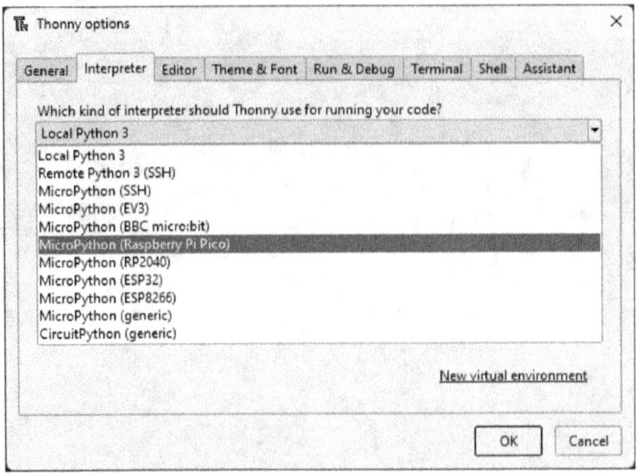

Fig 1-x. Thonny's Pico Interpreter

While on the Interpreter tab, also select the COM / tty port to which your Pico is attached. In Windows, the COM / tty port may look something like:

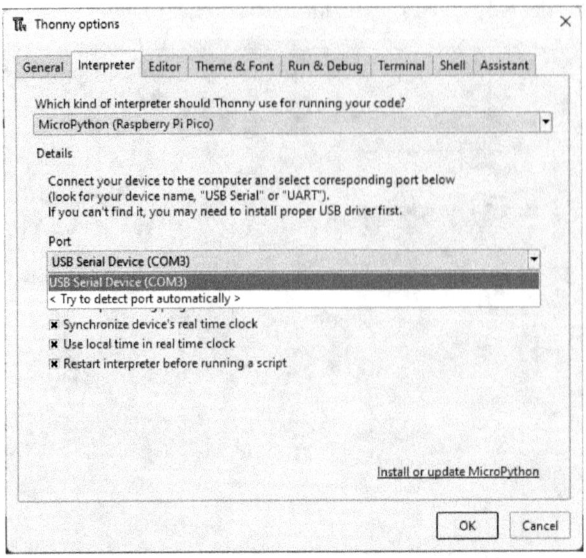

Fig 1-x. Thonny Selecting the Pico's COM Port

After selecting the OK button, the MicroPython interpreter should appear in the lower right hand corner of Thonny's main screen:

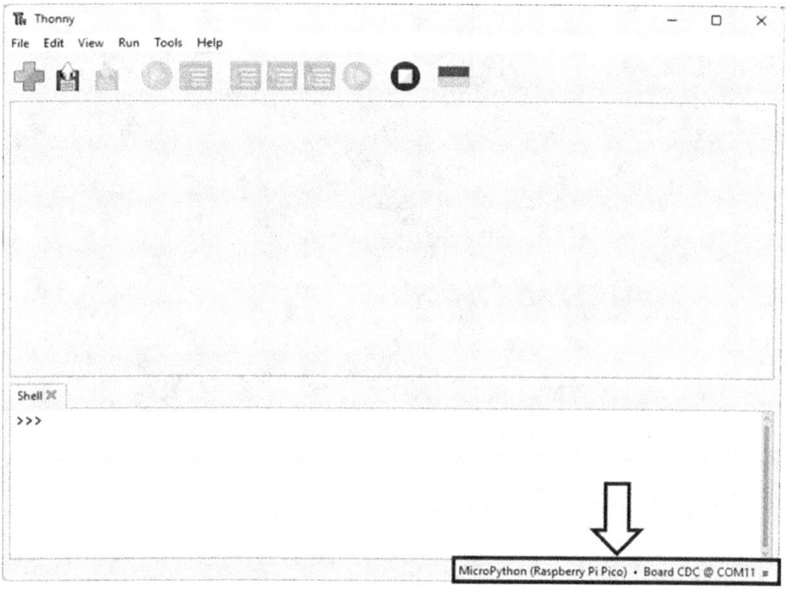

Fig 1-x. Thonny's MicroPython Interpreter on Windows COM port

On a Raspberry Pi, macOS or Linux host, this could look like:

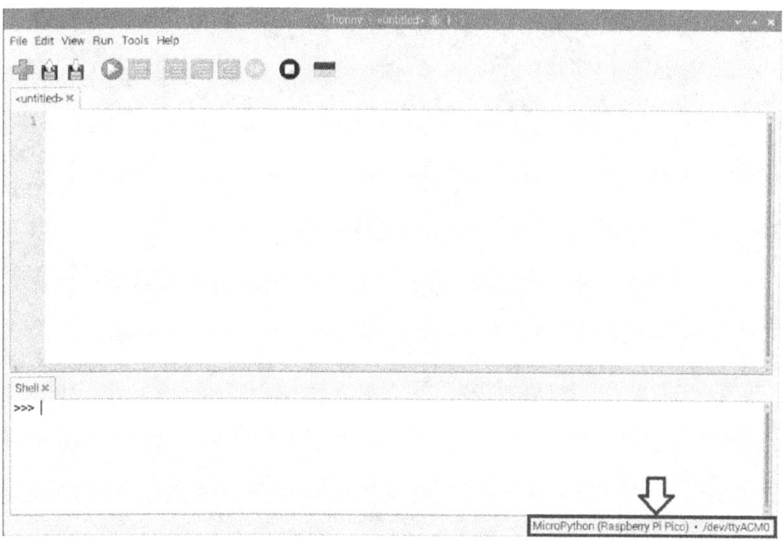

Fig 1-x. Thonny's MicroPython Interpreter: ttyACM0 on Raspberry Pi

If you don't see the port to which you connected your Pico, you can try detecting it with Thonny. If this doesn't work, you might try a different microUSB cable.

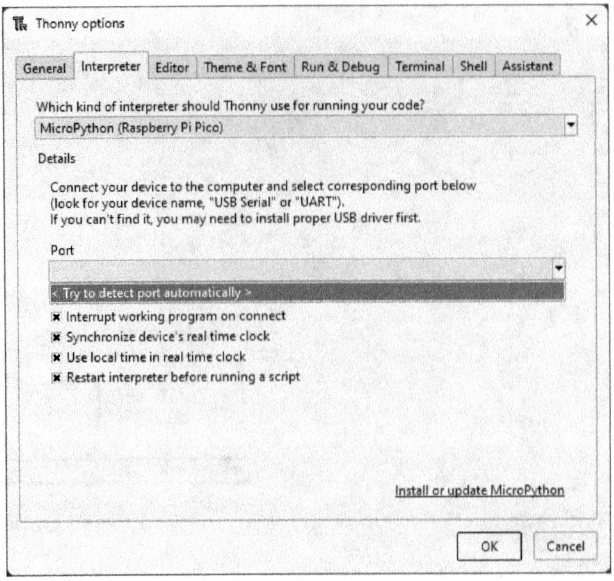

Fig 1-x. Thonny option to detect the Pico's COM port automatically

Hello, from your Pico!

In the Thonny Python Shell, type 'print("Hello, world!")' and hit the Enter key.

This time, instead of the Python interpreter on the host saying "Hello, world!", the MicroPython interpreter *on the Pico* says "Hello, world!".

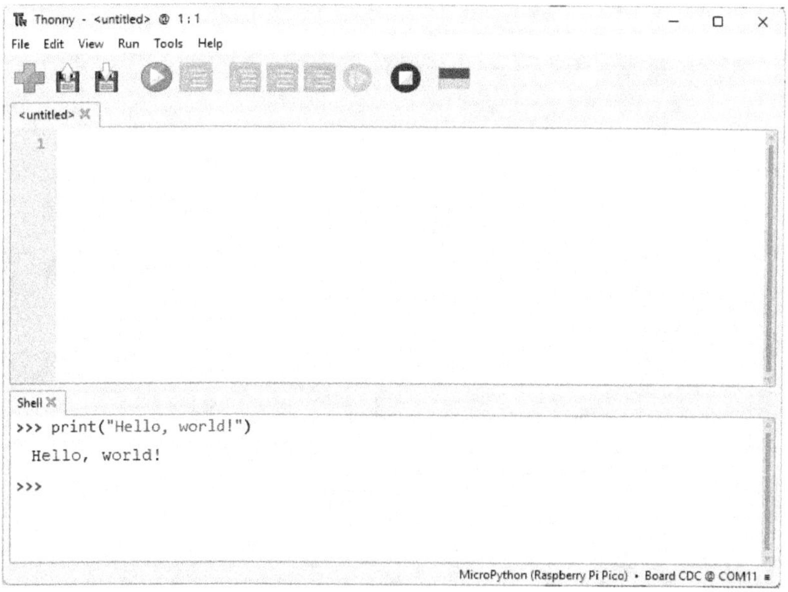

Fig 1-x. Thonny Python Shell: Hello, world!

Congratulations—you've run your first MicroPython program *on the Pico*!

Now let's open the hello_world.py program that you saved previously on your host computer with the File Open menu. The MicroPython interpreter on the Pico will ask you if you'd like to open it from your host computer or from the Pico:

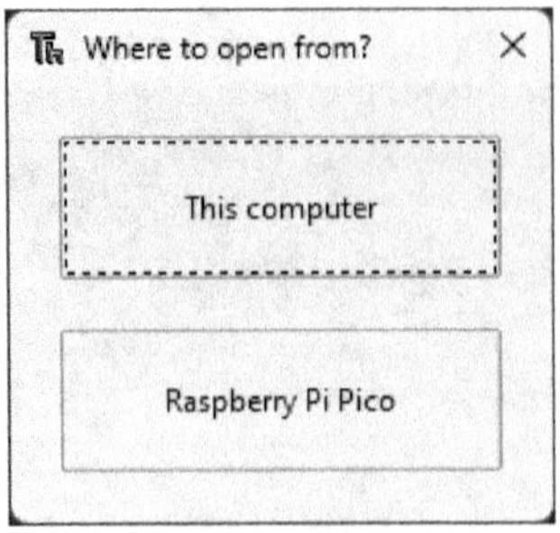

Fig 1-x. Thonny Open hello_world.py

First, open it from "This computer" (your host computer).

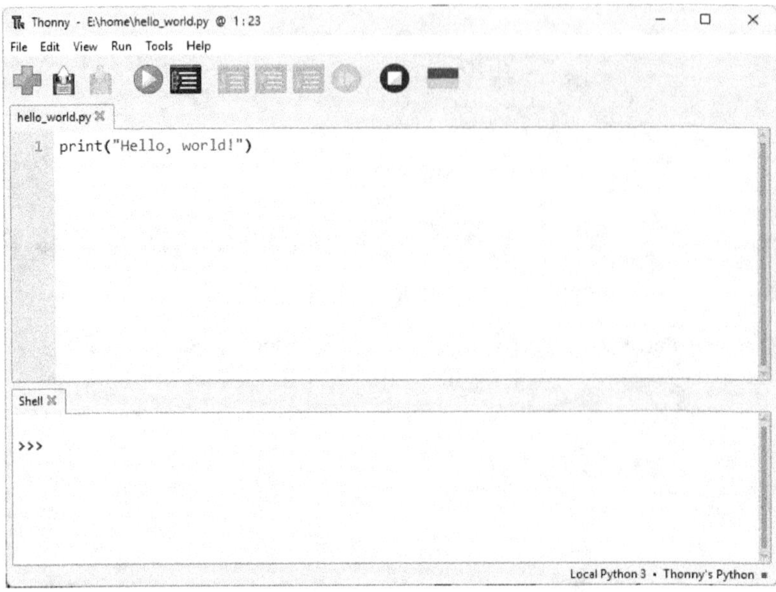

Fig 1-x. Thonny Open hello_world.py from "This computer"

You should see the following in Thonny's Program / Script Area:

```
print("Hello, world!")
```

Now switch to the MicroPython interpreter on the Pico and choose Save as... from the File menu. Select the "Raspberry Pi Pico" button in the message box.

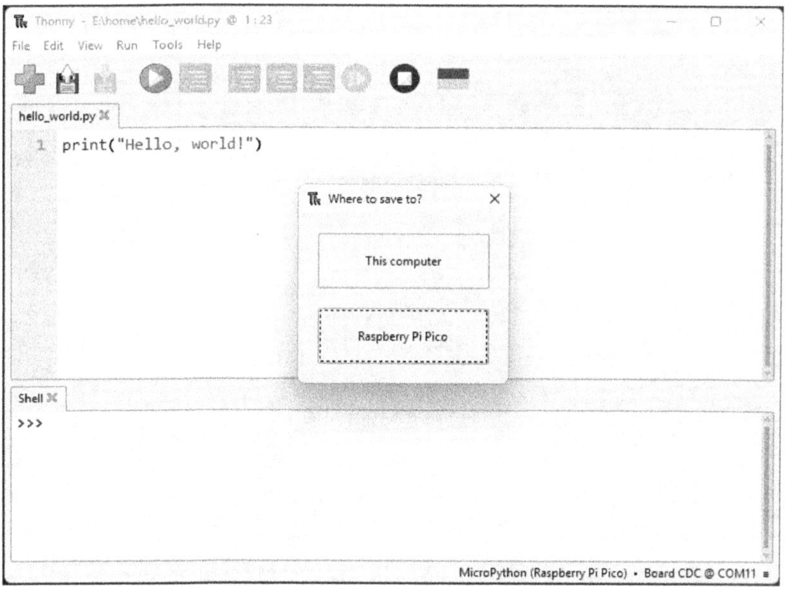

Fig 1-x. Thonny Save hello_world.py to the Pico

A dialog box opens asking you for a File name to save to *on the Pico*.

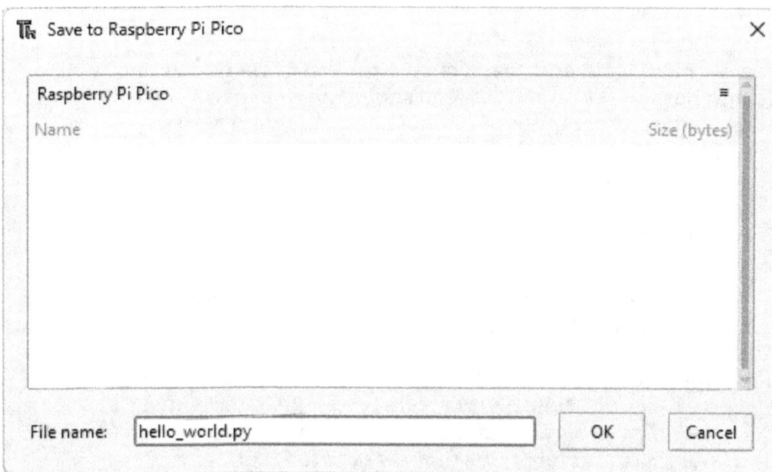

Fig 1-x. Thonny Save hello_world.py to the Pico

Save your program to the Pico by choosing OK.

This time when you run hello_world.py, the *MicroPython* interpreter *on the Pico* will execute the program that you just saved *on the Pico*!

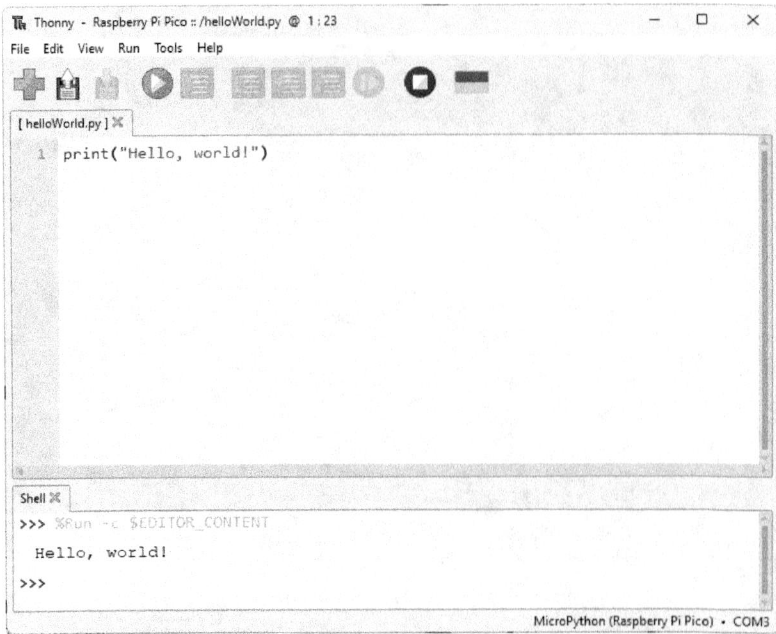

Fig 1-x. Thonny running the hello_world.py program on the Pico

Since Thonny has stored your program to the Pico's flash memory, you can re-run it again and again, even after you cycle power on the Pico. Just to be cautious, however, you should keep backup copies of your MicroPython programs on your host computer and possibly even in a code repository like GitHub. You never know when you might need to restore a backup!

Chapter Summary

In this chapter, we've covered how to install the Thonny IDE on a host computer and run MicroPython code in Thonny, both in its shell and in its program / script areas. MicroPython was then installed on a Pico and connected it to the host computer. After connecting Thonny to the Pico, we then ran MicroPython code on the Pico, reopened the hello_world.py program previously saved on the host computer, saved it to your Pico, and ran it this time *on the Pico*!

References and Further Exploration

Damien George

- https://dpgeorge.net/

Thonny

- https://thonny.org/

MicroPython

- https://www.kickstarter.com/projects/214379695/micro-python-python-for-microcontrollers
- https://micropython.org/

Raspberry Pi Pico W

- https://datasheets.raspberrypi.org/pico/getting_started_with_pico.pdf
- https://www.raspberrypi.com/documentation/microcontrollers/raspberry-pi-pico.html

Raspberry Pi Pico W: Datasheets

- https://datasheets.raspberrypi.org/pico/pico_datasheet.pdf
- https://datasheets.raspberrypi.org/rp2040/rp2040_datasheet.pdf
- https://datasheets.raspberrypi.org/rp2040/hardware_design_with_rp2040.pdf
- https://datasheets.raspberrypi.com/picow/RPi-PicoW-PUBLIC-20220607.zip
- https://datasheets.raspberrypi.com/picow/PicoW-step.zip

Raspberry Pi Pico 2W: Datasheets

- http://datasheets.raspberrypi.com/picow/pico-2-w-datasheet.pdf
- https://datasheets.raspberrypi.com/rp2350/rp2350-datasheet.pdf
- https://datasheets.raspberrypi.com/rp2350/hardware-design-with-rp2350.pdf

Chapter 2

Chapter Contents

1. Introduction

2. Programming Environment and Setup
    a. Introduction
    b. Setup and Construction
    c. Code

3. Evaluating the MicroPython environment
    a. Introduction
    b. Code
    c. Procedure / Steps
    d. Tests and Results
    e. Questions

4. Using a Web API with JSON
    a. Introduction
    b. Code
    c. Procedure / Steps
    d. Tests and Results
    e. Questions

5. Extracting and combining JSON Data
    a. Introduction
    b. Code
    c. Steps
    d. Tests and Results
    e. Questions

6. Chapter Summary

7. References and Further Exploration

Hello, world! (from the astronauts and JSON)

Become familiar with your Pico's computational and machine-to-machine (M2M) capabilities using JSON

MicroPython on the Pico executes the lines of code in a Python module from top to bottom just as if you typed them interactively at a Python prompt in the Thonny Python Shell area. You can keep this module as a text file stored on your host computer or stored on the Pico itself. Often, you'll want to do both because the files on the host can serve as a backup in case you inadvertently change or erase the files on the target. Even better: maintain a backup of your MicroPython code on GitHub or other source code repository.

A great place to begin programming in MicroPython is to try out some of the basics of MicroPython programming like lists and dictionaries (which are especially relevant for parsing JSON objects) and then to write a simple one-line program like "Hello, world!" that takes an input, like a person's name.

But sometimes, even before running your MicroPython code on the Pico, you'll want to try it on the host system first in order to debug it, develop an algorithm's logic, or even benchmark it. Python on the host has access to all of the libraries, tools, etc. that comes with a full-fledged Python installation. MicroPython doesn't. It's limited by the minimal hardware resources it's running on. Timing how long a particular function takes to run on your host computer, for instance, can help you decide how best to implement an algorithm on your target system.

Finally, you'll check out the wireless external communications interface on your Pico. For Entity Event-Driven Embedded Pico

Systems, the network is the medium whereby machine-to-machine (M2M) informational exchanges occur. In this chapter, if you have access to a secure wireless network, you can use your Pico's machine-to-machine (M2M) communications capabilities to retrieve JSON files from multiple web APIs, parse and integrate the information on your Pico.

But do not connect your Pico to an insecure network.
This cannot be emphasized enough.

> ⚠ **Warning: DO NOT connect your Pico to an insecure network!!!**

Programming Environment and Setup

For the examples in this chapter, you'll need the following.

Programming Environment
Host computer running either:
- Windows
- Raspberry Pi OS or Linux
- macOS
Host computer with the following installed:
- Python 3.10 or above
- Thonny (thonny.org)
Target microcontroller:
- Pico with MicroPython installed
micro USB cable

Plug your Pico into your host computer with a micro USB cable.

Setup and Construction

Installing the network requests module

The Python requests module (https://requests.readthedocs.io/) is intuitive and has a user-friendly API. It is one of the most widely used networking libraries for interacting with web services and APIs using HTTP requests. It should be installed for your host's Local Python 3 interpreter as well as for your Pico's MicroPython interpreter.

Local Python 3 interpreter

To install the network requests module for Thonny's Local Python 3 interpreter running on your host, first select "Options..." from the Tools menu and choose "Local Python 3" from the dropdown menu:

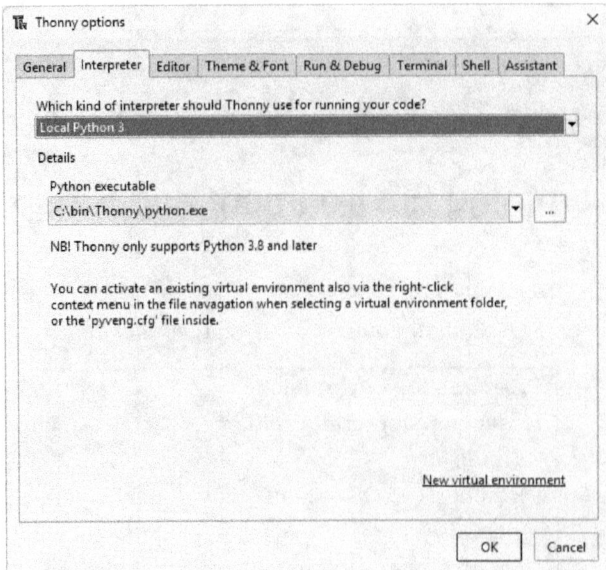

Fig 2-x. Thonny's Local Python 3 Interpreter

Then select "Manage packages..." from the Tools menu and search for "requests" to install the latest stable version of the package:

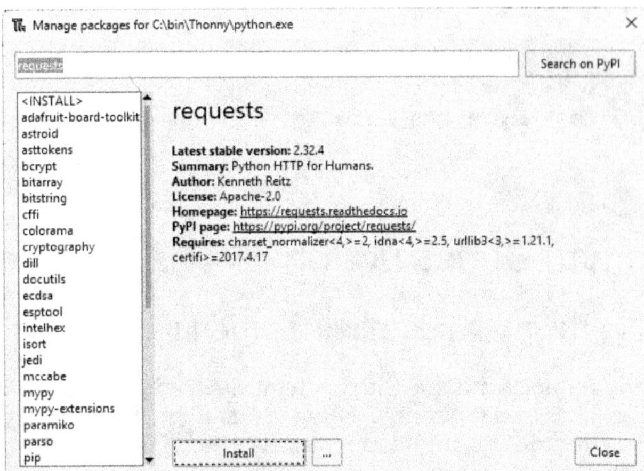

Fig 2-x. Installing CPython requests on Thonny

Pico MicroPython interpreter

To install the network requests module for Thonny's MicroPython interpreter, first select "Options..." from the Tools menu and choose "MicroPython (Raspberry Pi Pico)" from the dropdown menu:

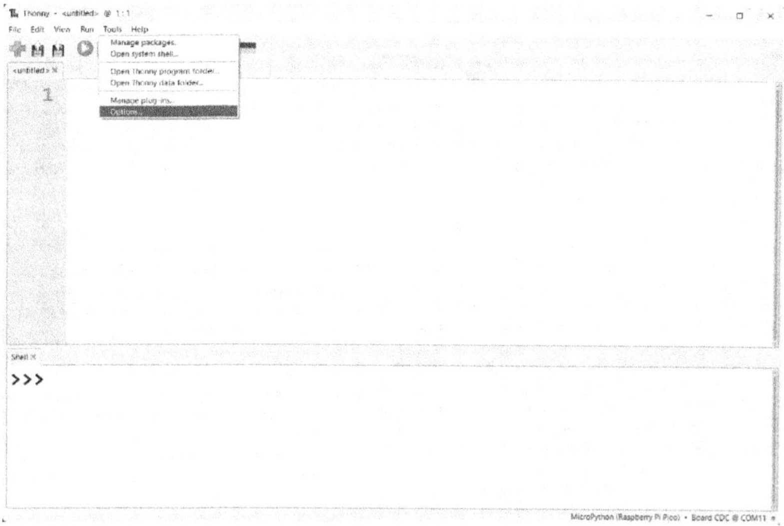

Fig 2-x. Thonny's MicroPython Interpreter

Then select "Manage packages..." from the Tools menu and search for "requests" to install the latest stable version of the package:

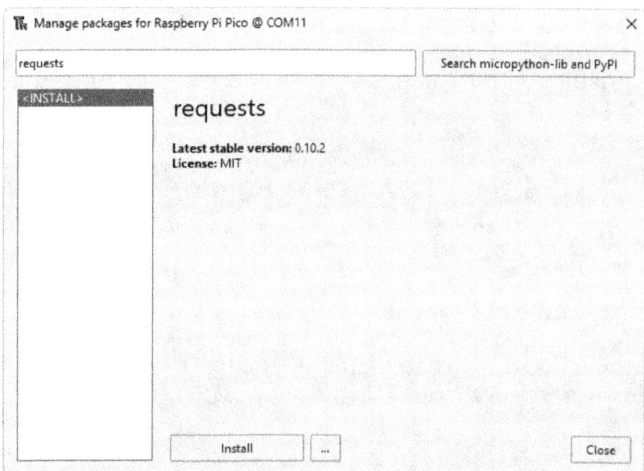

Fig 2-x. Installing MicroPython requests on Thonny

Code

Using Thonny (File > Save as), copy and save the Python modules below to your target Pico microcontroller.

my_secrets.py

This code separates sensitive information such as your WiFi credentials and other sensitive information from your application logic which helps prevent accidentally exposing sensitive information if you share your MicroPython code with others. It also makes your code more reusable since you can easily modify your authentication credentials in one place without having to change the Python programs that import it.

Keep this file in a directory accessible to the MicroPython interpreter's import path. If you use GitHub as a source code repository, make sure to add my_secrets.py to your .gitignore file so that my_secrets.py is not accidentally checked into GitHub.

```
# Add my_secrets.py to the .gitignore file to make sure
#   that my_secrets.py is never checked into GitHub
SSID     = 'MyNetwork'        # YOUR SSID (Network Name)
PASSWORD = 'MyPassword'       # YOUR WiFi PASSWORD
```

Fig 2-x. my_secrets_EXAMPLE.py

Code Explanation

Let's look at how to use the my_secrets.py module in your MicroPython code.

- The my_secrets module contains sensitive information such as your WiFi network's SSID and password. After importing it, you can access variables within the this module and assign their values to local variables.

```
import my_secrets
ssid = my_secrets.SSID             # Your SSID (Network Name)
password = my_secrets.PASSWORD  # Your WiFi PASSWORD
```

connect_wifi.py

You'll have to initiate a WiFi connection every time you use your Pico on a WiFi network. This module displays connection progress and handles connection failures. You can increase the max_retries variable if your Pico requires more time to establish a connection to your particular network.

> ⚠ **Warning: DO NOT connect your Pico to an insecure network!!!**

```
"""
connect_wifi.py
-----------
To connect to a wireless network,
    use the ``init_wlan()`` function
To obtain the IP address, use the ``get_ip()`` function

Example::
        >>> import connect_wifi
        >>> connect_wifi.init_wlan('Your Network Name',       \
                                    'Your Network Password' \
                                    max_retries=23)
        >>> connect_wifi.get_ip()

For information on MicroPython's WLAN built-in WiFi
    interfaces, see:
    docs.micropython.org/en/latest/library/network.WLAN.html
"""
import network
from time import sleep


# Network error messages
NETWORK_CONNECTION_ERROR = "Network connection failed"
SSID_ERROR = "Failed to obtain IP address"

# Create a WLAN network interface object in Station (STA) mode
wlan = network.WLAN(network.STA_IF)

def init_wlan(ssid, password, max_retries=10):
    """Initiate a wireless LAN connnection

    :param ssid: wireless network name
    :param password: wireless network password
    :param max_retries: number of connection attempts before
        giving up

    :raise RuntimeError: If the network connection failed

    :return: True (successful connection);
             False (unsuccessful connection)
    :rtype: bool
    """

    # Activate network interface
    wlan.active(True)

    # Connect to the specified wireless network, using the
    #   wireless network name and password
    wlan.connect(ssid, password)

    # Print a message to the console saying that the device
    #   is trying to connect
```

```
    print('Waiting for connection...')

    # Continue to loop as long as there are connection attempts
    while max_retries > 0:
        # wlan.status() < 0: connection failure
        # wlan.status() >= 3: connection successful
        #   or has a valid IP address
        if wlan.status() < 0 or wlan.status() >= 3:
            break
        print(max_retries, '.', sep='', end='', )
        max_retries -= 1
        sleep(1)  # delay before retrying

    # Check if the connection was unsuccessful
    if wlan.status() != network.STAT_GOT_IP:
        raise RuntimeError(NETWORK_CONNECTION_ERROR)
        return False # unsuccessful connection

    # Connection was successful and an IP address was obtained
    else:
        # Get the IP address
        ip = wlan.ifconfig()[0]

        # Print a confirmation message to console
        print( 'Connected: ip = {}'.format(ip))
        return True  # successful connection

def get_ip():
    """Get the IP address if WiFi is connected

    :raise RuntimeError: If not connected

    :return: IP Address (successful connection);
             SSID_ERROR (unsuccessful connection)
    :rtype: bool
    """
    if wlan.isconnected():
        return wlan.ifconfig()[0]
    else:
        print('\nNot connected')
        raise RuntimeError(SSID_ERROR)
        return None
```

Fig 2-x. connect_wifi.py

Code Explanation

Note: For more information on MicroPython's WLAN built-in WiFi interfaces, see https://docs.micropython.org/en/latest/library/network.WLAN.html.

Let's look at how the code works.

- The network module is used for configuring and controlling WiFi connectivity on the Pico.
  The sleep() module function is needed to introduce delays in the code execution.

```
import network
from time import sleep
```

- Define network error messages that are printed to the console if a Runtime Error is raised.
  NETWORK_CONNECTION_ERROR: Unsuccessful network connection.
  SSID_ERROR: Unable to obtain an IP address because there is not a network connection.

```
NETWORK_CONNECTION_ERROR = "Network connection failed"
SSID_ERROR = "Failed to obtain IP address"
```

- Create a WLAN network interface object in "Station" (STA) mode to connect to an existing WiFi access point (like a home router).

```
wlan = network.WLAN(network.STA_IF)
```

- Define a function init_wlan() to initiate a wireless LAN connection that returns True if the network connection is successful.
  If the network connection is not successful, init_wlan() raises a Runtime Error, printing the NETWORK_CONNECTION_ERROR message and returns False.

  The init_wlan() function takes three arguments:
  - ssid: wireless network name
  - password: wireless network password
  - max_retries: number of connection attempts before giving up

```
def init_wlan(ssid, password, max_retries=10):
    ...
```

- wlan.active(True) activates the network interface.

  ```
  wlan.active(True)
  ```

- wlan.connect(ssid, password) connects to the specified wireless network, using the wireless network name ssid and password.

  ```
  wlan.connect(ssid, password)
  ```

- A message is printed to the console saying that the device is attempting to connect.

  ```
  print('Waiting for connection...')
  ```

- As long as there are connection attempts as specified by the max_retries argument, init_wlan() continues to loop, printing a dot ('.') to the console showing progress and delaying for a second between each retry attempt.
  The loop breaks if the there is a connection failure (wlan.status() < 0); it also breaks if successfully connected or it obtains a valid IP address (wlan.status() >= 3):

  ```
  while max_retries > 0:
      if wlan.status() < 0 or wlan.status() >= 3:
          break
  ```

```
        print(max_retries, '.', sep='', end='', )
        max_retries -= 1
        sleep(1)  # delay before retrying
```

- If the connection was unsuccessful, a RuntimeError with the NETWORK_CONNECTION_ERROR error message is raised and init_wlan() returns False (unsuccessful connection).

```
    if wlan.status() != network.STAT_GOT_IP:
        raise RuntimeError(NETWORK_CONNECTION_ERROR)
        return False
```

- However, if the connection was successful and an IP address was obtained, the ip addressed is printed to the console and init_wlan() returns True (successful connection):

```
    else:
        ip = wlan.ifconfig()[0]

        print( 'Connected: ip = {}'.format(ip))
        return True
```

- The module function get_ip() returns the IP address if connected to the WiFi network. If not connected to the WiFi network, the function raises a Runtime Error, printing the SSID_ERROR message to the console.

  Note that the ifconfig() method returns a 4-tuple (IP address, subnet mask, gateway, DNS server), and that ifconfig()[0] accesses the IP address.

```
def get_ip():
    if wlan.isconnected():
        return wlan.ifconfig()[0]
    else:
        print('\nNot connected')
        raise RuntimeError(SSID_ERROR)
        return None
```

Evaluating the MicroPython environment

In this section, you'll first write a program for your host computer and the exact same program for your Pico. Both your host and Pico will execute the identical REPL (Read, Evaluate, Print, and Loop) code.

Then you'll write a "Hello, world!" program that accepts a person's name as an input, a program that determines whether a word or phrase is a palindrome, and one that converts temperatures from Fahrenheit to Celsius (and vice-versa). Running a test batch of these programs on both your host computer and your Pico with various inputs allows you to check if the actual outputs are the ones you expected. It's a quick sanity check which verifies that your embedded Pico system is up and running.

The Fibonacci sequence is defined as 0, 1, and the sum of the previous two Fibonacci numbers past that (https://en.wikipedia.org/wiki/Fibonacci_sequence):

$F_0 = 0$, $F_1 = 1$ and $F_n = F_{n-1} + F_{n-2}$ for $n > 1$

These numbers can be generated in Python both iteratively and recursively.

On a host computer, the iterative version executes *much, much faster* than the recursive version does when calculating the nth term in the series and n is greater than 30 (or so). By graphing the elapsed times for the recursive version, it will be clear that, given a choice between the two algorithms, you should choose the iterative version for the Pico over the recursive one—especially if calculational speed is a consideration.

When developing algorithms for the Pico, sometimes first trying out an algorithm on your host computer will tell you enough about which option to use. Or, if you don't have a choice, if you *must* use the recursive Fibonacci version, then at least you'll know that some adjustment (such as *memoization*) or workaround (such as lookup tables) should be employed. Without an adjustment, for example, the time to calculate each new term using the recursive Fibonacci algorithm grows exponentially, almost doubling the time it took to calculate the previous term.

We end this section with a *knock-knock* joke.

- *Knock-knock.*
- **Who's there?**
- *UUID.*
- **UUID who?**
- *If UUID generate an Apollo NCS string, I wouldn't have to keep track of everyone's unique IDs!*

The UUID (https://en.wikipedia.org/wiki/Universally_unique_identifier) was originally developed by Apollo Computer in the 1980s as part of their Network Computing System (NCS). Since then it has evolved into a 128-bit number that is often used to uniquely identify objects in computer systems. With just a few lines of code, you'll learn how easy it is to create high-quality, cryptographically secure UUIDs and also how to use Python to check whether a string a given string qualifies as a UUID or not. In later chapters, you'll use it to uniquely identify events that your Entity-Event Driven Embedded Pico System originates.

Code

Using Thonny (File > Save as), copy and save the Python modules (text files) below to a directory on your host computer and also to your target Pico.

REPL_script.py

The following code shows some Python basics working. You can run it on your host computer or on your target Pico.

```
''' Quick sanity check Python script '''

# Hello, world!
print("Hello, world!")
s1="Hello";s2=", again!"; print(s1+s2)

# Tuple
xTuple =('a','b','c')+('d','e','f')
print(f'\nxTuple = {xTuple}')

# List
yList  =[1,2,3]+[4,5,6]
print(f'\nyList = {yList}')

# Dictionary
D = {'0':0, 'a':1, 'b':2, 'c':3}
D['b'] = 52
D['d'] = 4
print(f"""\nDictionary:
```

```
    D = {D},
    len(D) = {len(D)},
    D.keys() = {D.keys()},
    D.values() = {D.values()}
    """)

# Palindrome
test_string='Are we not drawn onward, drawn onward to new era?'
input_string = "".join(c.upper() for c in test_string \
                       if c.isalpha())
reversed_string = ''.join(reversed(input_string))
if input_string == reversed_string:
    print(f'PALINDROME: {test_string}')
else:
    print(f'NOT a PALINDROME: {test_string}')

# Temperature Conversion
tempCelsius = 100.0
print(f"\nFahrenheit: {(9.0/5.0 * tempCelsius) + 32.0}")
```

Fig 2-x. REPL_script.py

hello_world_HOST.py

For general computing, CPython is the standard and most widely used implementation of Python. This Hello, world! program can be useful for debugging. It runs on most host computers with CPython installed and can be called to display information about the Python script's environment along with a friendly, personalized greeting.

```
import platform, sys

def say_hello(name="world"):
    '''Print info about the host computer and greeting'''
    mySoftwareVersion = "1.0"
    myPlatform = platform.uname()
    mySys = sys.implementation

    print(f'SoftwareVersion = {mySoftwareVersion}')
    print(f'myPlatform: {myPlatform}')
    print(f'mySys: {mySys}')
    print(f'Hello, {name}!\n')
```

Fig 2-x. hello_world_HOST.py

Code Explanation

Let's look at how the code works.

- The platform module gives you access to your host computer's operating system name, hardware information, etc. The sys module function provides access to system-specific parameters and functions.

```
import platform, sys
```

- Define a function named say_hello() that takes an optional argument name which defaults to "world" if none is provided when calling the function.

```
def say_hello(name="world"):
    ...
```

- Initialize the variable mySoftwareVersion to 1.0.
  ```
  mySoftwareVersion = 1.0
  ```
- Retrieve information about the current operating system and hardware.
  ```
  myPlatform = platform.uname()
  ```
- Retrieve information about implementation-specific data.
  ```
  mySys = sys.implementation
  ```
- print(...) variable values using an f-string for formatted output.
  ```
  print(f'SoftwareVersion = {mySoftwareVersion}')
  print(f'myPlatform: {myPlatform}')
  print(f'mySys: {mySys}')
  print(f'Hello, {name}!\n')"
  ```

hello_world_TARGET.py

MicroPython is a lightweight, efficient implementation of Python 3 optimized for microcontrollers and other resource-constrained devices; it is ideal for embedded systems. But it has some significant differences with the CPython implementation of Python 3. For example, even though the platform library in MicroPython mirrors some of the functionality found in CPython, the counterpart to platform.uname() in CPython is os.uname() in MicroPython.

This Hello, world! program for your target Pico can be useful for debugging. It runs on the Pico with MicroPython installed and can be called to display information about the MicroPython script's environment along with a friendly, personalized greeting.

```
import os, sys

def say_hello(name="world"):
    '''Print info about the system and greeting'''
    mySoftwareVersion = "1.0"
    myPlatform = os.uname()
    mySys = sys.implementation

    print(f'SoftwareVersion = {mySoftwareVersion}')
    print(f'myPlatform: {myPlatform}')
    print(f'mySys: {mySys}')
    print(f'Hello, {name}!\n')
```

Fig 2-x. hello_world_TARGET.py

Code Explanation

Let's look at how the code works.

- The os module gives you access to your host computer's operating system name, hardware information, etc. The sys module function provides access to system-specific parameters and functions.

```
import os, sys
```

- Define a function named say_hello() that takes an optional argument name which defaults to "world" if none is provided when calling the function.

```
def say_hello(name="world"):
    ...
```

- Initialize the variable mySoftwareVersion to 1.0.

```
    mySoftwareVersion = 1.0: This line initializes a variable
mySoftwareVersion to 1.0.
```

- Retrieve information about the current operating system and hardware.
  Note that os.uname() is not specific to MicroPython but is also a part of the standard Python os module on Unix-like systems.

```
    myPlatform = os.uname()
```

- Retrieve information about implementation-specific data.

```
    mySys = sys.implementation
```

- print(...) variable values using an f-string for formatted output.

```
    print(f'SoftwareVersion = {mySoftwareVersion}')
    print(f'myPlatform: {myPlatform}')
    print(f'mySys: {mySys}')
    print(f'Hello, {name}!\n')"
```

palindrome.py

This program determines whether the string argument passed to it is a palindrome or not.

```
def is_palindrome(s):
    ''' Determine whether s is a palindrome or not '''
    r1="".join(list([c for c in s.upper() if c.isalpha()]))
    r2="".join(reversed(r1))
    print(f'PALINDROME: {s}') if r1 == r2 else print(\
                                f'NOT a PALINDROME: {s}')
```

Fig 2-x. palindrome.py

convert_temperature.py

This MicroPython module defines two functions for converting temperatures between Celsius and Fahrenheit.

```
def CtoF(tempCelsius):
    ''' Convert Celsius to Fahrenheit '''
    return (9.0/5.0 * tempCelsius) + 32.0

def FtoC(tempFahrenheit):
    ''' Convert Fahrenheit to Celsius '''
    return 5.0/9.0 * (tempFahrenheit - 32.0)
```

Fig 2-x. convert_temperature.py

batch_test_HOST.py

This code quickly checks hello_world, palindrome, and convert_temperature modules on your host computer.

```
''' Quickly check hello_world, palindrome, \
    and convert_temperature modules '''

# hello_world
from hello_world_HOST import say_hello
say_hello()
say_hello("again")
say_hello("Young Rustwalker")

# palindrome
from palindrome import is_palindrome
is_palindrome("Was it a car or a cat I saw?")
is_palindrome("A man, a plan, a canal, Panama!")
is_palindrome("Are we not drawn onward, "
              "drawn onward to new era?")

is_palindrome("rotated")
is_palindrome("Mr. Robin ate my metal worm.")
is_palindrome("Anne, I vote more cars race Rome to Paris.")

# convert_temperature
from convert_temperature import CtoF, FtoC
print(f"\nCtoF(0.0) = {CtoF(0.0)}")
print(f"CtoF(100.0) = {CtoF(100.0)}")
print(f"\nFtoC(32.0) = {FtoC(32.0)}")
print(f"FtoC(212.0) = {FtoC(212.0)}")
```

Fig 2-x. batch_test_HOST.py

batch_test_TARGET.py

This code quickly checks hello_world, palindrome, and convert_temperature modules on your target Pico.

```
''' Quickly check hello_world, palindrome, \
    and convert_temperature modules '''
```

```
# hello_world
from hello_world_TARGET import say_hello
say_hello()
say_hello("again")
say_hello("Young Rustwalker")

# palindrome
from palindrome import is_palindrome
is_palindrome("Was it a car or a cat I saw?")
is_palindrome("A man, a plan, a canal, Panama!")
is_palindrome("Are we not drawn onward"
              "drawn onward to new era?")

is_palindrome("rotated")
is_palindrome("Mr. Robin ate my metal worm.")
is_palindrome("Anne, I vote more cars race Rome to Paris.")

# convert_temperature
from convert_temperature import CtoF, FtoC
print(f"\nCtoF(0.0) = {CtoF(0.0)}")
print(f"CtoF(100.0) = {CtoF(100.0)}")
print(f"\nFtoC(32.0) = {FtoC(32.0)}")
print(f"FtoC(212.0) = {FtoC(212.0)}")
```

Fig 2-x. batch_test_TARGET.py

fibonacci_n.py

This module defines iterative and recursive functions for finding the *nth* term in the Fibonacci Sequence.

```
# Iteratively find the nth in the Fibonacci Sequence
def fibonacci_iterative(n):
    ''' '''
    a, b = 0, 1
    for i in range(n):
        a, b = b, a+b
    return a

# Recursively find the nth in the Fibonacci Sequence
def fibonacci_recursive(n):
    if n in {0, 1}:  # Base case halting the recursion
        return n
    return fibonacci_recursive(n - 1) \
           + fibonacci_recursive(n - 2)
```

Fig 2-x. fibonacci_n.py

time_fibonacci_HOST.py

This code uses the time.perf_counter() module function to time the iterative and recursive functions for finding the *nth* term in the Fibonacci Sequence on your host computer.

```
import time
from fibonacci_n import fibonacci_iterative, fibonacci_recursive

# Time iterative Fibonacci algorithm
print("\nElapsed times in ms for iterative Fibonacci algorithm:")
for n in range(0, 36, 5):
    start = time.perf_counter()
    result = fibonacci_iterative(n)
    end = time.perf_counter()
    elapsed_ms = (end - start) * 1000  # convert to milliseconds
    print(f'F_i({n}): {result} = {elapsed_ms:.5f} ms')

# Time recursive Fibonacci algorithm
print("\nElapsed times in ms for recursive Fibonacci algorithm:")
for n in range(0, 36, 5):
    start = time.perf_counter()
    result = fibonacci_recursive(n)
    end = time.perf_counter()
    elapsed_ms = (end - start) * 1000  # convert to milliseconds
    print(f'F_r({n}): {result} = {elapsed_ms:.5f} ms')
```

Fig 2-x. time_fibonacci_HOST.py

time_fibonacci_TARGET.py

This code uses the time.ticks_ms() module function to time the iterative and recursive functions for finding the nth term in the Fibonacci Sequence on your Pico.

```
import time
from fibonacci_n import fibonacci_iterative, fibonacci_recursive

# Time iterative Fibonacci algorithm
print("\nElapsed times in ms for iterative Fibonacci algorithm:")
for n in range(0, 36, 5):
    start = time.ticks_ms()
    result = fibonacci_iterative(n)
    end = time.ticks_ms()
    elapsed_ms = end - start
    print(f'F_i({n}): {result} = {elapsed_ms} ms')

# Time recursive Fibonacci algorithm
print("\nElapsed times in ms for recursive Fibonacci algorithm:")
for n in range(0, 36, 5):
    start = time.ticks_ms()
    result = fibonacci_recursive(n)
```

```
    end = time.ticks_ms()
    elapsed_ms = end - start
    print(f'F_r({n}): {result} = {elapsed_ms} ms')
```

Fig 2-x. time_fibonacci_TARGET.py

my_uuid4.py

This code generates a random UUID compliant to IETF RFC 4122 using 16 high-quality, cryptographically secure random bytes and runs on a host computer with Python installed. It sets the "version" and "variant" bits to be compliant with RFC 4122 section 3 (https://datatracker.ietf.org/doc/html/rfc4122).

```
# my_uuid4.py - Generate a random UUID compliant to IETF RFC 4122
#
# See: https://datatracker.ietf.org/doc/html/rfc4122
#      https://datatracker.ietf.org/doc/html/rfc9562
#      https://docs.python.org/3/library/uuid.html
# ----------------------------------------------------------------

import os
import uuid

def my_uuid4():
    # Get 16 high-quality, cryptographically secure random bytes
    random_x = bytearray(os.urandom(16))

    # Set the "version" and "variant" bits per RFC 4122
    random_x[6] = (random_x[6] & 0x0F) | 0x40
    random_x[8] = (random_x[8] & 0x3F) | 0x80

    # Generate a 32-character hexadecimal string
    h = random_x.hex()

    # Return the string formatted as a UUID string with hyphens
    return str('-'.join((h[0:8], h[8:12], \
                         h[12:16], h[16:20], h[20:32])))

def is_rfc4122_UUID(test_string):
    # Try creating a valid UUID object from the string;
    #   raise ValueError if the format is invalid
    try:
        parsed_string = uuid.UUID(test_string)
        if parsed_string.variant == uuid.RFC_4122 and \
           parsed_string.version == 4:
            return True
        # The string is not in a valid UUID format
        else:
            return False
    # The string is not a UUID
    except ValueError:
        return False
```

```python
if __name__ == '__main__':
    for _ in range(5):
        x = my_uuid4()
        print(f"RFC version 4, 4122 compliant? " \
              f"{is_rfc4122_UUID(x)}: '{x}'")

    not_UUID = "not-a-good-uuid-string"
    print(f"\nnot_UUID = '{not_UUID}'")
    print(f"RFC version 4, 4122 compliant? " \
          f"{is_rfc4122_UUID(not_UUID)}")

    nil_UUID = "00000000-0000-0000-0000-000000000000"
    print(f"\nnil_UUID = '{nil_UUID}'")
    print(f"RFC version 4, 4122 compliant? " \
          f"{is_rfc4122_UUID(nil_UUID)}")

    omni_UUID = "FFFFFFFF-FFFF-FFFF-FFFF-FFFFFFFFFFFF"
    print(f"\nomni_UUID = '{omni_UUID}'")
    print(f"RFC version 4, 4122 compliant? " \
          f"{is_rfc4122_UUID(omni_UUID)}")
```

Fig 2-x. my_uuid4.py

Procedure / Steps

⚠ **Warning:** Do not connect your host or your Pico to the internet on an insecure network!!!

Run the Python code on your host computer

1. In Thonny, go to Tools > Options > Interpreter
   Select "Local Python 3"
2. Go to File > Open
   Select the copy of REPL_script.py on your host computer
3. Go to Run
   Select "Run current script"
4. Open and run:
   batch_test_HOST.py
5. Open and run:
   time_fibonacci_HOST.py

Run the MicroPython code on your target Pico

6. Go to Tools > Options > Interpreter
   Select "MicroPython (Pico)"
7. Go to File > Open
   Select the copy of REPL_script.py on your target Pico
8. Go to Run
   Select "Run current script"
9. Open and run:
   batch_test_TARGET.py

Note: time_fibonacci_TARGET.py takes a *lot* longer to run on your Pico than time_fibonacci_HOST.py does running on your host!

Run the Python code on your host computer

10. In Thonny, go to Tools > Options > Interpreter
    Select "Local Python 3"
11. Go to File > Open
    Select the copy of my_uuid4.py on your target Pico
12. Go to Run
    Select "Run current script"
13. Open and run:
    my_uuid4.py

Tests and Results

REPL_script.py

In Thonny's Python Shell, when REPL_script.py is run on the host computer using the "Local Python 3" interpreter and when REPL_script.py is re-run on the target using the "MicroPython (Pico)" interpreter, something like the following should appear in both instances:

```
Hello, world!
Hello, again!

xTuple = ('a', 'b', 'c', 'd', 'e', 'f')

yList = [1, 2, 3, 4, 5, 6]

Dictionary:
      D = {'0': 0, 'a': 1, 'b': 52, 'c': 3, 'd': 4},
      len(D) = 5,
      D.keys() = dict_keys(['0', 'a', 'b', 'c', 'd']),
      D.values() = dict_values([0, 1, 52, 3, 4])

PALINDROME: Are we not drawn onward, drawn onward to new era?

Fahrenheit: 212.0
```

batch_test_HOST.py on your host computer

In Thonny's Python Shell, when batch_test_HOST.py script is run on the host computer using the "Local Python 3" interpreter, something like the following should appear (your host computer's platform specific details will likely be different):

```
SoftwareVersion = 1.0
myPlatform: uname_result(...)
mySys: namespace(...)
Hello, world!

SoftwareVersion = 1.0
myPlatform: uname_result(...)
mySys: namespace(...)
Hello, again!

SoftwareVersion = 1.0
myPlatform: uname_result(...)
mySys: namespace(...)
Hello, Young Rustwalker!

PALINDROME: Was it a car or a cat I saw?
PALINDROME: A man, a plan, a canal, Panama!
```

```
PALINDROME: Are we not drawn onward, drawn onward to new era?
NOT a PALINDROME: rotated
NOT a PALINDROME: Mr. Robin ate my metal worm.
NOT a PALINDROME: Anne, I vote more cars race Rome to Paris.

CtoF(0.0)   = 32.0
CtoF(100.0) = 212.0

FtoC(212.0) = 100.0
FtoC(32.0)  = 0.0
```

batch_test_TARGET.py on your target Pico

In Thonny's Python Shell, when batch_test_TARGET.py is run on a target Pico microcontroller using the "MicroPython (Pico)" interpreter, something like the following should appear:

```
SoftwareVersion = 1.0
myPlatform: (sysname='rp2', ...)
mySys: (name='micropython', ...)
Hello, world!

SoftwareVersion = 1.0
myPlatform: (sysname='rp2', ...)
mySys: (name='micropython', ...)
Hello, again!

SoftwareVersion = 1.0
myPlatform: (sysname='rp2', ...)
mySys: (name='micropython', ...)
Hello, Young Rustwalker!

PALINDROME: Was it a car or a cat I saw?
PALINDROME: A man, a plan, a canal, Panama!
PALINDROME: Are we not drawn onward, drawn onward to new era?
NOT a PALINDROME: rotated
NOT a PALINDROME: Mr. Robin ate my metal worm.
NOT a PALINDROME: Anne, I vote more cars race Rome to Paris.

CtoF(0.0)   = 32.0
CtoF(100.0) = 212.0

FtoC(212.0) = 100.0
FtoC(32.0)  = 0.0
```

time_fibonacci_HOST.py on your host computer

For the last step which executes time_fibonacci_HOST.py on your host computer, Python will respond with something like (these elapsed times are taken from my host computer at the time of this writing):

```
Elapsed times in ms for iterative Fibonacci algorithm:
F_i(0): 0 = 0.00310 ms
F_i(5): 5 = 0.00580 ms
F_i(10): 55 = 0.00560 ms
F_i(15): 610 = 0.00660 ms
F_i(20): 6765 = 0.00590 ms
F_i(25): 75025 = 0.00590 ms
F_i(30): 832040 = 0.00670 ms
F_i(35): 9227465 = 0.00610 ms

Elapsed times in ms for recursive Fibonacci algorithm:
F_r(0): 0 = 0.00280 ms
F_r(5): 5 = 0.00510 ms
F_r(10): 55 = 0.02400 ms
F_r(15): 610 = 0.22890 ms
F_r(20): 6765 = 4.36650 ms
F_r(25): 75025 = 35.92960 ms
F_r(30): 832040 = 623.03760 ms
F_r(35): 9227465 = 8898.43010 ms
```

For the iterative Fibonacci algorithm, we see that it takes roughly about the same amount of time (~0.006 ms) to calculate any of the terms in the series.

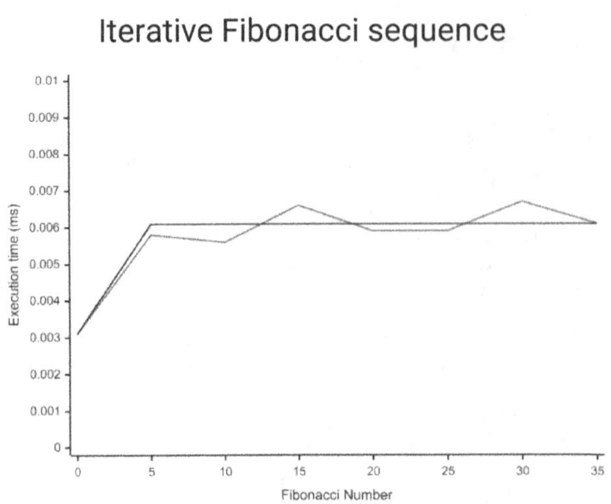

Fig 2-x. Elapsed times in ms for iterative Fibonacci algorithm

The recursive Fibonacci algorithm, however, is a different story. Dividing the elapsed time for the recursive version of $F_r(35)$ by the elapsed time for the iterative version $F_i(35)$, we see that the latter is 1.46 *million* times faster for that particular term:

$F_r(35) / F_i(35) = 8898.43010 / 0.00610 = 1,458,759.03279 \approx$ 1.46e+06

Here's a graph to illustrate how the recursive algorithm for the Fibonacci starts climbing exponentially once the calculation gets past the 30th term (or so).

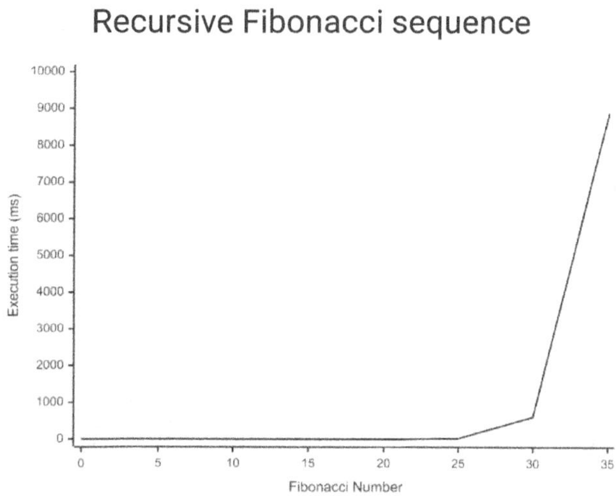

Fig 2-x. Elapsed times in ms for recursive Fibonacci algorithm

Algorithms matter. They can make the difference between a fast and responsive application on your Pico and one that takes a long time. Checking them out on your host system ahead of time is a good practice when deciding which to use.

Universally Unique Identifiers (UUIDs)

We can use the UUID module in Python's uuid library to check whether a string meets the requirements for UUID. How? First by checking the format of the string. Trying to create a valid UUID object from the string will raise a ValueError if it's in the wrong format. Example: 'not-a-good-uuid-string'. If, on the other hand, the string is well-formatted, it might be the wrong variant type or version. The uuid.UUID() object can tell you that, too, by examining its variant and version properties.

When you run the my_uuid4.py program using the Python interpreter on your host computer, you might see in Thonny's Python Shell something like:

```
>>> %Run my_uuid4.py
RFC version 4, 4122 compliant? True: 'cc5ab519-39c2-4cbb-971e-
92fdfd6208e5'
RFC version 4, 4122 compliant? True: '06357497-db21-438c-af59-
1126432e2000'
RFC version 4, 4122 compliant? True: 'dee4a10a-b09e-49a1-8ae1-
afc371953dfc'
RFC version 4, 4122 compliant? True: 'b26f8879-bcd1-46e4-b14a-
079396965dec'
RFC version 4, 4122 compliant? True: '3ad3636f-1489-4baf-a63f-
69628355ee9e'

not_UUID = 'not-a-good-uuid-string'
RFC version 4, 4122 compliant? False

nil_UUID = '00000000-0000-0000-0000-000000000000'
RFC version 4, 4122 compliant? False

omni_UUID = 'FFFFFFFF-FFFF-FFFF-FFFF-FFFFFFFFFFFF'
RFC version 4, 4122 compliant? False
```

Congratulations! You have explored MicroPython and gained insights into how algorithms can significantly affect the calculational times for your Pico. You've also learned how to create RFC 4122 version 4 compliant UUIDs which will be used in this book to uniquely identify events that an Entity Event-Driven Embedded Pico System can generate.

Questions

1. In interactive sessions, Python echoes expression results so you don't have to necessarily use print() statements. For example, Python will echo "Hello, world!" if you type "Hello, world!" at a Python command prompt.

    a) Why might it be advantageous to *not* use print() statements in some cases?

    b) How might scripts kept in Python modules be used as sanity checks if a microcontroller like the Pico isn't behaving or responding as expected?

2. What are some of the reasons for using default arguments in print() statements such as the hello_world.py program? Are there any disadvantages? Why might it be useful to print the software version of your code and the MicroPython os.uname() info in a program as simple as hello_world_TARGET.py running on the Pico?

3. Using Python modules saves you the trouble of typing the same thing over and over again. Python modules also allow you to structure and reuse code in functions, classes and as objects that can accept data, process information, return values, etc. Further, Python modules can be kept under configuration control with systems like git and run from your host computer.

    a) Identify some ways that Python modules can be used for testing microcontrollers like the Pico using various inputs under different scenarios.

    b) How might modules be used in Continuous Integration / Testing / Delivery systems?

4. How can expected outputs be used to test functionality given a set of known inputs? More specifically, how can arguments having different values be used to check microcontrollers like the Pico periodically throughout the system development lifecycle?

5. Convert the three strings above that are "NOT a PALINDROME" ("rotated", "Mr. Robin ate my metal ...", "Anne, I vote ...") into palindromes and check them with is_palindrome(). Why might "cleaning data" (in this case, fixing the palindromes) as much as possible before processing that data on a target microcontroller like the Pico be important to do?

6. What is the equivalent Fahrenheit temperature of -273.15 degrees Celsius? Express this in degrees Kelvin. Should temperature conversion programs be able to calculate values below this thermodynamic temperature? Why or why not?

7. The code for time_fibonacci_HOST.py that runs on your host computer uses time.perf_counter() whereas the code for time_fibonacci_TARGET.py that runs on the Pico uses time.ticks_ms(). Why?

   How does moving "business logic" such as the two types of Fibonacci algorithms into platform independent modules like fibonacci_n.py improve testability of an embedded system?

8. Using the iterative Fibonacci data above for the Pico, graph the elapsed times in ms for calculating the 8 terms shown of the Fibonacci sequence.

   a) When choosing which algorithm to use on a microcontroller like the Pico, why might it be sufficient to perform the two types of calculations, iterative and recursive, only on your host computer and not on the microcontroller itself?

   b) Should there be a limit placed on the value of *n* for the iterative Fibonacci algorithm?

   c) The Golden Ratio to 15 decimal places is 1.618033988749895. Calculate $F_i(1001)$ / $F_i(1000)$ to 15 decimal places. How much do these two numbers differ by? Can you use the Golden Ratio to calculate the nth term in the Fibonacci sequence for large *n*? (Hint: what is the exact value of the Golden Ratio?) Why or why not? How useful might this be for an embedded Pico system?

9. A Mersenne Prime is a prime number which has the form $M_n = 2^n - 1$ where *n* is an integer (https://en.wikipedia.org/wiki/Mersenne_prime). On Tuesday, January 19, 2038 at 3:14:07 AM (GMT) the UNIX timestamp in seconds will hit the 8th Mersenne Prime: $2147483647 = 2^{31} - 1$. This is the maximum value that can be represented by a signed, 32-bit integer. How might this pose a risk for some 32-bit microcontrollers?

10. Is 'f538cf88-9ed7-cafe-f00d-79b27f68673d' a RFC 4122 version 4 compliant UUID? (Hint: *no*). How can you find out using Thonny's Python interpreter? What about 'f538cf88-9ed7-41d6-ad14-79b27f68673d'? What are the risks associated with using this UUID string?

Using a Web API with JSON

Due to its ease of use and feature-richness, Python's requests library (https://requests.readthedocs.io/en/latest/) is one of the most widely adopted ways for interacting with web services and retrieving data from external sources on the internet. The corresponding requests library in MicroPython can be used to access publicly available web APIs that provide information in a data interchange format known as JSON (JavaScript Object Notation: https://www.json.org/json-en.html).

Two systems exchanging JSON data must cooperate when sending and receiving such data if they are to understand the contents of each other's messages. The 2017 international standard (ECMA-404 and ISO/IEC 21778:2017) defines the JSON data interchange syntax for valid JSON text. Because its lightweight and human readable format can also readily be parsed by computers, however, it's easy to connect your Pico to the internet with MicroPython and interface to web APIs using JSON.

Fig 2-x. Image source: https://www.nasa.gov/reference/international-space-station/

JSON is widely supported by a number of computer languages. It is simple and concise in its expression, fast and straightforward to parse. JSON is commonly used by machine-to-machine (M2M) applications and Internet of things (IoT) devices to communicate with each other over wireless network channels (such as wifi, Bluetooth, RFID, NFC, LoRa) employing M2M communication protocols (such as http(s), MQTT, CoAP, OPC UA, LwM2M).

Other data formats like XML can also be used for M2M communications. But since they are more self-descriptive, they generally are slower and more cumbersome to parse. They typically include metadata about themselves in the form of attributes about their content which make them more suitable for applications like spreadsheets and word processors than for M2M communications.

JSON data simply contain key-value pairs that map directly to Python dictionaries and lists. JSON *objects* are unordered sets of key / value pairs written inside of curly braces ('{ }'). While a JSON object key must be a string, the associated values can be made up of multiple data types that can contain strings, numbers and booleans, null—and other JSON objects and arrays. JSON *arrays* are ordered lists of values written inside of square brackets ('[ ]'). They also can contain combinations of any valid JSON data type including other JSON arrays and objects which allows for complex data structures such as multidimensional arrays since one array can be stored inside another.

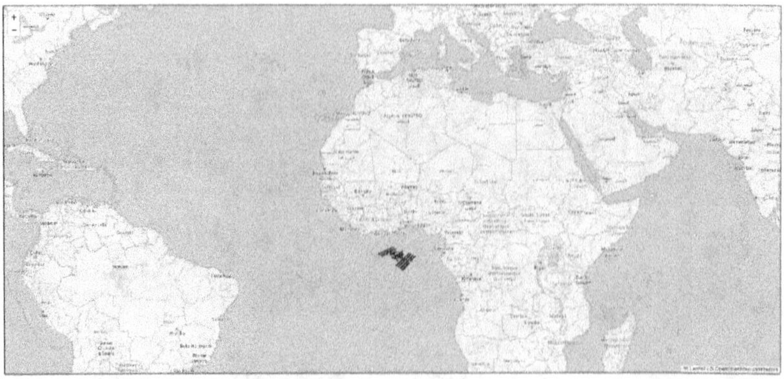

Fig 2-x. Image created using leaflet map data from OpenStreetMap (see Appendix F for details)

How many people are in space right now?

The *Open Notify API* website (http://open-notify.org/Open-Notify-API/) web API not only lists the names of the astronauts currently on the International Space Station (ISS) but it also gives their current location in latitude and longitude directly overhead (about 400km / 250 miles or so above the surface of the earth). This information originates from NASA in JSON format.

Open Notify's API (http://open-notify.org/Open-Notify-API/People-In-Space/) documentation specifies that it returns the number of people in space, their names and the spacecraft they're in—all in JSON format:

```
{
  "message": "success",
  "number":  NUMBER_OF_PEOPLE_IN_SPACE,
  "people":  [
    {"name": NAME, "craft": SPACECRAFT_NAME},
    ...
  ]
}
```

If you open a web browser on your host computer and call Open Notify's API in the address bar with http://api.open-notify.org/astros.json, the web API returns something like the following:

```
{
  "message": "success",
  "number":  7,
  "people":  [
    {"name": "Jasmin Moghbeli",     "craft": "ISS"},
    {"name": "Andreas Mogensen",    "craft": "ISS"},
    {"name": "Satoshi Furukawa",    "craft": "ISS"},
    {"name": "Konstantin Borisov", "craft": "ISS"},
    {"name": "Oleg Kononenko",      "craft": "ISS"},
    {"name": "Nikolai Chub",        "craft": "ISS"},
    {"name": "Loral O'Hara",        "craft": "ISS"}
  ]
}
```

The Open Notify API (http://open-notify.org/Open-Notify-API/ISS-Location-Now/) also returns the time and the location of the International Space Station (ISS) in JSON format:

```
{
  "message":        "success",
  "timestamp":      UNIX_TIME_STAMP,
  "iss_position": {
    "latitude":     CURRENT_LATITUDE,
    "longitude":    CURRENT_LONGITUDE
  }
}
```

If you open a web browser on your host computer and call its API in the address bar with http://api.open-notify.org/iss-now.json, the web API returns something like the following:

```
{
  "message":        "success",
  "timestamp":      1679250290,
  "iss_position": {
    "latitude":     "34.1509",
    "longitude":    "-9.2171"
  }
}
```

In this section, we'll request information from Open Notify's website containing the people currently in space as well of the location of the ISS. We'll do this first during an interactive session in the Thonny Python Shell, then with a MicroPython program that runs on your Pico.

This example shows how straightforward it is for your Pico to fetch JSON data from a web API.

Code

Using Thonny (File > Save as), copy and save the Python modules below to your Pico.

astronauts.py

The following code shows who's in space and their location (400km / ~250 miles overhead).

```
# astronauts.py - Show people in space and their location
#    (400km / ~250 miles overhead)
#    see: http://open-notify.org/,
#         https://github.com/open-notify/Open-Notify-API

import requests, sys

# Add my_secrets.py to the .gitignore file to make sure
#    that my_secrets.py is never checked into GitHub
import my_secrets
ssid = my_secrets.SSID             # Your SSID (Network Name)
password = my_secrets.PASSWORD   # Your WiFi PASSWORD

# Initialize the WiFi Interface
import connect_wifi
if not connect_wifi.init_wlan( \
                               ssid, \
                               password, \
                               max_retries=10):
    print('WiFi authentication error: {}'\
          .format(connect_wifi.SSID_ERROR))
    print('Exiting program')
    sys.exit(0)
else:
    ip_address = connect_wifi.get_ip()

# Request the JSON data for the astronauts currently in space
astronauts_URL = "http://api.open-notify.org/astros.json"
astronauts = requests.get(astronauts_URL, \
                           timeout=10)  # 10-second timeout
```

```
# Show people in space and their spacecraft if the HTTP \
#   response is successful
if astronauts.status_code == 200:  # (200 = OK)
    print(f"\nastronauts_in_space = {astronauts.json()}")
else:
    print("Unable to fetch astronaut data.")

# Close the connection to the server to release network resources
astronauts.close()

# Request the JSON data for the ISS location
iss_URL = "http://api.open-notify.org/iss-now.json"
iss_now = requests.get(iss_URL, timeout=10)  # 10-second timeout

# Show ISS location if the HTTP response is successful
if iss_now.status_code == 200:  # (200 = OK)
    print(f"\nISS_position_and_time = {iss_now.json()}")
else:
    print("Unable to fetch ISS position and time.")

# Close the connection to the server to release network resources
iss_now.close()
```

Fig 2-x. astronauts.py

Code Explanation

Let's look at how the code works.

- The requests library is used for making HTTP requests (like fetching JSON data from websites). The sys module is used to stop the execution of the current program if the WiFi network is unavailable.

```
import requests, sys
```

- The my_secrets module contains the name of your network (SSID) and your network password.

```
import my_secrets
ssid = my_secrets.SSID          # Your SSID (Network Name)
password = my_secrets.PASSWORD  # Your WiFi PASSWORD
```

- To initialize the WiFi interface, use the connect_wifi.init_wlan() and connect_wifi.get_ip() module functions.

```
# Initialize the WiFi Interface
if not connect_wifi.init_wlan(ssid, password, max_retries=10):
    print('WiFi authentication error: {}'.\
          format(connect_wifi.SSID_ERROR))
    print('Exiting program')
    sys.exit(0)
else:
    ip_address = connect_wifi.get_ip()
```

- Request the JSON data for the astronauts currently in space from the Open Notify website.

```
astronauts_URL = "http://api.open-notify.org/astros.json"
astronauts = requests.get(astronauts_URL, timeout=10)
```

- Show people in space and their spacecraft if the HTTP response is successful.

```
if astronauts.status_code == 200:  # (200 = OK)
    print(f"\nastronauts_in_space = {astronauts.json()}")
else:
    print("Unable to fetch astronaut data.")
```

- Close the connection to the server to release network resources.

```
astronauts.close()
```

- Request the JSON data for the ISS location from the Open Notify website.

```
iss_URL = "http://api.open-notify.org/iss-now.json"
iss_now = requests.get(iss_URL, timeout=10)  # 10-second timeout
```

- Show ISS location if the HTTP response is successful.

```
if iss_now.status_code == 200:  # (200 = OK)
    print(f"\nCurrent_ISS_position_and_time = {iss_now.json()}")
else:
    print("Unable to fetch ISS position and time.")
```

- Close the connection to the server to release network resources.

```
iss_now.close()
```

Procedure / Steps

> ⚠ **Warning:** Do not connect your host or your Pico to the internet on an insecure network!!!

Interactive session using CPython

We will first interact with the http://api.open-notify.org website using CPython running on your host. Select "Options..." from the Tools menu and choose "Local Python 3" from the dropdown menu.

1. In the the Python Shell area at the bottom of the Thonny window, click just to the right of the ">>>" symbols.
2. Import the requests and JSON libraries. Type the following and press **ENTER**:

   ```
   import requests, json
   ```
3. Get astronauts JSON data from Open Notify website. Type the following and press **ENTER**:

   ```
   astronauts_URL = "http://api.open-notify.org/astros.json"
   astronauts = requests.get(astronauts_URL, timeout=10)
   ```

4. Pretty print the JSON data on the console with an indent of 2 spaces. (Note: the CPython json.dumps() function has an indent argument but the corresponding MicroPython function does not.) Type the following and press **ENTER**:

```
print(json.dumps(astronauts, indent=2))
```

5. Get ISS location JSON data from Open Notify website. Type the following and press **ENTER**:

```
iss_URL = "http://api.open-notify.org/iss-now.json"
iss_now = requests.get(iss_URL, timeout=10)  # 10-second
timeout
```

6. Pretty print the JSON data on the console with an indent of 2 spaces. Type the following and press **ENTER**:

```
print(json.dumps(iss_now, indent=2))
```

astronauts.py

Run astonauts.py on your Pico.

1. In Thonny, go to Tools > Options > Interpreter
   Select "MicroPython (Raspberry Pi Pico)"
2. Go to File > Open
   Select astronauts.py
3. Go to Run
   Select "Run current script"

Tests and Results

Interactive session using CPython

In Thonny's Python Shell, when the astronauts JSON object is displayed, it will probably look something like:

```
{
  "people": [
    {
      "craft": "ISS",
      "name": "Tracy Caldwell Dyson"
    },
    ...
  ],
  "number": 12,
  "message": "success"
}
```

When the iss_now JSON object is displayed, it will probably look something like:

```
{
  "timestamp": 1753380593,
  "iss_position": {
    "longitude": "120.8612",
    "latitude": "-36.0439"
  },
  "message": "success"
}
```

astronauts.py

When astronauts.py is run, in Thonny's Python Shell window, something like the following should be displayed:

```
Waiting for connection...
10.9.8.7.6.5.Connected: ip = 192.168.0.100
```

After a short delay, this will be followed by something like:

```
astronauts_in_space =
{
  "people": [
    {
      "craft": "ISS",
      "name": "Zena Cardman"
    },
    ...
  ],
  "number": 7,
  "message": "success"
}

ISS_position_and_time =
{
  "timestamp": 1756843839,
  "iss_position": {
    "longitude": "-44.9900",
    "latitude": "48.2846"
  },
  "message": "success"
}
```

Congratulations!!! The example in this section shows how to retrieve JSON data from Open Notify's website on the people currently in space as well of the location of the ISS, first during an interactive session, then with a MicroPython program.

Questions

1. Why is "interface stability" important when an API becomes public? How can adding or removing parameters to an API request break compatibility with clients that use that API?

2. What are some of the services / resources provided by the WorldTimeAPI (https://worldtimeapi.org/)? Does the website recommend using its API for commercial applications? Why or why not? What are some of the things you can learn from its response schemas (https://worldtimeapi.org/pages/schema)?

3. What are some examples of other publicly accessible web APIs that use the JSON format? Can you find their documentation online? Which services / resources do they provide?

4. On your host computer, open Google Maps (https://www.google.com/maps/). In the search box, enter the latitude and longitude of the ISS in decimal degrees. Example: 41.40338, 2.17403. Where is this?

5. If the ISS orbits the earth approximately every 92 minutes at roughly 17,500 mph / 28,165 kilometers per hour (kph), how many times / day does the sun rise and set onboard the ISS? About how far does the ISS move in 1 second?

Extracting and combining JSON Data

The International Space Station (ISS) orbits the earth roughly at 28,165 kph / 17,500 mph every 92 minutes at an altitude of approximately 370-460 km / 230-285 miles with an inclination of 51.6 degrees (https://spotthestation.nasa.gov/).

Onboard, the crew experiences the sun rising and setting 16 times a day while everyone else living on earth between the Arctic Polar Circle at 66.6° N and the Antarctic Polar Circle at 66.6° S latitudes experience dawn and dusk just once per day. As large as a football field in size, the ISS reflects the sun, making it visible to the naked eye to those it passes below during the few hours before sunrise or the few hours after sunset.

The coordinates of the current location of the ISS directly overhead is given in latitude and longitude. For any location on the ground, the Sunrise-Sunset.org website (https://sunrise-sunset.org/) provides the day length, twilight, sunrise and sunset times.

Fig 2-x. Image source (NASA/Bill Ingalls):
https://spotthestation.nasa.gov/

In this section, we'll write a program that extracts the current latitude and longitude of the ISS from the Open Notify API in JSON format and use that positional information to get the sunrise and sunset times as well as the length of the day—all in JSON format—from the Sunrise-Sunset API at those coordinates on the surface of the earth.

Sunrise, sunset times for viewing the ISS

We'll use MicroPython's requests module to access the Open Notify API from your Pico as well to access the Sunrise-Sunset API which is also publicly available and documented. This is an example of one system (your Pico) communicating with two other systems that are online to answer the question: when does the sun rise and set on earth when the ISS is directly overhead at its current location? Note: because of its orbital inclination relative to the axis of the earth, the ISS will never be directly overhead further north of 51.6 degrees (London, England) or further south of -51.6 degrees (Port Stanley, Falkland Islands) latitude.

In combination, these web APIs can tell you when the sun rises and sets at a point on the earth's surface immediately below the ISS at its current location. Since the space station is visible to the naked eye a couple of hours before dawn and a couple of hours after sunset while passing overhead in the sky, this information can be useful if you know exactly when and where to look from your location. (NASA provides this information on its website: https://spotthestation.nasa.gov/.)

What is the current location of the ISS?

The Open Notify API (http://open-notify.org/Open-Notify-API/ISS-Location-Now/) returns the current location of the International Space Station (ISS) in JSON format:

```
{
  "message":        "success",
  "timestamp":      UNIX_TIME_STAMP,
  "iss_position": {
    "latitude":     CURRENT_LATITUDE,
    "longitude":    CURRENT_LONGITUDE
  }
}
```

If you open a web browser on your host computer and call its API in the address bar with http://api.open-notify.org/iss-now.json, something like the following should be displayed:

```
{
  "message":        "success",
  "timestamp":      1679250290,
  "iss_position": {
    "latitude":     "34.1509",
    "longitude":    "-9.2171"
  }
}
```

What are the sunrise and sunset times at that location on earth?

The Sunset and sunrise times API (https://sunrise-sunset.org/api) returns the sunrise and sunset times for a given location in JSON format:

```
{
  "results": {
    "sunrise": SUNRISE,
    "sunset":  SUNSET,
    "solar_noon": SOLAR_NOON,
    "day_length": DAY_LENGTH,
    ...
  },
  "status": "OK",
  "tzid": TIME_ZONE_ID
}
```

Open a web browser on your host computer and call its API in the address bar with https://api.sunrise-sunset.org/json?lat=34.1509&lng=-9.2171. Something like the following should appear:


```
{
  "results": {
    "sunrise": "6:58:29 AM",
    "sunset": "6:37:56 PM",
    "solar_noon": "12:48:12 PM",
    "day_length": "11:39:27",
    "civil_twilight_begin": "6:34:44 AM",
    "civil_twilight_end": "7:01:41 PM",
    "nautical_twilight_begin": "6:05:43 AM",
    "nautical_twilight_end": "7:30:42 PM",
    "astronomical_twilight_begin": "5:36:40 AM",
    "astronomical_twilight_end": "7:59:45 PM"
  },
  "status": "OK",
  "tzid": "UTC"
}
```


Request parameters

The Sunset and sunrise times API (https://sunrise-sunset.org/api) defines the following request parameters:

- **lat** (float): Latitude in decimal degrees. *Required.*
- **lng** (float): Longitude in decimal degrees. *Required.*
- **date** (string): Date in YYYY-MM-DD format. Also accepts other date formats and even relative date formats. If not present, date defaults to current date. *Optional.*
- **callback** (string): Callback function name for JSONP response. *Optional.*
- **formatted** (integer): 0 or 1 (1 is default). Time values in response will be expressed following ISO 8601 and day_length will be expressed in seconds. *Optional.*
- **tzid** (string): A timezone identifier. *Optional.*

In this section, we'll write a program that extracts the current latitude and longitude of the ISS from the Open Notify API (http://api.open-notify.org/iss-now.json) in JSON format and use that positional information to get the sunrise and sunset times as well as the length of the day–all in JSON format—from the Sunrise-Sunset API at those coordinates on the surface of the earth.
This program is a good example of how to use JSON objects to facilitate M2M (Machine-to-Machine) communications.

Code

Using Thonny (File > Save as), copy and save the Python module below to your Pico.

sunrise.py

The following code shows the current ISS location (latitude and longitude in decimal format), the sunrise and sunset times on the ground immediately below that location.

```
# sunrise.py - Show the current ISS location and the sunrise and
#   sunset times on the ground immediately below that location
import requests, sys

# Add my_secrets.py to the .gitignore file to make sure
#   that my_secrets.py is never checked into GitHub
import my_secrets
ssid = my_secrets.SSID          # Your SSID (Network Name)
password = my_secrets.PASSWORD  # Your WiFi PASSWORD

# Initialize the WiFi Interface
import connect_wifi
if not connect_wifi.init_wlan(ssid, password, max_retries=10):
    print('WiFi authentication error: {}'\
          .format(connect_wifi.SSID_ERROR))
    print('Exiting program')
    sys.exit(0)
else:
    ip_address = connect_wifi.get_ip()

try:
    # Request the JSON data for the ISS location
    iss_URL = "http://api.open-notify.org/iss-now.json"
    iss_now = requests.get(iss_URL, timeout=10)  # 10-sec timeout

    # Get ISS location if the HTTP response is successful
    if iss_now.status_code == 200:
        print("\nCurrent_ISS_position_and_time:")
        json_data = iss_now.json()

        # Format and display the JSON data
        json_niceify = "{\n"
        for key, value in json_data.items():
            json_niceify += f'  "{key}": "{value}",\n'
        json_niceify = json_niceify.rstrip(",\n") + "\n}"
        print(f"json_data = {json_niceify}")

        iss_latitude  = json_data["iss_position"]["latitude"]
```

```
        iss_longitude = json_data["iss_position"]["longitude"]
        iss_location = f"{iss_latitude},{iss_longitude}"

    else:
        print("Unable to fetch ISS position and time.")

    # Release network resources
    if iss_now:
        iss_now.close()

    # Get the sunrise and sunset times for the ISS location
    sunrise_URL = "https://api.sunrise-sunset.org/json?lat=" \
                + iss_latitude + "&lng=" + iss_longitude
    sunrise_now = requests.get(sunrise_URL, timeout=10)

    # Show the sunrise and sunset times
    #   if the HTTP response is successful
    if sunrise_now.status_code == 200:
        json_data = sunrise_now.json()
        print("\nSunrise and sunset times:")
        print("(JSON data from https://api.sunrise-sunset.org)")
        print(f"sunrise     = {json_data["results"]["sunrise"]}")
        print(f"sunset      = {json_data["results"]["sunset"]}")
        print(f"day length  = {\
                          json_data["results"]["day_length"]\
                          }")

    else:
        print("Unable to fetch sunrise and sunset times.")

    # Release network resources
    if sunrise_now:
        sunrise_now.close()

# Keyboard interrupt caught
except KeyboardInterrupt:
    print("\nUser interrupted the program")

# JSON decoding error?
except ValueError as e:
    print(f"JSON decoding error: {e}")

# Catch other potential errors, e.g., network errors
except Exception as e:
    print(f"An unexpected error occurred: {e}")

finally:
    print("\nProgram ended.")
```

Fig 2-x. sunrise.py

Code Explanation

Let's look at how the code works.

- The requests library is used for making HTTP requests (like fetching JSON data from websites). The sys module is used to stop the execution of the current program if the WiFi network is unavailable.

```
import requests, sys
```

- The my_secrets module contains the name of your network (SSID) and your network password.

```
import my_secrets
ssid = my_secrets.SSID           # Your SSID (Network Name)
password = my_secrets.PASSWORD   # Your WiFi PASSWORD
```

- To initialize the WiFi interface, use the connect_wifi.init_wlan() and connect_wifi.get_ip() module functions.

```
# Initialize the WiFi Interface
if not connect_wifi.init_wlan(ssid, password, max_retries=10):
    print('WiFi authentication error: {}'\
        .format(connect_wifi.SSID_ERROR))
    print('Exiting program')
    sys.exit(0)
else:
    ip_address = connect_wifi.get_ip()
```

- Request the JSON data for the ISS location from the Open Notify website.

```
    iss_URL = "http://api.open-notify.org/iss-now.json"
    iss_now = requests.get(iss_URL, timeout=10)  # 10-sec timeout
```

- Get ISS location (latitude and longitude) if the HTTP response is successful (200 = OK) and release the network resources.

```
    if iss_now.status_code == 200:
        print(f"\nCurrent_ISS_position_and_time:")
        json_data = iss_now.json()

        # Format and display the JSON data
        json_niceify = "{\n"
        for key, value in json_data.items():
            json_niceify += f'  "{key}": "{value}",\n'
        json_niceify = json_niceify.rstrip(",\n") + "\n}"
        print(f"json_data = {json_niceify}")

        iss_latitude  = json_data["iss_position"]["latitude"]
        iss_longitude = json_data["iss_position"]["longitude"]
        iss_location = f"{iss_latitude},{iss_longitude}"

    else:
        print("Unable to fetch ISS position and time.")

    # Release network resources
```

```
if iss_now:
    iss_now.close()
```

- Get the sunrise and sunset times for the ISS location.

```
sunrise_URL = "https://api.sunrise-sunset.org/json?lat=" \
            + iss_latitude + "&lng=" + iss_longitude
sunrise_now = requests.get(sunrise_URL, timeout=10)
```

- Show the sunrise and sunset times on the console for the ISS location if the HTTP response is successful (200 = OK) and release the network resources.

```
if sunrise_now.status_code == 200:
    json_data = sunrise_now.json()
    print("\nSunrise and sunset times:")
    print("(JSON data from https://api.sunrise-sunset.org)")
    print(f"sunrise     = {json_data["results"]["sunrise"]}")
    print(f"sunset      = {json_data["results"]["sunset"]}")
    print(f"day length  = {\
                           json_data["results"]["day_length"]\
                           }")
else:
    print("Unable to fetch sunrise and sunset times.")

# Release network resources
if sunrise_now:
    sunrise_now.close()
```

- The try-except fetches the JSON data (as explained above) but catches a user interrupt (e.g. Ctrl-C), JSON decoding and other errors. Finally, it prints the message "Program ended." to the console when the program stops.

```
# Fetch and display the time
try:
    ...

# Keyboard interrupt caught
except KeyboardInterrupt:
    print("\nUser interrupted the program")

# JSON decoding error?
except ValueError as e:
    print(f"JSON decoding error: {e}")

# Catch other potential errors, e.g., network errors
except Exception as e:
    print(f"An unexpected error occurred: {e}")

finally:
    print("Program ended.")
```

Procedure / Steps

> ⚠ **Warning:** Do not connect your host or your Pico to the internet on an insecure network!!!

Run the Python code on your target Pico.

sunrise.py

1. In Thonny, go to Tools > Options > Interpreter
   Select "MicroPython (Pico)"
2. Go to File > Open
   Select the copy of `sunrise.py` on the *host* computer
3. Go to Run
   Select "Run current script"

Tests and Results

sunrise.py

When you run the sunrise.py program using the "MicroPython (Pico)" interpreter, you might see in Thonny's Python Shell something like:

```
Current_ISS_position_and_time:
json_data = {
  "message": "success",
  "iss_position": "{'longitude': '143.1182', 'latitude':
'36.5183'}",
  "timestamp": "1756843428"
}

Sunrise and sunset times:
(JSON data from https://api.sunrise-sunset.org)
sunrise      = 7:58:15 PM
sunset       = 8:56:16 AM
day length   = 12:58:01

Program ended.
```

Congratulations!!! By collecting and combining JSON data pulled from multiple web APIs, we have seen how to use M2M (Machine-to-Machine) communications to create a data integrator.

This data integrator initiated requests to various web servers' APIs (http://api.open-notify.org/, https://api.sunrise-sunset.org) which responded by sending JSON data that your program combined automatically. A human being did not have to actively copy and paste information from various websites to determine when the ISS might be seen passing overhead. The Pico did all the work!

Questions

1. Why is good documentation specifying the JSON format for publicly accessible web APIs important?

2. What is an API key? What is API rate limiting used for?

3. On your host computer, determine your latitude and longitude on Google Maps (https://www.google.com/maps/) in decimal degrees. Now find out when and where to look for the ISS from your location. (NASA provides this information on its website: https://spotthestation.nasa.gov/.)

4. For a sighting opportunity in the future, open a web browser on your host computer and call the *Sunset and sunrise times API* in the address bar with your location information and a date parameter. Example:
   https://api.sunrise-sunset.org/json?lat=36.7201600&lng=-4.4203400&date=2025-09-21

Chapter Summary

In this chapter, you have explored your Pico's computational capabilities and learned how your Pico can extract and combine JSON data that it fetched from various web APIs.

At the time of this writing, NASA provides a number of public APIs, many of which respond with JSON data through its API portal https://api.nasa.gov/. Here's a sampling:

- **APOD:** Astronomy Picture of the Day
- **Asteroids NeoWs:** Near Earth Object Web Service
- **DONKI:** Space Weather Database Of Notifications, Knowledge, Information
- **EONET:** The Earth Observatory Natural Event Tracker
- **EPIC:** Earth Polychromatic Imaging Camera
- **Exoplanet:** Programmatic access to NASA's Exoplanet Archive database
- **GIBS:** Standardized web services that deliver global, full-resolution satellite imagery, enabling interactive exploration of Earth.
- **Insight:** Mars Weather Service API
- **Mars Rover Photos:** Image data gathered by NASA's Curiosity, Opportunity, and Spirit rovers on Mars
- **NASA Image and Video Library:** API to access the NASA Image and Video Library site at images.nasa.gov
- **Open Science Data Repository:** Programmatic interface for the Open Science Data Repository website
- **Satellite Situation Center:** System to cast geocentric spacecraft location information into a framework of (empirical) geophysical regions
- **SSD/CNEOS:** Solar System Dynamics and Center for Near-Earth Object Studies
- **Techport:** API to make NASA technology project data available in a machine-readable format
- **TechTransfer:** Patents, Software, and Tech Transfer Reports
- **TLE API:** Two line element data for earth-orbiting objects at a given point in time
- **Vesta/Moon/Mars Trek WMTS:** A Web Map Tile Service for the Vesta, Moon, and Mars Trek imagery projects

In the next chapter, you'll learn about how to start connecting and controlling the physical world with your Pico's pins.

References and Further Exploration

Universally Unique Identifiers (UUIDs)

- https://datatracker.ietf.org/doc/html/rfc4122
- https://datatracker.ietf.org/doc/html/rfc9562
- https://en.wikipedia.org/wiki/Universally_unique_identifier
- https://docs.python.org/3/library/uuid.html

JSON

- https://www.json.org/json-en.html
- https://docs.python.org/3/library/json.html

Connecting to the Internet with the Raspberry Pi Pico

- https://datasheets.raspberrypi.com/picow/connecting-to-the-internet-with-pico-w.pdf
- https://requests.readthedocs.io/
- https://docs.micropython.org/en/latest/library/os.html
- https://docs.micropython.org/en/latest/library/platform.html
- https://docs.micropython.org/en/latest/library/sys.html

MicroPython's WLAN built-in WiFi interfaces

- https://docs.micropython.org/en/latest/library/network.WLAN.html

Python requests module

- https://requests.readthedocs.io

Machine-to-machine (M2M) authentication and authorization

- https://stytch.com/blog/the-complete-guide-to-m2m-auth/

The NASA API portal (responses returned in JSON format!)

- https://api.nasa.gov/

The International Space Station Program

- https://www.nasa.gov/reference/international-space-station/
- https://spotthestation.nasa.gov/
- https://wsn.spaceflight.esa.int/iss/index_portal.php

People in space

- **Open Notify's "People In Space Now" API** http://api.open-notify.org/astros.json
- **The Launch Library 2 API (LL2)** https://github.com/TheSpaceDevs/Tutorials/blob/main/tutorials/getting_started_LL2/README.md
- https://projects.raspberrypi.org/en/projects/people-in-space-indicator
- https://github.com/raspberrypilearning/people-in-space-indicator/blob/master/worksheet.md

Sunrise-Sunset API

- https://sunrise-sunset.org/

Chapter 3

1. Chapter Introduction

2. Programming Environment and Setup
    a. Introduction
    b. Equipment and Components
    c. Setup and Construction
    d. Code

3. Blinking the Onboard LED
    a. Introduction
    b. Code
    c. Procedure / Steps
    d. Tests and Results

4. Timed Interrupts
    a. Introduction
    b. Code
    c. Procedure / Steps
    d. Tests and Results

5. Debouncing Buttons
    a. Introduction
    b. Code
    c. Procedure / Steps
    d. Tests and Results

6. References and Further Exploration

Hello, blinky! Physical computing with the Pico

Learn how to start connecting and controlling the physical world with your Pico's pins

Making an LED blink is the equivalent in physical computing to "Hello, world!". It demonstrates that your system can interact with the world and, with the help of a few connected parts, is well on its way to sensing and responding to it.

As you'll see in this chapter, you can easily make an LED blink at fixed intervals inside of a Python loop with the sleep() function. But looping is not the only way to toggle an LED. Sometimes it is useful to cause an *interrupt* that momentarily stops the execution of the main program in order to run a small section of code known as an ISR (interrupt service routine) and then resume executing the main program after the ISR has completed.

Configuring an interrupt on your Pico involves setting up a *trigger* that identifies an event which should interrupt whatever your Pico is currently doing, and a corresponding *interrupt handler*—the ISR—a callback function which runs when that event occurs. Example: a button press event that toggles an LED. Here, the interrupt trigger causes the microcontroller to pause its current task and execute the code inside an ISR to turn the LED on if it was off, or off if it was on.

MicroPython on the Pico provides two types of interrupts:

- *Timed Interrupts* using MicroPython's machine.Timer class which triggers callbacks to the ISR at regular, predetermined intervals.
- *External Interrupts* which are triggered by signals from a GPIO pin when, for example, the state of a pin changes.

Timed interrupts are based on a specified time interval. These can operate in "one-shot" mode where a timer runs for the duration of the interval then triggers the interrupt but just once and only once. This can be is useful for implementing a countdown timer or delaying a task for the specified time interval, such as turning an LED on for 10 seconds. Or they can operate in "periodic" mode for scheduling recurring actions. This can be useful for tasks that execute repeatedly, like blinking an LED, updating a display, or reading an environmental sensor in predefined time periods.

For time-sensitive interactions requiring immediate attention, however, *external interrupts* are useful for responding to events generated by push buttons, sensors, or other external devices connected to your Pico's GPIO pins. Without external interrupts, your program would need to poll a pin's state in an endless loop to react to these types of events. If the loop is busy with other tasks, there's a risk of missing a brief or quick event. External interrupts pause the execution of the main program when a designated event occurs, allowing you to capture and handle the event without delay and to run a specific ISR when a GPIO pin state changes.

In either case, ISRs need to be kept short and simple in order to minimize the disruption to the main program, doing only what's necessary immediately after the event causing it. This usually involves communicating with the main program by updating shared data (like a boolean flag) that indicates an interrupt occurred, then immediately returning. (Other tips and recommend practices can be found at https://docs.micropython.org/en/latest/reference/isr_rules.html). In this chapter, you'll see how to write such ISRs.

In the first section, you'll first blink the Pico's onboard LED, then blink an external LED which shows that your Pico can interact with the physical world.

You'll then implement an interrupt timer to blink the external LED periodically by scheduling an ISR to trigger in preset time intervals. Periodic timers facilitate event-driven programming by executing code at precise, regular intervals without the drawbacks of managing time-dependent actions by continuous polling.

Finally, you'll write a program that blinks an external LED with an external interrupt when you press a button. This shows how a global interrupt flag set in an ISR can be used to notify the main program that an external event occurred that requires immediate attention.

Programming Environment and Setup

For the examples in this chapter, you'll need the following.

Programming Environment
Host computer running either:
- Windows
- Raspberry Pi OS or Linux
- macOS
Host computer with the following installed:
- Python 3.10 or above
- Thonny (thonny.org)
Target microcontroller:
- Pico with MicroPython installed
micro USB cable

Equipment and Components

Components used in this chapter (see fritzing.org for components created with Fritzing):

Description	Image
Male-to-male jumper wires	
Half or full-sized Breadboard	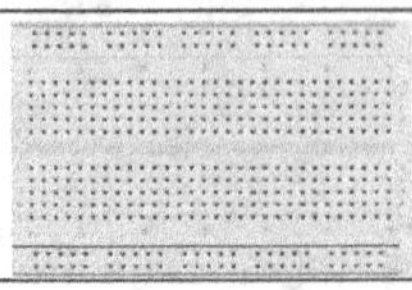
330 Ohm resistor (orange, orange, and brown stripes)	
Red LED - the anode (+ positive) lead is the longer lead - the cathode (- negative) lead is the shorter lead	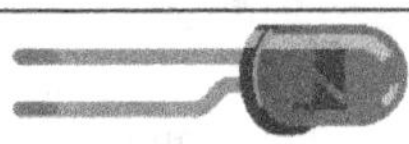
Push button switch	

Fig 3-x. Components used in this chapter

Setup and Construction

Refer to Appendix A for a pinout guide to the Raspberry Pi Pico W.
Refer to Appendix C for a pinout guide to the Raspberry Pi Pico 2W.

Before you begin constructing the circuit, make sure your Pico is unplugged from your host computer.

1. Connect one end of a 330 Ohm resistor to the same column as the Pico's GPIO16 pin (this should be column 20 on a numbered breadboard with the Pico's GPIO1 pin aligned to column 1). Connect the other end to column 24.
2. Connect the anode (the longer leg) of the LED to the same column as the end of the resistor.
3. Connect the cathode (the shorter leg) to the ground rail on the breadboard.
4. Add a push button switch so that it straddles the center divide. Connect one leg to pin GPIO15 and the other leg to a GND pin (Pin 18).
5. Finally, connect a GND pin (Pin 38) on the Pico with a jumper in column 3 to the ground rail on the breadboard.
6. Your finished circuit should look like Figure 3-x:

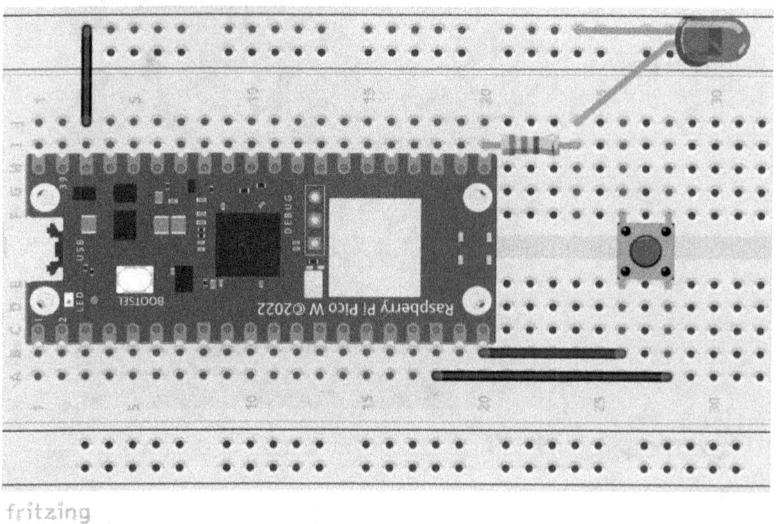

Fig 3-x. An external LED and a push button connected to the Pico

Now plug your Pico back into your host computer with a micro USB cable.

Blinking the Onboard LED

The small onboard LED on the Pico is a surface-mounted device in the top left corner of the board between the micro-USB port on the one side and the GPIO1 (pin 2) and GND (Ground: pin 3) on the other. It lights up when it's turned on; is dark, otherwise. When you toggle it, you know immediately that your Pico is getting power and that you're communicating with the microcontroller. The onboard LED provides a visible output without the need of additional components.

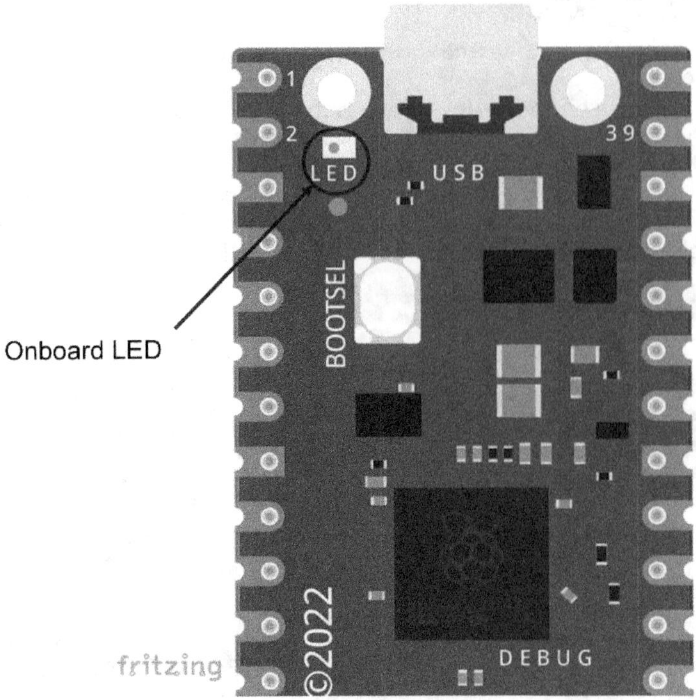

Fig 3-x. The onboard LED is in the top left corner of the Pico

Toggling an external LED connected to a GPIO pin is equally straightforward. Make sure to add a current-limiting resistor as shown in the wiring diagram or the LED will likely burn itself out and your Pico could be damaged in the process.

Code

Using Thonny (File > Save as), copy and save the Python modules below to your Pico.

hello_blinkyOnboard.py

The following blinks the Pico's onboard LED every second.

```
# hello_blinkyOnboard.py - Blink the onboard LED every second

from machine import Pin
from time import sleep

# Initialize the onboard LED
led = Pin("LED", Pin.OUT)
led.off()

# Toggle LED
def toggle_LED():
    while True:
        led.toggle()  # turn the LED on if it's off
                      # turn it off if it's on
        sleep(1)  # delay 1 second

if __name__ == '__main__':
    try:
        # Start blinking the LED
        toggle_LED()

    # Keyboard interrupt caught
    except KeyboardInterrupt:
        print("\nUser interrupted the program.")

    # Unexpected error
    except Exception as e:
        print(f"An unexpected error occurred: {e}")

    # End the program gracefully
    finally:
        # Turn off LED
        led.off()

        print("\nOnboard LED blinking program stopped.")
```

Fig 3-x. hello_blinkyOnboard.py

Let's look at how the code works.

- The Pin module allows you to configure and control GPIO pins on the Pico.

The sleep() module function is needed to introduce delays in the code execution.

```
from machine import Pin
from time import sleep
```

- led = Pin(...) initializes the onboard LED.

```
led = Pin("LED", Pin.OUT)
led.off()
```

- The toggle_LED() function blinks the onboard LED every second.

```
def toggle_LED():
    while True:
        led.toggle()  # turn the LED on if it's off
                      # turn it off if it's on
        sleep(1)  # delay 1 second
```

- the try-except block runs the toggle_LED() task but catches a user interrupt (e.g. Ctrl-C) and any unexpected errors, and finally turns off the LED when the program finishes.

```
try:
    # Start blinking the LED
    toggle_LED()

# Keyboard interrupt caught
except KeyboardInterrupt:
    print("\nUser interrupted the program.")

# Unexpected error
except Exception as e:
    print(f"An unexpected error occurred: {e}")

# End the program gracefully
finally:
    # Turn off LED
    led.off()

    print("\nOnboard LED blinking program stopped.")
```

hello_blinkyLED.py

The following blinks an external LED every second.

```
# hello_blinkyLED.py - Blink an external LED every second

from machine import Pin
from time import sleep

# Initialize the LED
led = Pin(16, Pin.OUT)  # GPIO16
led.off()

# Toggle LED
def toggle_LED():
    while True:
```

```
        led.toggle()  # turn the LED on if it's off
                      # turn it off if it's on
        sleep(1)  # delay 1 second

if __name__ == '__main__':
    try:
        # Start blinking the LED
        toggle_LED()

    # Keyboard interrupt caught
    except KeyboardInterrupt:
        print("\nUser interrupted the program.")

    # Unexpected error
    except Exception as e:
        print(f"An unexpected error occurred: {e}")

    # End the program gracefully
    finally:
        # Turn off LED
        led.off()

        print("\nExternal LED blinking program stopped.")
```

Fig 3-x. hello_blinkyLED.py

Code Explanation

Let's look at how the code works.

- The Pin module allows you to configure and control GPIO pins on the Pico.
  The sleep() module function is needed to introduce delays in the code execution.

```
from machine import Pin
from time import sleep
```

- led = Pin(...) initializes GPIO16 as an output pin for the external LED connected to it.

```
led = Pin(16, Pin.OUT)  # GPIO16
led.off()
```

- The toggle_LED() function blinks the LED every second.

```
def toggle_LED():
    while True:
        led.toggle()  # turn the LED on if it's off
                      # turn it off if it's on
        sleep(1)  # delay 1 second
```

- the try-except block runs the toggle_LED() task but catches a user interrupt (e.g. Ctrl-C) and any unexpected errors, and finally turns off the LED when the program finishes.

```
    try:
        # Start blinking the LED
```

```
    toggle_LED()

# Keyboard interrupt caught
except KeyboardInterrupt:
    print("\nUser interrupted the program.")

# Unexpected error
except Exception as e:
    print(f"An unexpected error occurred: {e}")

# End the program gracefully
finally:
    # Turn off LED
    led.off()

    print("\nExternal LED blinking program stopped.")
```

Procedure / Steps

Run the MicroPython code interactively to blink the onboard LED.

You can use Thonny's Python Shell on your host computer to blink the onboard LED on the Pico. Running REPL (Read, Evaluate, Print, and Loop) code in an interactive session can show that your Pico is up and running with MicroPython installed on it without even having to write a Python program to do so! This can be an important initial step when bringing up a microcontroller for the first time.

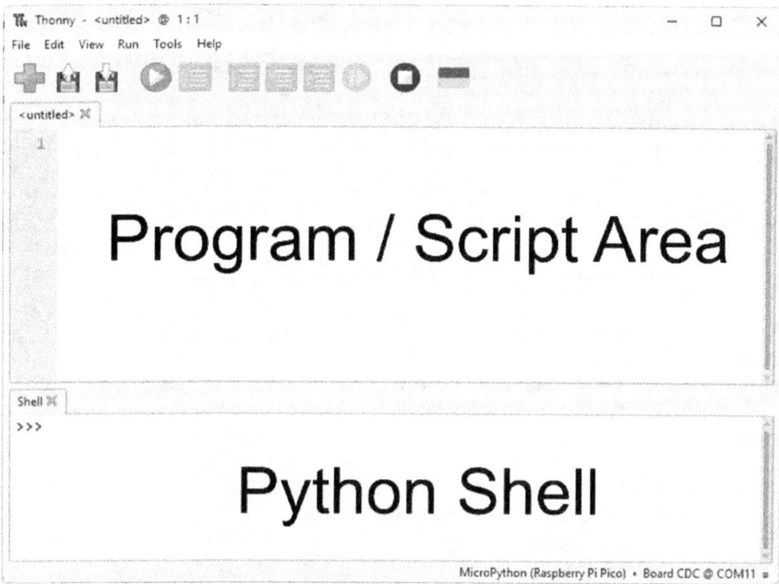

Fig 3-x. The Thonny IDE

An interactive MicroPython REPL session allows you to try things out, see if a line of code works (or doesn't!) almost immediately. It's a quick way to test some simple operations on your Pico and to clear up any doubt if there are any questions about its working correctly.

1. In the the Python Shell area at the bottom of the Thonny window, click just to the right of the ">>>" symbols
2. Type the following and press **ENTER**:
   ```
   from machine import Pin # import only the Pin function from the machine library
   ```
3. Type the following and press **ENTER**:
   ```
   led = Pin("LED", Pin.OUT)
   ```
4. Type the following and press **ENTER**:
   ```
   led.value(1) # turn the LED on
   ```
5. Type the following and press **ENTER**:
   ```
   led.value(0) # turn the LED off
   ```
6. Type the following and press **ENTER**:
   ```
   led.toggle() # turn the LED on if it's off; turn it off if it's on
   ```
7. Type the following and press **ENTER**:
   ```
   led.toggle() # turn the LED off if it's on; turn it on if it's off
   ```

The following should appear in the Thonny Python Shell area and the onboard LED will turn on and turn off twice:

```
>>> from machine import Pin  # import only the Pin function from
the machine library
>>> led = Pin("LED", Pin.OUT)
>>> led.value(1) # turn the LED on
>>> led.value(0) # turn the LED off
>>> led.toggle() # turn the LED on if it's off; turn it off if
it's on
>>> led.toggle() # turn the LED off if it's on; turn it on if
it's off
```

Importing what you need in MicroPython

You'll notice that we didn't import the entire machine library for toggling the onboard LED. Selectively importing just the module functions you need uses less memory which is a constrained resource on a microcontroller. It's a good habit to get into unless, of course, you need most or all of the functions in a given module!

When writing MicroPython code, you can use the dir() function to list all of the properties and methods of an object before using the object for the first time. Example:

```
>>> import machine
>>> dir(machine)
['__class__', '__name__', 'ADC', 'I2C', 'I2S', 'PWM',
'PWRON_RESET', 'Pin', 'RTC', 'SPI', 'Signal', 'SoftI2C',
'SoftSPI', 'Timer', 'UART', 'WDT', 'WDT_RESET', '__dict__',
'bitstream', 'bootloader', 'deepsleep', 'dht_readinto',
'disable_irq', 'enable_irq', 'freq', 'idle', 'lightsleep',
'mem16', 'mem32', 'mem8', 'reset', 'reset_cause', 'soft_reset',
'time_pulse_us', 'unique_id']
>>>
```

Since we're using the `Pin` function, you can drill down a little deeper to see its attributes:

```
>>> dir(Pin)
['__class__', '__name__', 'value', 'ALT', 'ALT_GPCK', 'ALT_I2C',
'ALT_PIO0', 'ALT_PIO1', 'ALT_PWM', 'ALT_SIO', 'ALT_SPI',
'ALT_UART', 'ALT_USB', 'IN', 'IRQ_FALLING', 'IRQ_RISING',
'OPEN_DRAIN', 'OUT', 'PULL_DOWN', 'PULL_UP', '__bases__',
'__dict__', 'board', 'cpu', 'high', 'init', 'irq', 'low', 'off',
'on', 'toggle']
>>>
```

Once you're familiar with an object's attributes, listing them every time becomes unnecessary. But it can sometimes be surprising which attributes an object has, especially when working with MicroPython.

Run the MicroPython code on your target Pico.

hello_blinkyOnboard.py

1. Using Thonny (File > Open), select hello_blinkyOnboard.py
2. Go to the Run menu
   Select "Run current script"

hello_blinkyLED.py

1. Using Thonny (File > Open), select hello_blinkyLED.py
2. Go to the Run menu
   Select "Run current script"

Tests and Results

Running MicroPython code interactively

Interactive sessions using the Thonny Python Shell like the example shown here is a great way to check that your Pico is up and running.

hello_blinkyOnboard.py

When you run hello_blinkyOnboard.py on the target, the onboard LED will keep turning on and off every second.

hello_blinkyLED.py

When you run hello_blinkyLED.py on the target, the external LED will keep turning on and off every second.

Congratulations! You have toggled both the onboard LED and an external LED in an infinite while loop.

Timed Interrupts

In addition to toggling an LED and sleeping for a set amount of time in an infinite loop, you can use the Timer class in MicroPython's machine library module to periodically interrupt an ongoing program without the need to call the sleep() function.

In this section, we'll toggle an external LED with a periodic Timer showing that other tasks in the main program can continue while the timer is running in the background. The timer_isr() ISR callback function is kept short and simple.

Code

Using Thonny (File > Save as), copy and save the Python module below to your Pico.

hello_blinkyTimerInterrupt.py

The following blinks an external LED with a periodic timer interrupt. Refer to:
https://docs.micropython.org/en/latest/library/machine.Timer.html

```
# hello_blinkyTimerInterrupt.py - Blink an external LED with a
#   periodic timer interrupt

from machine import Pin, Timer
from time import sleep

# Initialize the LED
led = Pin(16, Pin.OUT)  # GPIO16
led.off()

# Define an ISR callback function for when the timer triggers
def timer_isr(timer_obj):
    led.toggle()

# Initialize a periodic timer
led_timer = Timer(-1) # Create a virtual timer (id=-1)
led_timer.init(mode=Timer.PERIODIC, period=250, \
               callback=timer_isr)

# Perform main tasks while the timer is running in the background
def main_program():
    counter = 0
    while True:
        if counter % 5 != 0:
            print('.', end='')
        else:
            print(counter, end='')

        counter += 1
        sleep(1)

if __name__ == '__main__':
    try:
        # Start main program
        main_program()

    # Keyboard interrupt caught
    except KeyboardInterrupt:
        print("\nUser interrupted the program.")

    # Unexpected error
```

```
    except Exception as e:
        print(f"An unexpected error occurred: {e}")

    # End the program gracefully
    finally:
        # Stop the timer
        print('\nDeinitializing timer')
        led_timer.deinit()

        # Turn off LED
        led.off()

        print("\nPERIODIC timer interrupt program ended.")
```

Fig 3-x. hello_blinkyTimerInterrupt.py

Code Explanation

Let's look at how the code works.

- The Pin module allows you to configure and control GPIO pins on the Pico.
  The Timer class from the machine module is used to control timer functionality.
  The sleep() module function is needed to introduce delays in the code execution.

```
from machine import Pin, Timer
from time import sleep
```

- led = Pin(...) initializes GPIO 16 as an output pin connected to the external LED.

```
led = Pin(16, Pin.OUT)  # GPIO16
led.off()
```

- timer_isr() is an ISR callback function that toggles the LED when the timer triggers.

```
def timer_isr(timer_obj):
    led.toggle()
```

- led_timer = Timer(-1) creates a virtual software timer for the Pico.

```
led_timer = Timer(-1) # Create a virtual timer (id=-1)
```

- Configure the timer's behavior with the timer's init() method. The arguments for this example are:
  - mode = Timer.PERIODIC: The associated ISR callback function is executed repeatedly at a specified interval.
  - period = 250: The period of the timer is 250ms.
  - callback = timer_isr: The associated ISR callback function.

```
led_timer.init(mode=Timer.PERIODIC, period=250, \
               callback=timer_isr)
```

- The main_program() performs other tasks while the timer is running in the background. In this example, it prints out dots and numbers that progress in increments of 5.

```
counter = 0
while True:
    if counter % 5 != 0:
        print('.', end='')
    else:
        print(counter, end='')

    counter += 1
    sleep(1)
```

- the try-except block runs the main_program() task but catches a user interrupt (e.g. Ctrl-C) and any unexpected errors, and finally de-initializes the timer and turns off the LED when the program finishes.

```
try:
    # Start main program
    main_program()

# Keyboard interrupt caught
except KeyboardInterrupt:
    print("\nUser interrupted the program.")

# Unexpected error
except Exception as e:
    print(f"An unexpected error occurred: {e}")

# End the program gracefully
finally:
    # Stop the timer
    print('\nDeinitializing timer')
    led_timer.deinit()

    # Turn off LED
    led.off()

    print("\nPERIODIC timer interrupt program ended.")
```

Procedure / Steps

Run the MicroPython code on your target Pico.

hello_blinkyTimerInterrupt.py

1. Using Thonny (File > Open), select hello_blinkyTimerInterrupt.py
2. Go to the Run menu
   Select "Run current script"

Tests and Results

hello_blinkyTimerInterrupt.py

When you run hello_blinkyTimerInterrupt.py, the external LED will keep turning on and off every 0.25 seconds (250 ms). Using the Timer interrupt shows that the main program is minimally affected by toggling the LED, allowing it to do other things.

Congratulations! You have attached an electronic component, in this case an LED, to the Pico's GPIO pins, turning it on and off using MicroPython's machine.Timer interrupt class.

Debouncing Buttons

Configuring a GPIO pin on the Pico to catch an interrupt is usually more complex than setting an I/O pin as an input or an output. The corresponding ISR must be kept short and simple so that the CPU on the microcontroller can enter and exit it quickly and proceed with its main execution tasks with minimal delay.

To the Pico, a button push event doesn't just happen. When you initially press a button, the electrical contacts in the switch may rapidly make and break contact multiple times until they connect firmly. The button "bounces". It doesn't produce a clean signal. It can take a moment or two for the voltage transitions to finally settle down.

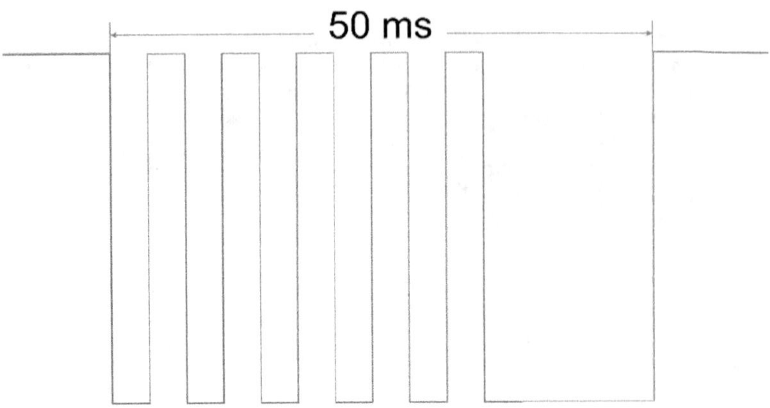

Fig 3-x. Bouncy digital signal of a push button switch

One way to get around the bouncy button problem is to create a forever loop in a separate thread that constantly is polling the state of the button, setting a global flag. But this can add considerable processor overhead.

But incessant polling is extremely wasteful of CPU cycles if you would rather use them for more interesting tasks in your embedded systems applications.

There are a number of debouncing algorithms, all of which have tradeoffs. Waiting for the bouncing to settle down and stop is perhaps the simplest. This approach works pretty well if you expect the bouncing will never last longer than a given time period.

Picking a debounce period in the 50ms range (1/20th of a second) for a mechanical push button switch is not an unreasonable place to start (although some adjusting may be required depending on your particular application). 50ms is about as fast as a person typing at 120 words per minute, if they average 5 characters per word. 50ms is also “good enough” in many real-world situations. Example: a pedestrian pressing a crosswalk button at a traffic light.

In this section, you’ll implement a delay-based debouncer in an ISR to turn an LED on and off. The primary drawback to this approach is that you have to know in advance the duration of the longest bounce event. But it’s otherwise easy and straightforward to implement: check if the button has been held down for at least 50ms. If the button is held down for that long, set a global interrupt flag in the ISR to 1 that tells the main program to handle the event which it does by toggling the LED and resetting the flag to 0, ready for another push of the button.

Note that button_isr() is kept short and simple: when triggered by a button press event, it’s only task is to set the interrupt flag when the button signal has settled into a stable, unambiguous state.

Code

Using Thonny (File > Save as), copy and save the Python module below to your Pico.

hello_blinkyButtonInterrupt.py

This example shows how to use an external interrupt that is triggered by a button press.

```
# hello_blinkyButtonInterrupt.py - Blink an external LED with
#   a button interrupt
from machine import Pin
from time import sleep, ticks_ms, ticks_diff

# Initialize the LED
led = Pin(16, Pin.OUT)  # GPIO16
led.off()

# Initialize the button pin
button = Pin(15, Pin.IN, Pin.PULL_UP)  # GPIO15

# Define an ISR callback function for a button press
interrupt_flag = 0
last_debounce_time = 0
def button_isr(pin):
    global interrupt_flag, last_debounce_time
```

```
    current_time = ticks_ms()  # get current time in milliseconds

    # Debounce: Has the button been held down for at least 50ms?
    if ticks_diff(current_time, last_debounce_time) > 50:
        interrupt_flag = 1  # set interrupt flag
        last_debounce_time = current_time

# Initialize the IRQ
button.irq(trigger = Pin.IRQ_FALLING, handler = button_isr)

# Perform main tasks while the IRQ is running in the background
def main_program():
    global interrupt_flag
    while True:
        # Button pressed?
        if interrupt_flag == 1:
            print("Button press detected!")
            led.toggle()  # toggle LED
            interrupt_flag = 0  # reset interrupt flag
        sleep(1)  # delay

if __name__ == '__main__':
    try:
        # Start main program
        main_program()

    # Keyboard interrupt caught
    except KeyboardInterrupt:
        print("\nUser interrupted the program.")

    # Unexpected error
    except Exception as e:
        print(f"An unexpected error occurred: {e}")

    # End the program gracefully
    finally:
        # Turn off LED
        led.off()

        print("\nButton interrupt program ended.")
```

Fig 3-x. hello_blinkyButtonInterrupt.py

Code Explanation

Let's look at how the code works.

- The Pin module allows you to configure and control GPIO pins on the Pico.
  The sleep() module function is needed to introduce delays in the code execution.
  The ticks_ms() and ticks_diff() module functions are used to

measure how long it takes for specific code blocks or functions to execute.

```
from machine import Pin
from time import sleep, ticks_ms, ticks_diff
```

- led = Pin(...) initializes an output pin (GPIO 16) for the external LED connected to GPIO16.

```
led = Pin(16, Pin.OUT)  # GPIO16
led.off()
```

- button = Pin(...) initializes the push button connected to GPIO15 as an input pin with a pull-up resistor enabled that reads HIGH when the button is not pressed.

```
button = Pin(15, Pin.IN, Pin.PULL_UP)  # GPIO15
```

- button_isr() is an ISR callback function that executes when the interrupt is triggered by a button press. The pin argument is the specific pin that triggered the interrupt.

```
def button_isr(pin):
    ...
```

- The global interrupt_flag is a boolean flag signaling to the main program that a button press event has occurred. The global last_debounce_time saves the time of the last valid button event. This timestamp is used to determine whether the button has been held down for at least 50ms.

```
    global interrupt_flag, last_debounce_time
```

- When the button interrupt is triggered, the time in milliseconds (ms) is captured.

```
    current_time = ticks_ms()
```

- Check if the time elapsed since the previous valid button event (last_debounce_time) is greater than 50 milliseconds. This logic helps prevent multiple triggers when a mechanical button "bounces" (makes and breaks contact multiple times rapidly) before settling into a stable state during a single button press. If a stable button press has been detected–the debounce condition is met–the interrupt flag is set to 1 indicating to the main program that a valid button press has occurred. A new reference point for debouncing the next button press event is then established by updating the last_debounce_time to the current_time.

```
    if ticks_diff(current_time, last_debounce_time) > 50:
        interrupt_flag = 1  # set interrupt flag
        last_debounce_time = current_time
```

- button.irq() attaches an interrupt to the button pin.
    - trigger=Pin.IRQ_FALLING specifies that the interrupt should be triggered when the button is released, going from HIGH to LOW (i.e. on a falling edge).
    - handler = button_isr: The associated ISR callback function when the interrupt is triggered.

```
button.irq(trigger = Pin.IRQ_FALLING, handler = button_isr)
```

- The main_program() can perform other tasks while the IRQ is running in the background.
  In this example, it prints 'Button press detected!' when the button has been pressed (the interrupt flag is set to 1), toggles the led, and resets the interrupt flag.

```
def main_program():
    global interrupt_flag
    while True:
        # Button pressed?
        if interrupt_flag == 1:
            print("Button press detected!")
            led.toggle()  # toggle LED
            interrupt_flag = 0  # reset interrupt flag
        sleep(1)  # delay
```

- The try-except block runs the main_program() task but catches a user interrupt (e.g. Ctrl-C) and any unexpected errors, and finally turns off the LED when the program finishes.

```
try:
    # Start main program
    main_program()

# Keyboard interrupt caught
except KeyboardInterrupt:
    print("\nUser interrupted the program.")

# Unexpected error
except Exception as e:
    print(f"An unexpected error occurred: {e}")

# End the program gracefully
finally:
    # Turn off LED
    led.off()

    print("\nButton interrupt program ended.")
```

Procedure / Steps

Run the MicroPython code on your Pico.

hello_blinkyButtonInterrupt.py

1. Using Thonny (File > Open), select hello_blinkyButtonInterrupt.py
2. Go to the Run menu
   Select "Run current script"

Tests and Results

hello_blinkyButtonInterrupt.py

When you run hello_blinkyButtonInterrupt.py on your Pico, the external LED will turn on and off every time you press the button. At the same time, the main program continues in a loop. Using the IRQ shows that the this main loop is minimally affected by toggling the LED, allowing the Pico to do other things.

When writing interrupt service routines like button_isr(), it is important to keep the code in the ISR itself as short as possible so that the Pico can quickly get back to the main program.

It is tempting to put Python print() statements in the ISR. Don't—unless you're debugging. And even then. Conserve CPU cycles for the main task(s).

Congratulations! You have attached an electronic component, in this case an LED, to the Pico's GPIO pins, turning it on and off using MicroPython's machine IRQ interrupt class and a button.

References and Further Exploration

Jack Ganssle's "Guide to Debouncing"

- Pt 1: https://www.ganssle.com/debouncing.htm
- Pt 2: http://www.ganssle.com/debouncing-pt2.htm

MicroPython Documentation

- Timer Class https://docs.micropython.org/en/latest/library/machine.Timer.html
- ISR Rules https://docs.micropython.org/en/latest/reference/isr_rules.html

Raspberry Pi Code Club: Use digital inputs and outputs

- https://projects.raspberrypi.org/en/projects/getting-started-with-the-pico/7

Fritzing

- https://fritzing.org/

Chapter 4

1. Chapter Introduction

2. Programming Environment and Setup
    a. Introduction
    b. Equipment and Components
    c. Setup and Construction
    d. Code

3. Reading the Pico's internal temperature sensor
    a. Introduction
    b. Code
    c. Procedure / Steps
    d. Tests and Results

4. Creating a simple web server with sockets
    a. Introduction
    b. Code
    c. Procedure / Steps
    d. Tests and Results

5. Communicating JSON objects via a RESTful API
    a. Introduction
    b. Code
    c. Procedure / Steps
    d. Tests and Results
    e. Questions

6. References and Further Exploration

Web API Hosting with Sockets

Discover how to transform your wireless-enabled Pico into an Entity Event-Driven Embedded System with socket programming

Event-Driven Embedded Systems are about *Events*—data acquired from sensing or controlling the embedded system itself and / or the physical world that may have implicit or explicit metadata associated with the data. These metadata provide context about what happened and who or what was involved. They also mark an Event by a unique identifier like a UUID (Universally Unique Identifier).

So far we have seen that an embedded Pico system can use its WiFi capabilities to pull JSON information (like which astronauts are currently on the ISS and their location overhead) from the web. We have also seen how a Pico can control the physical world with attached components like a button switch and an LED. We will now look at a simple example of how a Pico can both control and sense the physical world and convey this information as an *Entity Event*—something of interest (to a microservice or other data consumer / AI Agent) that happened which is associated with a specific entity (like a system component).

RESTful APIs

In recent years, the Representational State Transfer (REST) architectural style for providing web services has become a popular choice for client-server and microservice architectures. Built on the HTTP protocol, a server that implements a RESTful API is comparatively simpler and easier to implement than its predecessors such as XML-RPC and its derivative, the Simplified Object Access Protocol (SOAP).

RESTful web services use common HTTP methods like GET, POST, PUT, PATCH and DELETE to perform operations. These services can be used on a public network like the World Wide Web, and they can be used on a private network to facilitate communications between different internal systems that allow for secure data exchange without exposing the API to the public internet.

There is some controversy about what exactly constitutes a RESTful API, however. Strictly speaking, a *RESTful API* is an application programming interface (API) that conforms to a set of six defining criteria of a RESTful architectural style for building and integrating application software on a network. While everyone agrees that codification and standardization of the World Wide Web helps drive its progress forward, there are many instances of "RESTful APIs" that do not meet all six criteria. For example, one such RESTful principle that frequently is not met is the *HATEOAS* (Hypermedia as the Engine of Application State) requirement which allows clients to navigate all of the endpoints of an API, essentially as a state machine by following hyperlinks between resources.

In this beginning book on learning how to construct Entity Event-Driven Embedded Pico Systems, the debate over what exactly constitutes a RESTful API is made somewhat irrelevant by the fact that these systems are "origin servers" that are highly constrained in terms of resources and which may never participate on a public network like the web. Indeed, their entire lifecycles may exist on private networks where the standardization of web APIs is relevant only to client data consumers on the same networks.

For the purposes of our examples, then, we define a *RESTful API* as one that allows a client to perform a function and / or retrieve information from a resource like an embedded Pico system that provides an API as a communications interface mediating these interactions. Bounded contexts help delineate a separation of concerns throughout an Entity Event-Driven architecture. One can think of a RESTful API as a type of contract between an information provider (the responder—i.e. the embedded Pico system) and an information consumer (the requestor). The RESTful API determines access control to web services and information resources that the "origin server", the embedded Pico system, shares with the client consumer.

Although a basic web page can provide a user-friendly interface in a web browser, a Pico running MicroPython can also communicate via a RESTful API in JSON, a human-readable message exchange format that other computer systems can easily understand and generate themselves. In this chapter, with a couple of quick edits to a "Hello, world!" web page, a RESTful API for an Event-Driven Embedded Pico System can readily be constructed using the Pico's built-in WiFi network capabilities.

Simply by changing the API endpoint on a Pico from "/light_on" to "/light_off", the Pico's external LED can be turned on and off without a person even pressing a physical or virtual (HTML) button! In addition to physically reacting to the request, the Pico can respond with its local time, internal temperature and available RAM, formatting its response that contains meta information in key / value pairs in JSON format. In other words, a Pico can both control and sense the physical world and convey this information through its WiFi communications interface. By doing so, the Pico thus becomes an Entity Event-Driven Embedded System.

The Pico has an internal temperature sensor located inside its microcontroller. This sensor reads the core temperature of the CPU which is a little higher than the ambient temperature because the Pico draws power when it's turned on. Power generates heat. In fact, the more work that the CPU does—for instance, when performing lots and lots of complicated calculations—the more power it draws, the higher the temperature of the chip. We'll first write a Python program to print this temperature to the console.

Using sockets, the Pico can be transformed into a very basic web server that can host web pages in HTML starting with "Hello, world!". From there, it is easy to view the Pico's internal temperature over a network, along with some other useful pieces of information about the Pico such as its local time and the amount of available free RAM. After that, it's straightforward to add a couple of buttons to the body of the web page that turn an external LED on and off.

By adding the API endpoints "/light_on" and "/light_off" and responding with Event details, a Pico web server can be transformed into an Entity Event-Driven Embedded System. Microservices and other data consumers / AI agents connecting to this web server will be able to read JSON objects through its *RESTful API* interface and readily understand details about a uniquely identified event—particulars about data the Pico senses (like temperature) and actions it might have taken (such as turning an external LED on or off).

Programming Environment and Setup

For the examples in this chapter, you'll need the following.

Programming Environment
Host computer running either:
- Windows
- Raspberry Pi OS or Linux
- macOS
Host computer with the following installed:
- Python 3.10 or above
- Thonny (thonny.org)
Target microcontroller:
- Pico with MicroPython installed
micro USB cable

Equipment and Components

Components used in this chapter (see fritzing.org for components created with Fritzing):

Description	Image
Male-to-male jumper wires	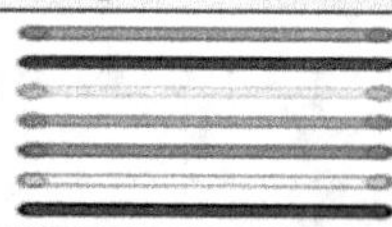
Half or full-sized Breadboard	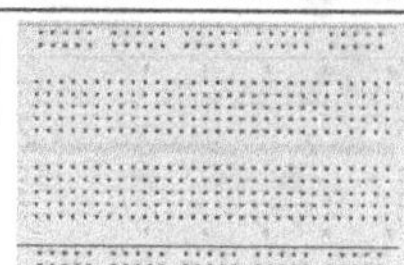
330 Ohm resistor (orange, orange, and brown stripes)	
Red LED - the anode (+ positive) lead is the longer lead - the cathode (- negative) lead is the shorter lead	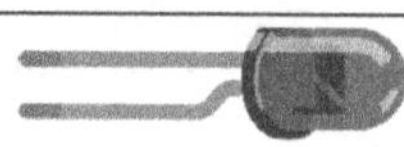

Fig 4-x. Components used in this chapter

Setup and Construction

Refer to Appendix A for a pinout guide to the Raspberry Pi Pico W.
Refer to Appendix C for a pinout guide to the Raspberry Pi Pico 2W.

Before you begin constructing the circuit, make sure your Pico is unplugged from your host computer.

1. Connect one end of a 330 Ohm resistor to the same column as the Pico's GP16 pin (this should be column 20 on a numbered breadboard with the Pico's GP01 pin aligned to column 1). Connect the other end to column 24.
2. Connect the anode (the longer leg) of the LED to the same column as the end of the resistor.
3. Connect the cathode (the shorter leg) to the ground rail on the breadboard.
4. Connect a GND pin (Pin 38) on the Pico with a jumper in column 3 to the ground rail on the breadboard.
5. Your finished circuit should look like Figure 4-x:

Fig 4-x. An external LED connected to the Pico

Now plug your Pico back into your host computer with a micro USB cable.

Synchronizing the Pico's Real Time Clock using Thonny

To synchronize the Pico's Real Time Clock using Thonny, select "Options..." from the Tools menu:

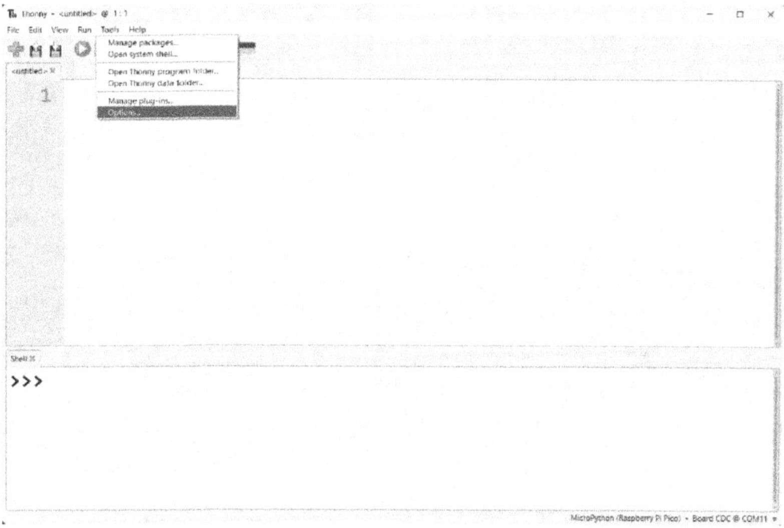

Fig 4-x. Thonny's Tools Options Menu

Choose the Interpreter tab and check the box labeled "Synchronize device's real time clock" to enable this feature.

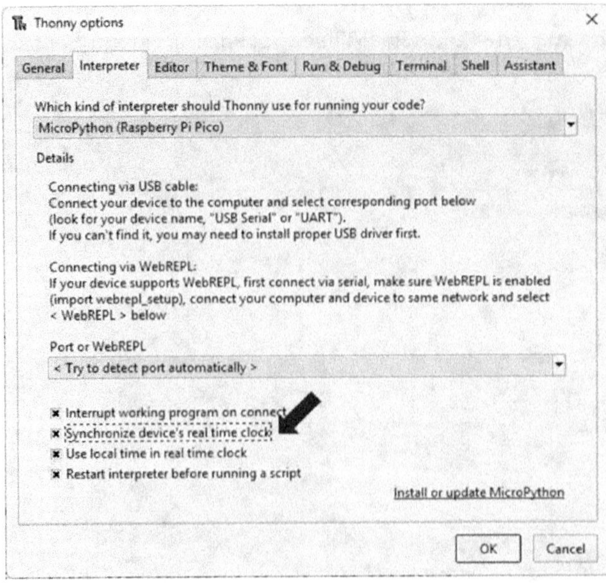

Fig 4-x. Synchronizing the Pico's RTC using Thonny

Code

Using Thonny (File > Save as), copy and save the Python modules below to your target Pico microcontroller.

my_secrets.py

This code separates sensitive information such as your WiFi credentials and other sensitive information from your application logic which helps prevent accidentally exposing sensitive information if you share your MicroPython code with others. It also makes your code more reusable since you can easily modify your authentication credentials in one place without having to change the Python programs that import it.

Keep this file in a directory accessible to the MicroPython interpreter's import path. If you use GitHub as a source code repository, make sure to add my_secrets.py to your .gitignore file so that my_secrets.py is not accidentally checked into GitHub.

```
# Add my_secrets.py to the .gitignore file to make sure
#   that my_secrets.py is never checked into GitHub
SSID     = 'MyNetwork'         # YOUR SSID (Network Name)
PASSWORD = 'MyPassword'        # YOUR WiFi PASSWORD
```

Fig 4-x. my_secrets_EXAMPLE.py

Code Explanation

Let's look at how to use the my_secrets.py module in your MicroPython code.

- The my_secrets module contains sensitive information such as your WiFi network's SSID and password. After importing it, you can access variables within the this module and assign their values to local variables.

```
import my_secrets
ssid = my_secrets.SSID              # Your SSID (Network Name)
password = my_secrets.PASSWORD  # Your WiFi PASSWORD
```

connect_wifi.py

You'll have to initiate a WiFi connection every time you use your Pico on a WiFi network. This module displays connection progress and handles connection failures. You can increase the max_retries variable if your Pico requires more time to establish a connection to your particular network.

> ⚠ **Warning: DO NOT connect your Pico to an insecure network!!!**

```
"""
connect_wifi.py
-----------
To connect to a wireless network,
    use the ``init_wlan()`` function
To obtain the IP address, use the ``get_ip()`` function

Example::
        >>> import connect_wifi
        >>> connect_wifi.init_wlan('Your Network Name',      \
                                       'Your Network Password' \
                                       max_retries=23)
        >>> connect_wifi.get_ip()

For information on MicroPython's WLAN built-in WiFi
    interfaces, see:
    docs.micropython.org/en/latest/library/network.WLAN.html
"""
import network
from time import sleep
```

```
# Network error messages
NETWORK_CONNECTION_ERROR = "Network connection failed"
SSID_ERROR = "Failed to obtain IP address"

# Create a WLAN network interface object in Station (STA) mode
wlan = network.WLAN(network.STA_IF)

def init_wlan(ssid, password, max_retries=10):
    """Initiate a wireless LAN connnection

    :param ssid: wireless network name
    :param password: wireless network password
    :param max_retries: number of connection attempts before
        giving up

    :raise RuntimeError: If the network connection failed

    :return: True (successful connection);
             False (unsuccessful connection)
    :rtype: bool
    """

    # Activate network interface
    wlan.active(True)

    # Connect to the specified wireless network, using the
    #   wireless network name and password
    wlan.connect(ssid, password)

    # Print a message to the console saying that the device
    #   is trying to connect
    print('Waiting for connection...')

    # Continue to loop as long as there are connection attempts
    while max_retries > 0:
        # wlan.status() < 0: connection failure
        # wlan.status() >= 3: connection successful
        #   or has a valid IP address
        if wlan.status() < 0 or wlan.status() >= 3:
            break
        print(max_retries, '.', sep='', end='', )
        max_retries -= 1
        sleep(1)  # delay before retrying

    # Check if the connection was unsuccessful
    if wlan.status() != network.STAT_GOT_IP:
        raise RuntimeError(NETWORK_CONNECTION_ERROR)
        return False  # unsuccessful connection

    # Connection was successful and an IP address was obtained
    else:
        # Get the IP address
```

```
        ip = wlan.ifconfig()[0]

        # Print a confirmation message to console
        print( 'Connected: ip = {}'.format(ip))
        return True  # successful connection

def get_ip():
    """Get the IP address if WiFi is connected

    :raise RuntimeError: If not connected

    :return: IP Address (successful connection);
             SSID_ERROR (unsuccessful connection)
    :rtype: bool
    """
    if wlan.isconnected():
        return wlan.ifconfig()[0]
    else:
        print('\nNot connected')
        raise RuntimeError(SSID_ERROR)
        return None
```

Fig 4-x. connect_wifi.py

Code Explanation

Note: For more information on MicroPython's WLAN built-in WiFi interfaces, see https://docs.micropython.org/en/latest/library/network.WLAN.html.

Let's look at how the code works.

- The network module is used for configuring and controlling WiFi connectivity on the Pico.
  The sleep() module function is needed to introduce delays in the code execution.

```
import network
from time import sleep
```

- Define network error messages that are printed to the console if a Runtime Error is raised.
  NETWORK_CONNECTION_ERROR: Unsuccessful network connection.
  SSID_ERROR: Unable to obtain an IP address because there is not a network connection.

```
NETWORK_CONNECTION_ERROR = "Network connection failed"
SSID_ERROR = "Failed to obtain IP address"
```

- Create a WLAN network interface object in "Station" (STA) mode to connect to an existing WiFi access point (like a home router).

```
wlan = network.WLAN(network.STA_IF)
```

- Define a function init_wlan() to initiate a wireless LAN connection that returns True if the network connection is successful.
  If the network connection is not successful, init_wlan() raises a Runtime Error, printing the NETWORK_CONNECTION_ERROR message and returns False.

  The init_wlan() function takes three arguments:
  - ssid: wireless network name
  - password: wireless network password
  - max_retries: number of connection attempts before giving up

```
def init_wlan(ssid, password, max_retries=10):
    ...
```

- wlan.active(True) activates the network interface.

```
wlan.active(True)
```

- wlan.connect(ssid, password) connects to the specified wireless network, using the wireless network name ssid and password.

```
wlan.connect(ssid, password)
```

- A message is printed to the console saying that the device is attempting to connect.

```
print('Waiting for connection...')
```

- As long as there are connection attempts as specified by the max_retries argument, init_wlan() continues to loop, printing a dot ('.') to the console showing progress and delaying for a second between each retry attempt.
  The loop breaks if the there is a connection failure (wlan.status() < 0); it also breaks if successfully connected or it obtains a valid IP address (wlan.status() >= 3):

```
while max_retries > 0:
    if wlan.status() < 0 or wlan.status() >= 3:
        break
    print(max_retries, '.', sep='', end='', )
    max_retries -= 1
    sleep(1)  # delay before retrying
```

- If the connection was unsuccessful, a RuntimeError with the NETWORK_CONNECTION_ERROR error message is raised and init_wlan() returns False (unsuccessful connection).

```
if wlan.status() != network.STAT_GOT_IP:
    raise RuntimeError(NETWORK_CONNECTION_ERROR)
    return False
```

- However, if the connection was successful and an IP address was obtained, the ip addressed is printed to the console and init_wlan() returns True (successful connection):

```
else:
    ip = wlan.ifconfig()[0]

    print( 'Connected: ip = {}'.format(ip))
    return True
```

- The module function get_ip() returns the IP address if connected to the WiFi network. If not connected to the WiFi network, the function raises a Runtime Error, printing the SSID_ERROR message to the console.

  Note that the ifconfig() method returns a 4-tuple (IP address, subnet mask, gateway, DNS server), and that ifconfig()[0] accesses the IP address.

```
def get_ip():
    if wlan.isconnected():
        return wlan.ifconfig()[0]
    else:
        print('\nNot connected')
        raise RuntimeError(SSID_ERROR)
        return None
```

get_socket.py

The following code creates a socket object and returns it.

```
"""
get_socket.py
-------------
To create a socket, use the ``get_socket.init()`` function:

Example::
        >>> import get_socket
        >>> s = get_socket.init(80, muted=False)

Refer to:
  https://docs.micropython.org/en/latest/library/socket.html
"""
import socket

def init(port=80, muted=False):
    """Initialize a socket connection object

    :param port: Optional port (80 is the default)
    :type port: port number or None
    :param muted: False (default)
    :type muted: bool

    :return: socket
    :rtype: socket object

    """
    # Define the socket address tuple, listening for
    #    connections on all available network interfaces
    addr = socket.getaddrinfo('0.0.0.0', port)[0][-1]

    # Create a socket object
    s = socket.socket()
```

```
    # Enable address reuse for restarts
    s.setsockopt(socket.SOL_SOCKET, socket.SO_REUSEADDR, 1)

    # Bind server socket to IP address and port
    s.bind(addr)

    # Listen for any incoming client connections
    s.listen(1)

    # Display the address the socket is listening on,
    #   if not muted
    if not muted:
        print('listening on: {}'.format(addr))

    return s
```

Fig 4-x. get_socket.py

Code Explanation

Let's look at how the code works.

- The socket module provides a low-level interface for creating and managing network connections using sockets.

```
import socket
```

- The init(port, muted) function creates a socket object and returns it.
  The port argument specifies the port for the socket to listen on.
  The muted argument determines whether to display to the console the address that the socket is listening on.

```
def init(port=80, muted=False):
    ...
```

- The socket.getaddrinfo(...) defines the socket address tuple and specifies that the socket should listen for connections on all available network interfaces.

```
addr = socket.getaddrinfo('0.0.0.0', port)[0][-1]
```

- socket.socket() creates a socket object 's'.

```
s = socket.socket()
```

- s.setsockopt(...) enables reuse of the socket address for restarts.

```
s.setsockopt(socket.SOL_SOCKET, socket.SO_REUSEADDR, 1)
```

- s.bind(...) binds the socket to the IP address and port.

```
s.bind(addr)
```

- s.listen() tells the socket to listen for any incoming client connections.

```
s.listen(1)
```

- The address that the socket is listening on should be displayed on the console, if the muted argument is False.

```
if not muted:
    print('listening on: {}'.format(addr))
```

- The init() function returns the socket object that it created.

```
return s
```

Reading the Pico's internal temperature sensor

The output of the internal temperature sensor on the Pico is a variable voltage that changes with the core temperature of the microcontroller. You can read this voltage through the fifth analogue-to-digital converter (ADC) channel (machine.ADC.CORE_TEMP) that is connected to the temperature sensor.

In Thonny's Python Shell, you can see the ADC channel for the internal temperature if your Pico is connected to your host computer:

```
>>> print('ADC channel: {}'.format(machine.ADC.CORE_TEMP))

ADC channel: 4
```

Note that the numbering for the ADC channels starts with zero.

The voltage is expressed as an unsigned 16-bit integer which ranges between 0 and 65,535. To find the temperature in Celsius, you multiply that number by a conversion factor 3.3V / (65535) to get the `ADC_voltage` as a temperature reading:

```
temperature_sensor = machine.ADC(machine.ADC.CORE_TEMP)
conversion_factor = 3.3 / (65535)
temp_reading = temperature_sensor.read_u16() * conversion_factor
```

and then plug the resulting reading into the following equation given in the Pico's datasheet (see Section "4.9.5. Temperature Sensor" for the RP2040 and Section "12.4.6. Temperature Sensor" for the RP2350) to calculate the temperature in Celsius:

```
tempCelsius = 27 - (temp_reading - 0.706)/0.001721
```

We'll first try things out in Thonny's Python Shell; then we'll write a Python program to print the Unix and local times as well as the temperature both in degrees Celsius and Fahrenheit. Because an Embedded Pico System is tight on resources, it is helpful to know when developing your system how much are available, in particular, how much memory—both volatile and non-volatile—you have to work with.

Code

Using Thonny (File > Save as), copy and save the Python module below to your target Pico microcontroller.

get_temperature.py

The `get_temperature.py` program displays flash info, time, and temperature of the microcontroller.

```
# get_temperature.py - Display flash info, time, and temperature
#   of the microcontroller

import gc
from os import statvfs
from machine import ADC
from time import sleep, time, localtime

# Get the number of bytes of available heap RAM
gc.collect()
free_memory = gc.mem_free()

# Display the amount of free RAM on the console
KB = 1024
print("Free Memory Size: {:,} bytes, {:,.1f} KB".\
      format(free_memory, free_memory / KB))

# Get flash memory size and storage consumption
flash_status = statvfs("/")
flash_size = flash_status[1] * flash_status[2]
flash_free = flash_status[0] * flash_status[3]
flash_used = flash_size - flash_free

# Display the flash file system stats on the console
print("File System Size: {:,} bytes, {:,.1f} KB".\
      format(flash_size, flash_size / KB))
print("File System Used: {:,} bytes, {:,.1f} KB".\
      format(flash_used, flash_used / KB))
print("File System Free: {:,} bytes, {:,.1f} KB\n".\
      format(flash_free, flash_free / KB))

# Set up ADC internal temperature reading
temperature_sensor = ADC(ADC.CORE_TEMP)
conversion_factor = 3.3 / (65535)

while True:
    # Get the Unix time and Local time
    time_unix  = time() # Unix epoch time
    time_local = "%4d/%02d/%02d %02d:%02d:%02d" \
                 % localtime(time_unix)[:6]

    # Get the core temperature of the microcontroller
```

```
    temp_reading = temperature_sensor.read_u16() \
                   * conversion_factor
    tempCelsius = 27 - (temp_reading - 0.706)/0.001721
    tempFahrenheit = 1.8 * tempCelsius + 32

    # Display temperature on the console
    print("{}, {}, {:,.1f} C, {:,.1f} F". \
      format(time_unix, time_local, tempCelsius, tempFahrenheit))

sleep(1)  # delay
```

Fig 4-x. get_temperature.py

Code Explanation

Let's look at how the code works.

- The gc module provides an interface to the garbage collector.
  The statvfs() module function retrieves information about the file system.
  The ADC module provides an interface to the Analog-to-Digital Converter (ADC) on the Pico.
  The sleep() module function is needed to introduce delays in the code execution.
  The time() module function returns the current time in seconds since the Epoch.
  The localtime() module function converts the time in seconds since the Epoch into a human-readable date and time format.

```
import gc
from os import statvfs
from machine import ADC
from time import sleep, time, localtime
```

- Getting an accurate number of bytes of available heap RAM requires first using MicroPython's garbage collector to reclaim memory from objects that are no longer actively used by your MicroPython program. This is followed by the garbage collector's mem_free() function.

  ```
  gc.collect()
  free_memory = gc.mem_free()
  ```

- The amount of free RAM is shown on the console in bytes and kilobytes.

```
KB = 1024
print("Free Memory Size: {:,} bytes, {:,.1f}
KB".format(free_memory, free_memory / KB))
```

- The statvfs() module function tells you the flash memory size and storage consumption on the Pico.
  flash_size = fragment size * size of fs in f_frsize units
  flash_free = file system block size * number of free blocks

  ```
  flash_status = statvfs("/")
  flash_size = flash_status[1] * flash_status[2]
  ```

```
flash_free = flash_status[0] * flash_status[3]
flash_used = flash_size - flash_free
```

- The flash memory size and storage consumption are displayed on the console in bytes and in kilobytes.

````
print("File System Size: {:,} bytes, {:,.1f} KB".\
      format(flash_size, flash_size / KB))
print("File System Used: {:,} bytes, {:,.1f} KB".\
      format(flash_used, flash_used / KB))
print("File System Free: {:,} bytes, {:,.1f} KB\n".\
      format(flash_free, flash_free / KB))```

* The internal temperature is read using the Pico's built-in
Analog-to-Digital Converter (ADC).
```python
temperature_sensor = ADC(ADC.CORE_TEMP)
conversion_factor = 3.3 / (65535)
````

- Getting the Unix time and the local time.

```
time_unix  = time() # Unix epoch time
time_local = "%4d/%02d/%02d %02d:%02d:%02d" \
             % localtime(time_unix)[:6]
```

- Getting the core temperature of the microcontroller. You can use the Pico's ADC to determine this temperature by reading the Pico's internal temperature sensor and converting that digital value to a temperature.

```
temp_reading = temperature_sensor.read_u16() \
               * conversion_factor
temp_celsius = 27 - (temp_reading - 0.706)/0.001721
tempFahrenheit = 1.8 * tempCelsius + 32
```

- The Unix time and local time are displayed on the console along with the core temperature in degrees Celsius and degrees Fahrenheit.

```
print("{}, {}, {:,.1f} C, {:,.1f} F".\
      format(time_unix, time_local, tempCelsius,
tempFahrenheit))
```

- A delay is added to make it easier to read the console display.

```
time.sleep(1)  # delay
```

Procedure / Steps

Interactive Session in Thonny's Python Shell

Run the following MicroPython code interactively to read the core temperature of the Pico.

1. In the the Python Shell area at the bottom of the Thonny window, click just to the right of the “>>>” symbols
```

2. Type the following and press **ENTER**:
   `import machine`
3. Type the following and press **ENTER**:
   `print('ADC channel: {}'.format(machine.ADC.CORE_TEMP))`
4. Type the following and press **ENTER**:
   `temperature_sensor = machine.ADC(machine.ADC.CORE_TEMP)`
5. Type the following and press **ENTER**:
   `conversion_factor = 3.3 / (65535)`
6. Type the following and press **ENTER**:
   `temp_reading = temperature_sensor.read_u16() * conversion_factor`
7. Type the following and press **ENTER**:
   `tempCelsius = 27 - (temp_reading - 0.706)/0.001721`
8. Type the following and press **ENTER**:
   `print("Temperature: {} C".format(tempCelsius))`

Something like the following will appear in the Thonny Python Shell area:

```
>>> import machine
>>> print("ADC channel: {}".format(machine.ADC.CORE_TEMP))
ADC channel: 4
>>> temperature_sensor = machine.ADC(machine.ADC.CORE_TEMP)
>>> conversion_factor = 3.3 / (65535)
>>> temp_reading = temperature_sensor.read_u16() *
conversion_factor
>>> tempCelsius = 27 - (temp_reading - 0.706)/0.001721
>>> print("Temperature: {} C".format(tempCelsius))
Temperature: 26.10811 C
>>>
```

get_temperature.py

Run the MicroPython code on your target Pico.

1. Using Thonny (File > Open), select get_temperature.py
2. Go to the Run menu
   Select "Run current script"

Tests and Results

MicroPython itself occupies around 1MB of non-volatile flash memory. The original Pico has 256KB of RAM and 2MB of flash; the Pico 2W twice those amounts. That leaves about 1MB for you to store programs and save data on the original Pico or 3Mb on the Pico 2W. If you run getTemperature.py on the original Pico, you should see the amount of available memory and a list of times and temperatures separated by commas. Example:

```
Free Memory Size: 200,432 bytes, 195.7 KB
File System Size: 868,352 bytes, 848.0 KB
File System Used: 561,152 bytes, 548.0 KB
File System Free: 307,200 bytes, 300.0 KB

1758489600, 2025/09/21 21:09:20, 31.3 C, 88.3 F
1758489601, 2025/09/21 21:09:21, 32.7 C, 90.8 F
1758489602, 2025/09/21 21:09:22, 32.7 C, 90.8 F
...
```

The first column in the list of temperatures is the number of seconds that have elapsed since the Unix epoch, 00:00:00 UTC (Coordinated Universal Time) on January 1, 1970. The second column is today's local date and time. The third and fourth columns are the core temperature of the Pico in degrees Celsius and Fahrenheit, respectively.

You could open a CSV file on the Pico itself to log these temperatures. But be aware that logging data to its non-volatile file system risks *wearing out* the original Pico's 2Mb and the Pico 2W's 4Mb of flash memory over time since flash cannot be rewritten indefinitely. Plus, 2Mb / 4Mb might initially seem like plenty of storage for MicroPython, your programs and data to occupy, but it may turn out to be a limiting factor depending on your particular application. For example, assuming your Pico stored the above times and temperatures in the example above in a CSV file every second (3600 seconds / hour), the 2Mb flash file system on the original Pico would fill up in just over a half a day or so:

```
47 bytes / second * 3600 seconds / hour * 12 hours = 2,030,400
bytes
```

As an embedded system, a Pico's hardware resources are constrained (unless other "fixes" can be found such as adding an SD card that does robust wear-levelling). On the other hand, as an *Entity Event-Driven Embedded Pico System*, a Pico can communicate information to a data consumer through a RESTful API over a network and let the *client* determine whether and how to store the data. In other words, make data storage the data consumer's problem. (Compared to your Embedded Pico System, a microservice or other data consumer / AI agent will usually have greater storage capabilities.)

To make a Pico a data producer to which a client, a separate computer system or device, can easily exchange information, we'll set up the Pico as a web server with a RESTful interface. But before we get there, let's first set up a Pico as a web server just hosting a basic web page.

Creating a simple web server with sockets

Using *sockets*, turning a Pico into a web server is straightforward. If you have access to a secure wireless local area network (WLAN), establishing a network connection to it is a matter of initiating a WiFi connection and then running about a dozen or so lines of Python code to start hosting a simple web page.

Sockets interface an embedded Pico system's application to the network. Sockets were originally developed in C in the 1980s with Berkeley Unix that later became BSD, the "Berkeley Software Distribution" (which is the basis for the macOS). Sockets provide bi-directional communication for sending and receiving data between two systems such as a client and a server.

To set up a web server on a Pico, the Pico must first connect to a WLAN using the SSID ("Service Set Identifier") name of your WiFi network and a WiFi password. After your wireless router and the Pico perform a handshake, your router will assign your Pico a network address which your Pico then uses to open a network socket and begin listening for connections. When a client such as your web browser or another device connects a socket to the server, communications proceed until the client disconnects, leaving the Pico to wait for another connection.

At a high level, it's a 3-stage process:

1. Connect your Pico to a WLAN
2. Open a socket
3. Serve your webpage

Let's first start with a "Hello, world!" web page that displays the local time, the temperature of the microcontroller, and the amount of available RAM on your Pico. Then using the "Hello, Blinky!" setup presented in the previous chapter, we'll add a couple of buttons to the HTML to turn the external LED on and off. This shows that a Pico can be controlled over a wireless network!

Code

Using Thonny (File > Save as), copy and save the Python modules below to your Pico.

webserver_HelloWorld.py

This web server uses sockets to serve an HTML page that displays the local time, temperature of the microcontroller and the amount of free memory.

```
"""
webserver_HelloWorld.py
--------
Socket-based web server that displays the local time, temperature
  of the microcontroller and the amount of free memory

"""
import gc, sys, socket
from machine import ADC, reset
from time import sleep, time, localtime
import connect_wifi, get_socket

# Add my_secrets.py to the .gitignore file to make sure
#   that my_secrets.py is never checked into GitHub
import my_secrets
ssid = my_secrets.SSID            # Your SSID (Network Name)
password = my_secrets.PASSWORD  # Your WiFi PASSWORD

# Initialize the WiFi Interface
if not connect_wifi.init_wlan(ssid, password, max_retries=10):
    print('WiFi authentication error: {}'.\
          format(connect_wifi.SSID_ERROR))
    print('Exiting program')
    sys.exit(0)
else:
    # Use Port 80 = default network port number for HTTP
    s = get_socket.init(port=80)

# Construct HTML page
def webpage(time_local, temp_celsius, free_memory):
    html = f"""
        <!DOCTYPE html>
        <html>
        <head> <title>Pico W</title> </head>
        <body> <h1>Hello, world!</h1>
        <p>Local Date/Time: {time_local}</p>
        <p>Temperature: {temp_celsius}</p>
        <p>Memory Available: {free_memory}</p>
        </body>
        </html>
        """
    return str(html)

# Set up ADC internal temperature reading
temperature_sensor = ADC(ADC.CORE_TEMP)
conversion_factor = 3.3 / (65535)
```

```
# Web server using sockets
def handle_client(s):
    # Listen for connections
    while True:
        # Accept incoming connections
        client_socket, client_address = s.accept()

        # Receive data from the client
        request = client_socket.recv(1024)
        request = str(request)
        # print("\n{}".format(request))

        # Get the time
        time_unix  = time() # Unix epoch time
        time_local = "%4d/%02d/%02d %02d:%02d:%02d" \
                     % localtime(time_unix)[:6]

        # Get the core temperature of the microcontroller
        temp_reading = temperature_sensor.read_u16() \
                       * conversion_factor
        temp_celsius = 27 - (temp_reading - 0.706)/0.001721
        temp_celsius = "{:,.1f} C".format(temp_celsius)

        # Get the number of bytes of available heap RAM
        gc.collect()
        free_memory = gc.mem_free()

        # Generate the HTML page
        html = webpage(time_local, temp_celsius, free_memory)

        # Respond to the HTTP request with the HTML page
        #   HTTP status code: 200 for OK
        #   Content is an HTML markup document
        client_socket.send('HTTP/1.1 200 OK\r\n')
        client_socket.send('Content-type: text/html\r\n\r\n')
        client_socket.send(html)

        # Close the socket connection with the client
        client_socket.close()
        sleep(1)  # delay

if __name__ == '__main__':
    try:
        # Start web server
        handle_client(s)

    # Keyboard interrupt caught
    except KeyboardInterrupt:
        print("\nUser interrupted the program.")

    # Handle the network error
    except OSError as e:
        print("OSError: errno={} {}", format(e.errno, e.args[0]))
```

```
    # End the program gracefully
    finally:
        print("\nWeb server stopped.")
```

Fig 4-x. webserver_HelloWorld.py

Code Explanation

Let's look at how the code works.

- The gc module provides an interface to the garbage collector. The sys module is used to stop the execution of the current program if the WiFi network is unavailable. The socket module provides a low-level interface for creating and managing network connections using sockets. The ADC module provides an interface to the Analog-to-Digital Converter (ADC) on the Pico. The reset() module function performs a hard reset of the microcontroller's hardware and restarts the MicroPython environment. The sleep() module function is needed to introduce delays in the code execution. The time() module function returns the current time in seconds since the Epoch. The localtime() module function converts the time in seconds since the Epoch into a human-readable date and time format. The connect_wifi module uses its `init_wlan()` function to connect to a wireless network and its `get_ip()` function to obtain an IP address for your Pico. The get_socket module creates a socket object and returns it.

```
import gc, sys, socket
from machine import ADC, reset
from time import sleep, time, localtime
import connect_wifi, get_socket
```

- The my_secrets module contains the name of your network (SSID) and your network password.

```
import my_secrets
ssid = my_secrets.SSID            # Your SSID (Network Name)
password = my_secrets.PASSWORD  # Your Wi-Fi PASSWORD
```

You should add my_secrets.py to your .gitignore file to make sure that my_secrets.py is never checked into a GitHub code repository.

```
# Add my_secrets.py to the .gitignore file to make sure
#   that my_secrets.py is never checked into GitHub
SSID     = 'MyNetwork'        # YOUR SSID (Network Name)
PASSWORD = 'MyPassword'       # YOUR WiFi PASSWORD
```

- To initialize the WiFi interface, use the connect_wifi.init_wlan() and connect_wifi.get_ip() module functions.

```
# Initialize the WiFi Interface
if not connect_wifi.init_wlan(ssid, password, max_retries=10):
    print('WiFi authentication error: {}'.\
          format(connect_wifi.SSID_ERROR))
    print('Exiting program')
    sys.exit(0)
else:
    ip_address = connect_wifi.get_ip()
```

- The webpage(...) function returns an HTML page with the following arguments inserted into the HTML page body.
    - time_local: The local time
    - temp_celsius: The core temperature of the microcontroller in degrees Celsius
    - free_memory: The amount of available RAM

```
def webpage(time_local, temp_celsius, free_memory):
    html = f"""
        <!DOCTYPE html>
        <html>
        <head> <title>Pico W</title> </head>
        <body> <h1>Hello, world!</h1>
        <p>Local Date/Time: {time_local}</p>
        <p>Temperature: {temp_celsius}</p>
        <p>Memory Available: {free_memory}</p>
        </body>
        </html>
        """
    return str(html)
```

- The internal temperature is read using the Pico's built-in Analog-to-Digital Converter (ADC).

```
temperature_sensor = ADC(ADC.CORE_TEMP)
conversion_factor = 3.3 / (65535)
```

- The handle_client() web server listens for connections in an infinite while loop and responds with an HTML page when a client connects with it.

```
def handle_client(s):
    # Listen for connections
    while True:
        ...
```

- The socket accept() function listens for an incoming connection from a client on the socket 's' that was previously created on the address and port.
  When a client successfully connects, accept() creates a new socket and assigns it to client_socket for handling communications with the client. It also assigns an IP address and port number of the connected client to client_address.

```
        client_socket, client_address = s.accept()
```

- The socket recv() function attempts to read up to 1024 bytes from the socket's receive buffer, blocking execution until data are received from the client or the client closes the connection with an empty bytes object (`b''`).
  Since the received data are assigned to request as a bytes object, request is then converted to a string for handling by the web server.

```
request = client_socket.recv(1024)
request = str(request)
```

- Getting the Unix time and the local time for the HTML page.

```
time_unix  = time() # Unix epoch time
time_local = "%4d/%02d/%02d %02d:%02d:%02d" \
             % localtime(time_unix)[:6]
```

- Getting the core temperature of the microcontroller.
  You can use the Pico's ADC to determine this temperature by reading the Pico's internal temperature sensor and converting that digital value to a temperature.

```
temp_reading = temperature_sensor.read_u16() \
               * conversion_factor
temp_celsius = 27 - (temp_reading - 0.706)/0.001721
temp_celsius = "{:,.1f} C".format(temp_celsius)
```

- Getting an accurate number of bytes of available heap RAM requires first using MicroPython's garbage collector to reclaim memory from objects that are no longer actively used by the MicroPython program. This is followed by the garbage collector's mem_free() function.

```
gc.collect()
free_memory = gc.mem_free()
```

- The handle_client() web server generates an HTML page showing the time, core temperature of the microcontroller, and the amount of RAM available, and sends it to the client with a header that specifies the HTTP protocol version being used and status code that the client's request was successfully received and processed. It also tells the client that the content being delivered is in HTML format before sending the HTML page on to the client.

```
html = webpage(time_local, temp_celsius, free_memory)

client_socket.send('HTTP/1.1 200 OK\r\n')
client_socket.send('Content-type: text/html\r\n\r\n')
client_socket.send(html)
```

- After returning the HTML page to the client, the connection to the client is closed and a delay added before listening for another client connection request.

```
client_socket.close()
sleep(1)  # delay
```

- The try-except block starts the web server but catches a user interrupt (e.g. Ctrl-C) and other OS errors, and prints the message "Web server stopped." to the console when the program stops.

```
    try:
        # Start web server
        handle_client(s)

    # Keyboard interrupt caught
    except KeyboardInterrupt:
        print("\nUser interrupted the program.")

    # Handle the network error
    except OSError as e:
        print("OSError: errno={} {}", format(e.errno, e.args[0]))

    # End the program gracefully
    finally:
        print("\nWeb server stopped.")
```

webserver_HelloBlinky.py

This web server uses sockets to serve an HTML form with buttons that turn an external LED on and off. It also displays the local time, temperature of the microcontroller and the amount of free memory.

```
"""
webserver_HelloBlinky.py
--------
Socket-based web server for turning an LED ON and OFF

"""
import gc, sys, socket
from machine import Pin, ADC, reset
from time import sleep, time, localtime
import connect_wifi, get_socket

# Add my_secrets.py to the .gitignore file to make sure
#   that my_secrets.py is never checked into GitHub
import my_secrets
ssid = my_secrets.SSID          # Your SSID (Network Name)
password = my_secrets.PASSWORD  # Your WiFi PASSWORD

# Initialize the WiFi Interface
if not connect_wifi.init_wlan(ssid, password, max_retries=10):
    print('WiFi authentication error: {}'.\
          format(connect_wifi.SSID_ERROR))
    print('Exiting program')
    sys.exit(0)
else:
    # Use Port 80 = default network port number for HTTP
    s = get_socket.init(port=80)

# Construct HTML page
def webpage(time_local, temp_celsius, free_memory, led_state):
    # Template HTML
    html = f"""
```

```
    <!DOCTYPE html>
    <html>
    <head> <title>Pico W</title> </head>
    <body> <h1>Hello, Blinky!!</h1>
    <form action="./light_on">
    <input type="submit" value="Turn LED on" />
    </form>
    <form action="./light_off">
    <input type="submit" value="Turn LED off" />
    </form>
    <p>LED is {led_state}</p>
    <p>Local Date/Time: {time_local}</p>
    <p>Temperature: {temp_celsius}</p>
    <p>Memory Available: {free_memory}</p>
    </body>
    </html>
    """
  return str(html)

# Set up external LED
led = Pin(16, Pin.OUT)  # GPIO16

# Set up ADC internal temperature reading
temperature_sensor = ADC(ADC.CORE_TEMP)
conversion_factor = 3.3 / (65535)

# Web server using sockets
def handle_client(s):
    # Listen for connections
    while True:
        # Accept incoming connections
        client_socket, client_address = s.accept()

        # Receive data from the client
        request = client_socket.recv(1024)
        request = str(request)
        # print("\n{}".format(request))

        # Get the time
        time_unix  = time() # Unix epoch time
        time_local = "%4d/%02d/%02d %02d:%02d:%02d" \
                     % localtime(time_unix)[:6]

        # Get the core temperature of the microcontroller
        temp_reading = temperature_sensor.read_u16() \
                       * conversion_factor
        temp_celsius = 27 - (temp_reading - 0.706)/0.001721
        temp_celsius = "{:,.1f} C".format(temp_celsius)

        # Get the number of bytes of available heap RAM
        gc.collect()
        free_memory = gc.mem_free()
```

```
        # Check if led has been turned on or off
        led_on  = request.find('/light_on')
        led_off = request.find('/light_off')

        led_state = ""
        if led_on == 6:
            # print("Led on")
            led.value(1)
            led_state = "ON"

        if led_off == 6:
            # print("Led off")
            led.value(0)
            led_state = "OFF"

        # Generate the HTML page
        html = webpage(time_local, \
                       temp_celsius, \
                       free_memory, \
                       led_state)

        # Respond to the HTTP request with the HTML page
        #   HTTP status code: 200 for OK
        #   Content is an HTML markup document
        client_socket.send('HTTP/1.1 200 OK\r\n')
        client_socket.send('Content-type: text/html\r\n\r\n')
        client_socket.send(html)

        # Close socket connection with the client
        client_socket.close()
        sleep(1)  # delay

if __name__ == '__main__':
    try:
        # Start web server
        handle_client(s)

    # Keyboard interrupt caught
    except KeyboardInterrupt:
        print("\nUser interrupted the program.")

    # Handle the network error
    except OSError as e:
        print("OSError: errno={} {}", format(e.errno, e.args[0]))

    # End the program gracefully
    finally:
        print("\nWeb server stopped.")
```

Fig 4-x. webserver_HelloBlinky.py

Code Explanation

Let's look at how the code works.

- The gc module provides an interface to the garbage collector.
  The sys module is used to stop the execution of the current program if the WiFi network is unavailable.
  The socket module provides a low-level interface for creating and managing network connections using sockets.
  The Pin module allows you to configure and control GPIO pins on the Pico.
  The ADC module provides an interface to the Analog-to-Digital Converter (ADC) on the Pico.
  The reset() module function performs a hard reset of the microcontroller's hardware and restarts the MicroPython environment.
  The sleep() module function is needed to introduce delays in the code execution.
  The time() module function returns the current time in seconds since the Epoch.
  The localtime() module function converts the time in seconds since the Epoch into a human-readable date and time format.
  The connect_wifi module uses its `init_wlan()` function to connect to a wireless network and its `get_ip()` function to obtain an IP address for your Pico.
  The get_socket module creates a socket object and returns it.

```
import gc, sys, socket
from machine import Pin, ADC, reset
from time import sleep, time, localtime
import connect_wifi, get_socket
```

- The my_secrets module contains the name of your network (SSID) and your network password.

```
import my_secrets
ssid = my_secrets.SSID          # Your SSID (Network Name)
password = my_secrets.PASSWORD  # Your Wi-Fi PASSWORD
```

You should add my_secrets.py to your .gitignore file to make sure that my_secrets.py is never checked into a GitHub code repository.

```
# Add my_secrets.py to the .gitignore file to make sure
#   that my_secrets.py is never checked into GitHub
SSID     = 'MyNetwork'         # YOUR SSID (Network Name)
PASSWORD = 'MyPassword'        # YOUR WiFi PASSWORD
```

- To initialize the WiFi interface, use the connect_wifi.init_wlan() and connect_wifi.get_ip() module functions.

```
# Initialize the WiFi Interface
if not connect_wifi.init_wlan(ssid, password, max_retries=10):
    print('WiFi authentication error: {}'.\
          format(connect_wifi.SSID_ERROR))
    print('Exiting program')
```

```
    sys.exit(0)
else:
    ip_address = connect_wifi.get_ip()
```

- The webpage(...) function returns an HTML page with the following arguments inserted into the HTML page body.
    - time_local: The local time
    - temp_celsius: The core temperature of the microcontroller in degrees Celsius
    - free_memory: The amount of available RAM
    - led_state: Whether the attached LED is ON or OFF

```
def webpage(time_local, temp_celsius, free_memory, led_state):
    html = f"""
        <!DOCTYPE html>
        <html>
        <head> <title>Pico W</title> </head>
        <body> <h1>Hello, Blinky!!</h1>
        <form action="./light_on">
        <input type="submit" value="Turn LED on" />
        </form>
        <form action="./light_off">
        <input type="submit" value="Turn LED off" />
        </form>
        <p>LED is {led_state}</p>
        <p>Local Date/Time: {time_local}</p>
        <p>Temperature: {temp_celsius}</p>
        <p>Memory Available: {free_memory}</p>
        </body>
        </html>
        """
    return str(html)
```

- led = Pin(...) sets up the LED on the designated GPIO pin.

```
led = Pin(16, Pin.OUT)  # GPIO16
```

- The internal temperature is read using the Pico's built-in Analog-to-Digital Converter (ADC).

```
temperature_sensor = ADC(ADC.CORE_TEMP)
conversion_factor = 3.3 / (65535)
```

- The handle_client() web server listens for connections in an infinite while loop and responds with an HTML page when a client connects with it.

```
def handle_client(s):
    # Listen for connections
    while True:
        ...
```

- The socket accept() function listens for an incoming connection from a client on the socket 's' that was previously created on the address and port.
  When a client successfully connects, accept() creates a new socket and assigns it to client_socket for handling communications with

the client. It also assigns an IP address and port number of the connected client to client_address.

```
client_socket, client_address = s.accept()
```

- The socket recv() function attempts to read up to 1024 bytes from the socket's receive buffer, blocking execution until data are received from the client or the client closes the connection with an empty bytes object (`b''`).
Since the received data are assigned to request as a bytes object, request is then converted to a string for handling by the web server.

```
request = client_socket.recv(1024)
request = str(request)
```

- Getting the Unix time and the local time for the HTML page.

```
time_unix  = time() # Unix epoch time
time_local = "%4d/%02d/%02d %02d:%02d:%02d" \
             % localtime(time_unix)[:6]
```

- Getting the core temperature of the microcontroller.
You can use the Pico's ADC to determine this temperature by reading the Pico's internal temperature sensor and converting that digital value to a temperature.

```
temp_reading = temperature_sensor.read_u16() \
               * conversion_factor
temp_celsius = 27 - (temp_reading - 0.706)/0.001721
temp_celsius = "{:,.1f} C".format(temp_celsius)
```

- Getting an accurate number of bytes of available heap RAM requires first using MicroPython's garbage collector to reclaim memory from objects that are no longer actively used by the MicroPython program. This is followed by the garbage collector's mem_free() function.

```
gc.collect()
free_memory = gc.mem_free()
```

- Checking if the led has been turned on or off.
The find() method is a built-in Python string method used to locate the starting index of the substring '/light_on' and the substring '/light_off' within the request string.
For example, if the request string is "b'GET /light_on HTTP/1.1", find('/light_on') would return 6 (the index where /light_on starts).
The led would be turned on and the led_state set to "ON".
If the '/light_on' is not found, find() returns -1.

```
led_on  = request.find('/light_on')
led_off = request.find('/light_off')

led_state = ""
if led_on == 6:
    # print("Led on")
    led.value(1)
    led_state = "ON"

if led_off == 6:
```

```
            # print("led off")
            led.value(0)
            led_state = "OFF"
```

- The handle_client() web server generates an HTML page showing the time, core temperature of the microcontroller, and the amount of RAM available, and sends it to the client with a header that specifies the HTTP protocol version being used and status code that the client's request was successfully received and processed. It also tells the client that the content being delivered is in HTML format before sending the HTML page on to the client.

```
    html = webpage(time_local, \
                   temp_celsius, \
                   free_memory, \
                   led_state)

    client_socket.send('HTTP/1.1 200 OK\r\n')
    client_socket.send('Content-type: text/html\r\n\r\n')
    client_socket.send(html)
```

- After returning the HTML page to the client, the connection to the client is closed and a delay added before listening for another client connection request.

```
    client_socket.close()
    sleep(1)  # delay
```

- The try-except block starts the web server but catches a user interrupt (e.g. Ctrl-C) and other OS errors, and prints the message "Web server stopped." to the console when the program stops.

```
try:
    # Start web server
    handle_client(s)

# Keyboard interrupt caught
except KeyboardInterrupt:
    print("\nUser interrupted the program.")

# Handle the network error
except OSError as e:
    print("OSError: errno={} {}", format(e.errno, e.args[0]))

# End the program gracefully
finally:
    print("\nWeb server stopped.")
```

Procedure / Steps

> ⚠ **Warning:** Do not connect your host or your Pico to the internet on an insecure network!!!

Run the MicroPython code on your target Pico.

webserver_HelloWorld.py

1. Using Thonny (File > Open), select webserver_HelloWorld.py
2. Go to the Run menu
   Select "Run current script"

webserver_HelloBlinky.py

1. Using Thonny (File > Open), select webserver_HelloBlinky.py
2. Go to the Run menu
   Select "Run current script"

Tests and Results

1. When you run WebServer_HelloWorld.py, something like the following should appear in the Thonny Python Shell area. The ip address will likely be different for your particular wireless network:

```
Waiting for connection...
10.9.8.7.6.5.4.Connected:
ip = 192.168.1.100
listening on: ('0.0.0.0', 80)
```

2. If you open a browser to the ip address after starting the "Hello, world!" (WebServer_HelloWorld.py) web server, you should see something like:

> **Hello, world!**
>
> Local Date/Time: 2025/09/14 13:54:56
>
> Temperature: 33.59845 C
>
> Memory Available: 182928

3. If you open a browser to the ip address after starting the "Hello, Blinky!" (WebServer_HelloBlinky.py) web server, you should see something like:

> **Hello, Blinky!**
>
> [Turn LED on]
>
> [Turn LED off]
>
> LED is ON
>
> Local Date/Time: 2025/09/14 13:54:56
>
> Temperature: 33.59845 C
>
> Memory Available: 182928

By clicking the "Turn LED on" and "Turn LED off" buttons, the Pico's external LED should turn on and off. Doing so shows that a Pico can be controlled over a wireless network via an interactive web page. We're now ready to set up a Pico as a web server with a *RESTful API*, more specifically as an Event-Driven Embedded Pico System that can communicate with other computer systems and devices over a wireless network.

Communicating JSON objects via a RESTful API

Given what you've learned so far in this chapter, hosting a web server on your Pico that communicates via a RESTful API using JSON as the interchange format is straightforward:

1. Convert a Python dictionary to a JSON formatted string using json.dumps()
2. Send a "HTTP/1.1 201 Created Content-type: application/json" to the client via socket.send()
3. Return the JSON string to the client also via a socket.send()

JSON is natively supported by most modern programming languages like Python. The json module included with MicroPython converts JSON objects to Python objects and vice versa. JSON objects are formatted in key-value pairs and resemble a Python dictionary. JSON keys are strings; JSON values are any supported type like dictionaries, arrays, strings, numbers, booleans, etc. (see https://www.json.org/):

JSON	Python
object	dict
array	list
string	str
number (int)	int
number (real)	float
true	True
false	False
null	None

Fig 4-x. JSON to Python mapping

JSON is also supported by databases such as Amazon RDS, Oracle, Microsoft SQL Server, MySQL / MariaDB, SQLite, and so forth, making it an ideal interchange format for Event-Driven Embedded Pico Systems since client data consumers can easily pull JSON information through a RESTful API hosted by your Pico.

To make the individual Entity Events uniquely identifiable for a client data consumer, you'll include the machine unique ID (which is the serial number of the flash on the Pico) and you'll add an event ID (as a randomly generated unique universal ID). Along with the time, the client will therefore know the answers to the questions *Who?*, *What?*, and *When?*—the essentials for describing an Entity Event.

Code

Using Thonny (File > Save as), copy and save the Python module below to your target Pico microcontroller.

webserver_HelloPico.py

This program adds event information to a socket-based web server's responses with minimal overhead. This allows the application to communicate events through its RESTful API as data that it senses from the physical world and as actions that it performs in it, transforming the embedded Pico system into an Entity-Event Driven one!

```
"""
webserver_HelloPico.py
--------
Socket-based web server that turns an LED ON and OFF
  and responds with an Event
"""
import gc, sys, socket
from machine import Pin, unique_id, ADC, reset
from time import sleep, time, localtime
from os import urandom
from json import dumps
import connect_wifi, get_socket

# Add my_secrets.py to the .gitignore file to make sure
#   that my_secrets.py is never checked into GitHub
import my_secrets
ssid = my_secrets.SSID            # Your SSID (Network Name)
password = my_secrets.PASSWORD  # Your WiFi PASSWORD

# Initialize the WiFi Interface
if not connect_wifi.init_wlan(ssid, password, max_retries=10):
    print('WiFi authentication error: {}'.\
          format(connect_wifi.SSID_ERROR))
    print('Exiting program')
    sys.exit(0)
else:
    # Use Port 80 = default network port number for HTTP
    s = get_socket.init(port=80)

"""Generate a version 4 UUID compliant to RFC 4122"""
def uuid4():
    random_x = bytearray(urandom(16))
    random_x[6] = (random_x[6] & 0x0F) | 0x40
    random_x[8] = (random_x[8] & 0x3F) | 0x80
    h = random_x.hex()
    return str('-'.join((h[0:8], h[8:12], \
                         h[12:16], h[16:20], h[20:32])))
```

```
# Set up external LED
led = Pin(16, Pin.OUT)

# Set up ADC internal temperature reading
temperature_sensor = ADC(ADC.CORE_TEMP)
conversion_factor = 3.3 / (65535)

# Web server using sockets
def handle_client(s):
    # Listen for connections
    while True:
        # Accept incoming connections
        client_socket, client_address = s.accept()

        # Receive data from the client
        request = client_socket.recv(1024)
        request = str(request)
        # print("\n{}".format(request))

        # Get a unique id for this event
        event_id = uuid4()
        # print (event_id)

        # Get the time
        time_unix  = time() # Unix epoch time
        time_local = "%4d/%02d/%02d %02d:%02d:%02d" \
                     % localtime(time_unix)[:6]

        # Get the core temperature of the RP2040
        temp_reading = temperature_sensor.read_u16() \
                       * conversion_factor
        temp_celsius = 27 - (temp_reading - 0.706)/0.001721
        temp_celsius = "{:,.1f} C".format(temp_celsius)

        # Check the number of bytes of available heap RAM
        KB = 1024
        gc.collect()
        free_memory = gc.mem_free()
        free_memory = "{:,.1f} KB".format(free_memory/KB)

        # Check if led has been turned on or off
        led_on  = request.find('/light_on')
        led_off = request.find('/light_off')

        led_state = ""
        if led_on == 6:
            print("led on")
            led.value(1)
            led_state = "ON"

        if led_off == 6:
            print("led off")
            led.value(0)
```

```
            led_state = "OFF"

        # Create an Event as a MicroPython dictionary
        xDict = {
            "event_id": event_id,
            "version": 1.01,
            "machine_unique_id": unique_id().hex(),
            "time_unix":    time_unix,
            "time_local":   time_local,
            "temp_celsius": temp_celsius,
            "free_memory":  free_memory,

            "led_state":    led_state
        }

        # Convert the Event dictionary into a JSON UTF-8 string
        resp = dumps(xDict).encode()

        # Send response back to client
        client_socket.send('HTTP/1.0 200 OK\r\n')
        client_socket.send(\
            'Content-type: application/json\r\n\r\n')
        client_socket.send(resp)

        # close socket connection with the client
        client_socket.close()
        sleep(1)


if __name__ == '__main__':
    try:
        # Start web server
        handle_client(s)

    # Keyboard interrupt caught
    except KeyboardInterrupt:
        print("\nUser interrupted the program.")

    # Handle the network error
    except OSError as e:
        print("OSError: errno={} {}", format(e.errno, e.args[0]))

    # End the program gracefully
    finally:
        print("\nWeb server stopped.")
```

Fig 4-x. webserver_HelloPico.py

Code Explanation

Let's look at how the code works.

- The gc module provides an interface to the garbage collector.
  The sys module is used to stop the execution of the current program if the WiFi network is unavailable.
  The socket module provides a low-level interface for creating and managing network connections using sockets.
  The Pin module allows you to configure and control GPIO pins on the Pico.
  The unique_id module function returns a unique identifier for the Pico.
  The ADC module provides an interface to the Analog-to-Digital Converter (ADC) on the Pico.
  The reset() module function performs a hard reset of the microcontroller's hardware and restarts the MicroPython environment.
  The sleep() module function is needed to introduce delays in the code execution.
  The time() module function returns the current time in seconds since the Epoch.
  The localtime() module function converts the time in seconds since the Epoch into a human-readable date and time format.
  The urandom() module function generates a string of random bytes suitable for creating unique identifiers.
  The json dumps module is used for serialization, converting MicroPython dictionaries, lists, and other basic data types into JSON formatted strings-data that can be easily transmitted over networks and readily understood by data consumers.
  The connect_wifi module uses its init_wlan() function to connect to a wireless network and its get_ip() function to obtain an IP address for your Pico.
  The get_socket module creates a socket object and returns it.

```
import gc, sys, socket
from machine import Pin, unique_id, ADC, reset
from time import sleep, time, localtime
from os import urandom
from json import dumps
import connect_wifi, get_socket
```

- The my_secrets module contains the name of your network (SSID) and your network password.

```
import my_secrets
ssid = my_secrets.SSID          # Your SSID (Network Name)
password = my_secrets.PASSWORD  # Your Wi-Fi PASSWORD
```

- To initialize the WiFi interface, use the connect_wifi.init_wlan() and connect_wifi.get_ip() module functions.

```
# Initialize the WiFi Interface
if not connect_wifi.init_wlan(ssid, password, max_retries=10):
```

```
    print('WiFi authentication error: {}'.\
          format(connect_wifi.SSID_ERROR))
    print('Exiting program')
    sys.exit(0)
else:
    ip_address = connect_wifi.get_ip()
```

- The uuid4() function returns a version 4 UUID compliant to RFC 4122.
  This UUID uniquely identifies an Event.

```
def uuid4():
    ...
```

- random_x = bytearray(). This line gets 16 high-quality, cryptographically secure random bytes.

```
    random_x = bytearray(urandom(16))
```

- random_x[6] = () and random_x[8] = (). These lines set the "version" and "variant" bits per RFC 4122.

```
    random_x[6] = (random_x[6] & 0x0F) | 0x40
    random_x[8] = (random_x[8] & 0x3F) | 0x80
```

- h = random_x.hex() generates a 32-character hexadecimal string from the byte array.

```
    h = random_x.hex()
```

- return str(). This line returns the UUID string correctly formatted with hyphens.

```
    return str('-'.join((h[0:8], h[8:12], \
                         h[12:16], h[16:20], h[20:32])))
```

- led = Pin(...) sets up the LED on the designated GPIO pin.

```
led = Pin(16, Pin.OUT)  # GPIO16
```

- The internal temperature is read using the Pico's built-in Analog-to-Digital Converter (ADC).

```
temperature_sensor = ADC(ADC.CORE_TEMP)
conversion_factor = 3.3 / (65535)
```

- The handle_client() web server listens for connections in an infinite while loop and responds with a JSON response object when a client connects with it.

```
def handle_client(s):
    # Listen for connections
    while True:
        ...
```

- The socket accept() function listens for an incoming connection from a client on the socket 's' that was previously created on the address and port.
  When a client successfully connects, accept() creates a new socket and assigns it to client_socket for handling communications with the client. It also assigns an IP address and port number of the connected client to client_address.

```
        client_socket, client_address = s.accept()
```

- The socket recv() function attempts to read up to 1024 bytes from the socket's receive buffer, blocking execution until data are received from the client or the client closes the connection with an empty bytes object (`b''`).
  Since the received data are assigned to request as a bytes object, request is then converted to a string for handling by the web server.

  ```
  request = client_socket.recv(1024)
  request = str(request)
  ```

- Get a unique id for this event.

  ```
  event_id = uuid4()
  ```

- Getting the Unix time and the local time for the HTML page.

  ```
  time_unix  = time() # Unix epoch time
  time_local = "%4d/%02d/%02d %02d:%02d:%02d" \
               % localtime(time_unix)[:6]
  ```

- Getting the core temperature of the microcontroller.
  You can use the Pico's ADC to determine this temperature by reading the Pico's internal temperature sensor and converting that digital value to a temperature.

  ```
  temp_reading = temperature_sensor.read_u16() \
                 * conversion_factor
  temp_celsius = 27 - (temp_reading - 0.706)/0.001721
  temp_celsius = "{:,.1f} C".format(temp_celsius)
  ```

- Getting an accurate number of bytes of available heap RAM requires first using MicroPython's garbage collector to reclaim memory from objects that are no longer actively used by the MicroPython program. This is followed by the garbage collector's mem_free() function.

  ```
  gc.collect()
  free_memory = gc.mem_free()
  ```

- Checking if the led has been turned on or off.
  The find() method is a built-in Python string method used to locate the starting index of the substring '/light_on' and the substring '/light_off' within the request string.
  For example, if the request string is "b'GET /light_on HTTP/1.1", find('/light_on') would return 6 (the index where /light_on starts).
  The led would be turned on and the led_state set to "ON".
  If the '/light_on' is not found, find() returns -1.

  ```
  led_on  = request.find('/light_on')
  led_off = request.find('/light_off')

  led_state = ""
  if led_on == 6:
      print("led on")
      led.value(1)
      led_state = "ON"

  if led_off == 6:
      print("led off")
  ```

```
        led.value(0)
        led_state = "OFF"
```

- An Event answers the questions Who? What? and When? In this case, your Pico returns an Event as a JSON response object converted from a MicroPython dictionary that includes a unique id for the event, the event version, the Pico's flash serial number, the time, core temperature of the microcontroller, and the amount of RAM available. The Event can include not only data your Pico senses (like temperature), but actions it might have taken (such as turning an external LED ON or OFF).

```
    # Create the Event as a MicroPython dictionary
    xDict = {
        "event_id": event_id,
        "version": 1.01,
        "machine_unique_id": unique_id().hex(),
        "time_unix":    time_unix,
        "time_local":   time_local,
        "temp_celsius": temp_celsius,
        "free_memory":  free_memory,

        "led_state":    led_state
    }
```

- The Event dictionary should first be converted to a JSON response object–in this case a JSON string in UTF-8–when MicroPython returns it to the client.

```
    resp = dumps(xDict).encode()
```

- The handle_client() web server sends the Event to the client with a header that specifies the HTTP protocol version being used and status code that the client's request was successfully received and processed. It also tells the client that the content being delivered is in JSON format before sending the response on to the client.

```
    client_socket.send('HTTP/1.0 200 OK\r\n')
    client_socket.send(\
        'Content-type: application/json\r\n\r\n')
    client_socket.send(resp)
```

- After returning the JSON response object to the client, the connection to the client is closed and a delay added before listening for another client connection request.

```
    client_socket.close()
    sleep(1)  # delay
```

- The try-except block starts the web server but catches a user interrupt (e.g. Ctrl-C) and other OS errors, and prints the message "Web server stopped." to the console when the program stops.

```
try:
    # Start web server
    handle_client(s)

# Keyboard interrupt caught
except KeyboardInterrupt:
    print("\nUser interrupted the program.")
```

```
    # Handle the network error
    except OSError as e:
        print("OSError: errno={} {}", format(e.errno, e.args[0]))

    # End the program gracefully
    finally:
        print("\nWeb server stopped.")
```

Procedure / Steps

> ⚠ **Warning:** Do not connect your host or your Pico to the internet on an insecure network!!!

Run the MicroPython code on your target Pico.

webserver_HelloPico.py

1. Using Thonny (File > Open), select webserver_HelloPico.py
2. Go to the Run menu
   Select "Run current script"

Tests and Results

1. If you open a browser to the ip address with the API endpoint set to "light_on" (example: http://192.168.1.100/light_on) after starting the "Hello, Pico!" web server, you should see something like:


```
{
  "led_state": "ON",
  "temp_celsius": "35.0 C",
  "time_local": "2025/09/14 15:40:39",
  "event_id": "dbf543d4-c16e-4d20-b4f8-ad76e6b755ed",
  "free_memory": "178.2 KB",
  "time_unix": 1726409621,
  "machine_unique_id": "314159265358979323846zza",
  "version": 1.01
}
```


2. Now open your browser to the ip address with the API endpoint set to "light_off" (example: http://192.168.1.100/light_off). You should see something like:


```
{
  "led_state": "OFF",
  "temp_celsius": "34.5 C",
  "time_local": "2025/09/14 15:40:58",
  "event_id": "7f97f1b7-2b41-4458-92c9-1da193f06d28",
  "free_memory": "178.2 KB",
  "time_unix": 1726410228,
  "machine_unique_id": "314159265358979323846zza",
  "version": 1.01
}
```


Congratulations! By providing Event details to the web server responses, you've transformed your Pico into an Entity Event-Driven Embedded System. Microservices and other data consumers / AI agents that connect to your web server can read JSON objects through its *RESTful API* interface and readily understand details about a uniquely identified event-particulars about data your Pico senses (like temperature) and actions it might have taken (such as turning an external LED on or off).

References and Further Exploration

Event-Driven Architectures

- *Building Event Driven Microservices* by Adam Bellemare (O'Reilly, 2020, ISBN-13: 978-1492057895)

JSON

- https://www.json.org/json-en.html
- https://docs.python.org/3/library/json.html

RESTful web API design

- Best practices for RESTful web API design https://learn.microsoft.com/en-us/azure/architecture/best-practices/api-design

Roy Fielding

- Architectural Styles and the Design of Network-based Software Architectures https://ics.uci.edu/~fielding/pubs/dissertation/rest_arch_style.htm
- REST APIs must be hypertext-driven https://roy.gbiv.com/untangled/2008/rest-apis-must-be-hypertext-driven

Flask

- https://pypi.org/project/Flask/
- *Flask Web Development* 2nd ed. by Miguel Grinberg (O'Reilly: 2018, ISBN-13: 978-1491991732)
- The New and Improved Flask Mega-Tutorial https://courses.miguelgrinberg.com/p/flask-mega-tutorial

Universally Unique Identifiers (UUIDs)

- https://datatracker.ietf.org/doc/html/rfc4122
- https://datatracker.ietf.org/doc/html/rfc9562
- https://en.wikipedia.org/wiki/Universally_unique_identifier
- https://docs.python.org/3/library/uuid.html

Chapter 5

1. Chapter Introduction

2. Programming Environment and Setup
    a. Introduction
    b. Equipment and Components
    c. Setup and Construction
    d. Code

3. Introducing Microdot
    a. Introduction
    b. Code
    c. Procedure / Steps
    d. Tests and Results

4. Parsing Route (URL) Converters and Query Parameters
    a. Introduction
    b. Code
    c. Procedure / Steps
    d. Tests and Results

5. Performing actions via a RESTful API
    a. Introduction
    b. Code
    c. Procedure / Steps
    d. Tests and Results

6. Entity Event-Driven Embedded Pico Systems
    a. Introduction
    b. Code
    c. Procedure / Steps
    d. Tests and Results

7. References and Further Exploration

Web API Hosting with Microdot

Transform your Pico into an Entity Event-Driven Embedded System using Microdot

Using sockets to implement a web API on an embedded system is sometimes the only viable solution for creating an external communications interface for your Entity Event-Driven Embedded Pico System. The needs of your embedded application, for instance, can severely limit the memory and file storage available to operate a network interface. But resorting to sockets as a data transfer technology is at best a low-level solution and can be tricky to program for a beginning learner when developing applications more complicated than simply blinking an LED.

In this chapter we introduce *Microdot*, "the impossibly small web framework for Python and MicroPython" (https://microdot.readthedocs.io/en/latest/). Microdot is an *ultra* lightweight web application framework with a Flask-like syntax that can run on the highly constrained resources of a typical microcontroller.

Because of its relatively small code footprint, Flask (https://pypi.org/project/Flask/) is one of the most popular Python lightweight micro web frameworks used in Event-Driven microservices architectures today. Flask operates at a higher level of abstraction than a socket layer. Its core feature set consists of routing, request handling and blueprint modules. Flask's modular but extensible design makes it nearly ideal for creating lightweight microservices with RESTful APIs.

However, given the limited amount of memory and file storage on the Pico, a Flask deployment is unfortunately just too big for it. Thankfully, Miguel Grinberg, has created Microdot—an ultra lightweight microframework inspired by Flask but which is significantly lighter than Flask. Starting with its version 2.0 release in December of 2023, Microdot is fully asynchronous, thus improving web-server responsiveness for microcontrollers that lack threading support. Just like Flask, Microdot automatically converts HTTP responses to JSON format when returning Python dictionaries. Also like Flask, Microdot uses decorated functions to write web routes.

Microdot has a small footprint.

If you're only using its basic web routing features, then the core Microdot web server, microdot.py, is about *one twentieth* the size of Flask 3.0. Excluding comments and blank lines, the current version of Microdot—as of this writing—has 766 lines of code:

Microdot 2.3.2	files	blank	comment	code
microdot.py (minimal)	1	234	532	766

Fig 5-x. How big is Microdot?

In its full configuration with everything installed, Microdot 2.x is still only about *one tenth* the size of Flask. With an even lighter footprint than Flask, Microdot is therefore ideal for creating Pico-based API endpoints quickly that can be used for machine-to-machine (M2M) data exchanges.

Similar to Flask, Microdot uses route decorators to define and associate URL routes with specific view functions. These decorators specify how a view function should respond to an HTTP verb (method) corresponding to a particular URL path. Because Microdot 2.x is designed specifically for asynchronous operations, you should define your view functions with the keywords 'async def' since regular functions just block for however long they run.

View functions in Microdot receive a request object as their first positional argument. This object enables access to various request-related details headers, body data, and the HTTP method used. Like Flask, Microdot automatically applies default headers and status codes to the body of the response sent to the client as the return value of a view function.

Examples of primary HTTP verbs and their corresponding decorated view functions in Microdot:

GET: @app.get('/path')
Used to retrieve data from the Microdot server.

```
@app.get('/data')
async def get_data(request):
    return "The requested data."
```

POST: @app.post('/path')
Used to send data to the Microdot server for processing. (Often used for creating new resources or for form submissions.)

```
@app.post('/submit')
async def submit_form(request):
    return "Form submitted."
```

PUT: @app.put('/path')
Used to update or replace an existing resource on the Microdot server with the uploaded content. (The entire resource is typically updated.)

```
@app.put('/update_employee/<int:employee_id>')
async def update_employeee(request, employee_id):
    return f"Employee updated: {employee_id}."
```

PATCH: @app.patch('/path')
Used to make partial modifications to an existing resource on the Microdot server.

```
@app.patch('/invoices/<int:invoice_id>')
async def update_invoice_partial(request, invoice_id):
    return f"Invoice updated: {invoice_id}."
```

DELETE: @app.delete('/path')
Used to remove the specified resource from the Microdot server.

```
@app.delete('/delete_item/<int:item_id>')
async def delete_item(request, item_id):
    return f"Item deleted: {item_id}."
```

Multiple HTTP Verbs: @app.route('/path', methods=[...])
Also like Flask, Microdot can handle multiple HTTP verbs for a single URL path using the optional methods argument in the more general `app.route()` decorator.

```
@app.route('/items', methods=['GET', 'POST', 'PUT', \
                              'PATCH', 'DELETE'])
async def handle_items(request):
    if request.method == 'GET':
        return 'Retrieving item(s).'
    elif request.method == 'POST':
        return 'Creating a new item.'
    elif request.method == 'PUT':
        return "Updating item."
    elif request.method == 'PATCH':
        return "Modifying item."
    elif request.method == 'DELETE':
        return "Deleting item."
```

After working through the Microdot examples in this chapter, you'll be able to easily create web interfaces with RESTful APIs that communicate Entity Events about your Pico controlling and sensing the physical world to client data consumers in JSON format. While there may not be a way to completely isolate an application's code from its web framework for a given Entity Event-Driven Embedded

System, you'll find that Microdot can significantly contribute to a separation of concerns in your overall designs making them more flexible and extensible than designs that rely solely on low-level socket programming.

In the first section of this chapter, you'll write a 'Hello, world!' program using the Microdot web server with various view functions that handle web requests and return web responses for different URL routes. This straightforward program shows that, like Flask, Microdot can automatically convert Python dictionaries and lists to JSON objects when returning them as HTTP responses.

Like Flask, Microdot can parse URL parameters with Route (URL) Converters or Query Parameters. In the next section, you'll demonstrate both types of parsing with a 'Hello, <name>!' program.

In the third section, you'll use the HTTP verbs GET and POST in the methods argument of the @app.route() route decorator to handle an HTML form with buttons that turn an external LED on and off. But you'll also blink the LED by defining the HTTP endpoints '/light/on' and '/light/off' or by using URL parameters and adding the relevant view function to each route decorator in your 'Hello, Blinky!' program.

Finally, you'll see how to add event information to your Microdot web server responses with minimal overhead. This allows your application to communicate events through its RESTful API as data that it senses from the physical world and as actions that it performs in it, transforming your embedded Pico system into an Entity-Event Driven one!

Programming Environment and Setup

For the examples in this chapter, you'll need the following.

Programming Environment
Host computer running either:
- Windows
- Raspberry Pi OS or Linux
- macOS
Host computer with the following installed:
- Python 3.10 or above
- Thonny (thonny.org)
Target microcontroller:
- Pico with MicroPython installed
micro USB cable

Equipment and Components

Components used in this chapter (see fritzing.org for components created with Fritzing):

Description	Image
Male-to-male jumper wires	
Half or full-sized Breadboard	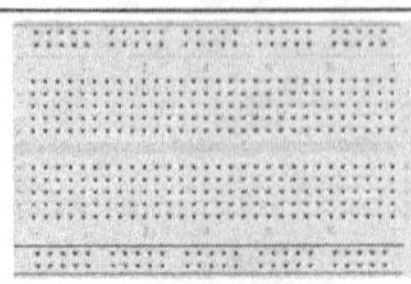
330 Ohm resistor (orange, orange, and brown stripes)	
Red LED - the anode (+ positive) lead is the longer lead - the cathode (- negative) lead is the shorter lead	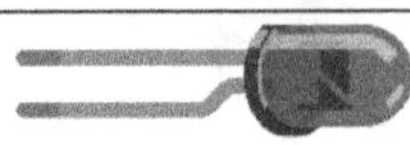

Fig 5-x. Components used in this chapter

Setup and Construction

Refer to Appendix A for a pinout guide to the Raspberry Pi Pico W.
Refer to Appendix C for a pinout guide to the Raspberry Pi Pico 2W.

Before you begin constructing the circuit, make sure your Pico is unplugged from your host computer.

1. Connect one end of a 330 Ohm resistor to the same column as the Pico's GP16 pin (this should be column 20 on a numbered breadboard with the Pico's GP01 pin aligned to column 1). Connect the other end to column 24.
2. Connect the anode (the longer leg) of the LED to the same column as the end of the resistor.
3. Connect the cathode (the shorter leg) to the ground rail on the breadboard.
4. Connect a GND pin (Pin 38) on the Pico with a jumper in column 3 to the ground rail on the breadboard.
5. Your finished circuit should look like Figure 5-x:

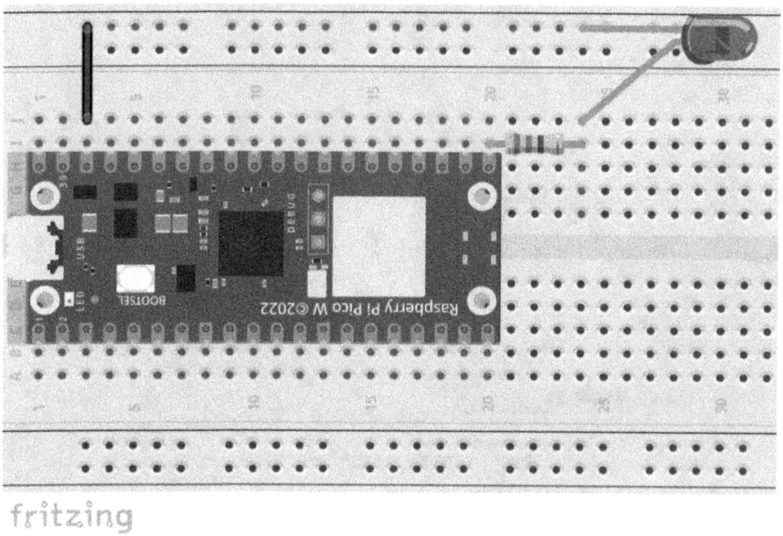

Fig 5-x. An external LED connected to the Pico

Now plug your Pico back into your host computer with a micro USB cable.

Installing Microdot

To install Microdot on your Pico using Thonny, select "Manage packages..." from the Tools menu:

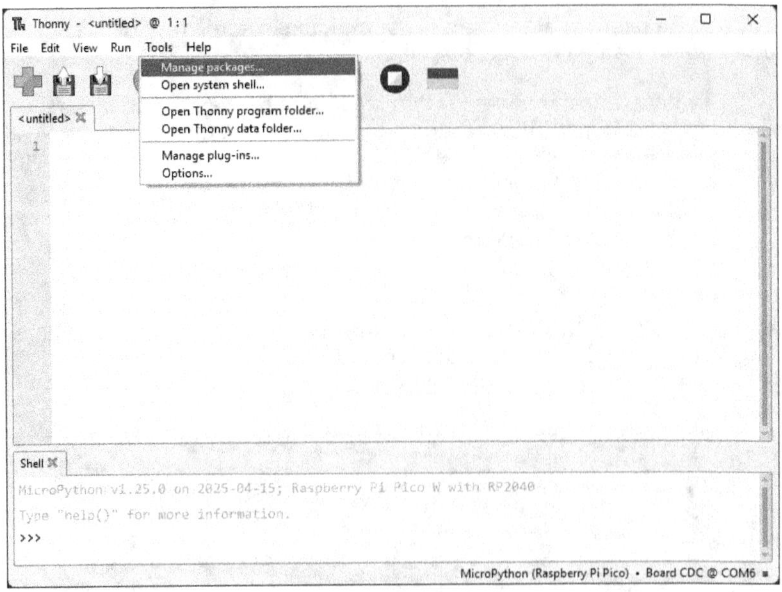

Fig 5-x. Thonny's Package Manager

Search for "microdot" and install the latest stable version of the package:

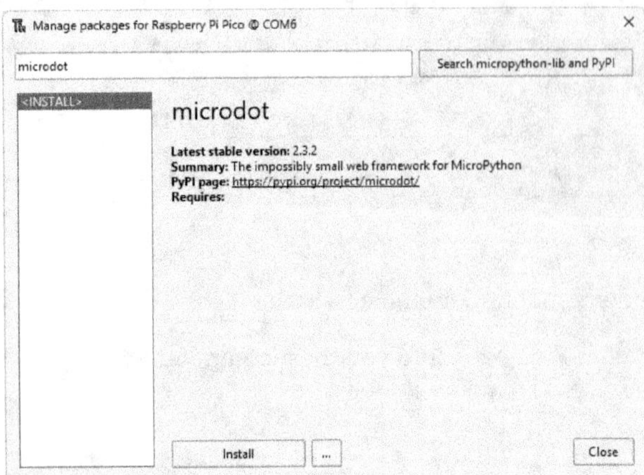

Fig 5-x. Installing Microdot with Thonny

Synchronizing the Pico's Real Time Clock using Thonny

To synchronize the Pico's Real Time Clock using Thonny, select "Options..." from the Tools menu:

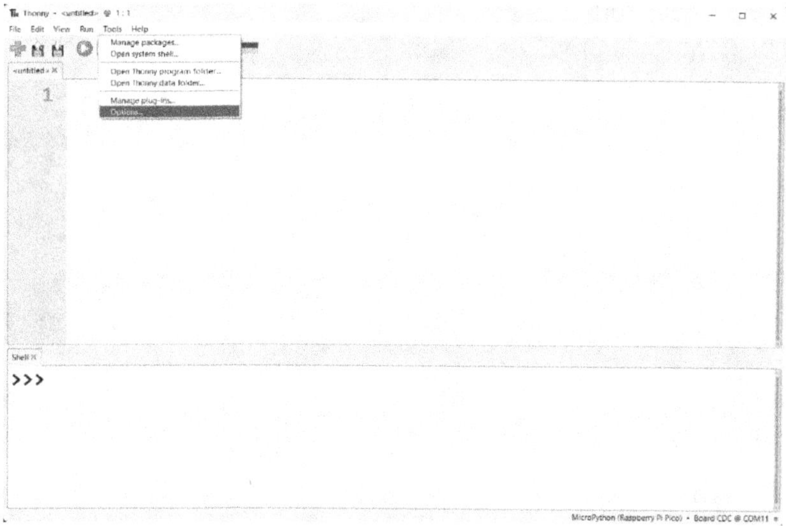

Fig 5-x. Thonny's Tools Options Menu

Choose the Interpreter tab and check the box labeled "Synchronize device's real time clock" to enable this feature.

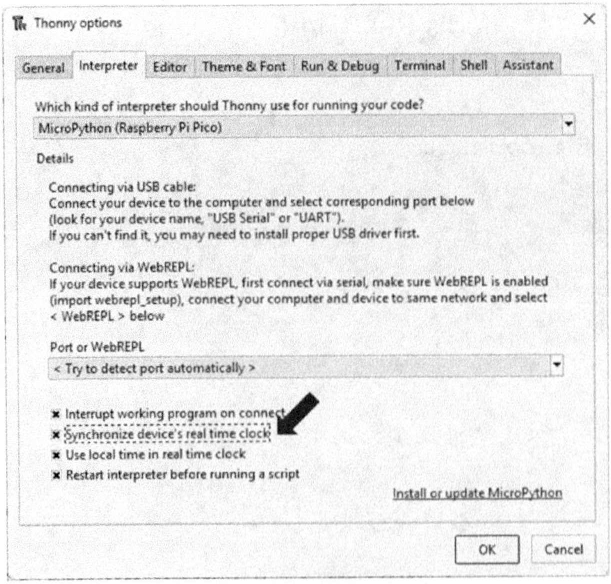

Fig 5-x. Synchronizing the Pico's RTC using Thonny

Code

Using Thonny (File > Save as), copy and save the Python modules below to your target Pico microcontroller.

my_secrets.py

This code separates sensitive information such as your WiFi credentials and other sensitive information from your application logic which helps prevent accidentally exposing sensitive information if you share your MicroPython code with others. It also makes your code more reusable since you can easily modify your authentication credentials in one place without having to change the Python programs that import it.

Keep this file in a directory accessible to the MicroPython interpreter's import path. If you use GitHub as a source code repository, make sure to add my_secrets.py to your .gitignore file so that my_secrets.py is not accidentally checked into GitHub.

```
# Add my_secrets.py to the .gitignore file to make sure
#   that my_secrets.py is never checked into GitHub
SSID     = 'MyNetwork'        # YOUR SSID (Network Name)
PASSWORD = 'MyPassword'       # YOUR WiFi PASSWORD
```

Fig 5-x. my_secrets_EXAMPLE.py

Code Explanation

Let's look at how to use the my_secrets.py module in your MicroPython code.

- The my_secrets module contains sensitive information such as your WiFi network's SSID and password. After importing it, you can access variables within the this module and assign their values to local variables.

```
import my_secrets
ssid = my_secrets.SSID          # Your SSID (Network Name)
password = my_secrets.PASSWORD  # Your WiFi PASSWORD
```

connect_wifi.py

You'll have to initiate a WiFi connection every time you use your Pico on a WiFi network. This module displays connection progress and handles connection failures. You can increase the max_retries variable if your Pico requires more time to establish a connection to your particular network.

> ⚠ **Warning: DO NOT connect your Pico to an insecure network!!!**

```
"""
connect_wifi.py
-----------
To connect to a wireless network,
    use the ``init_wlan()`` function
To obtain the IP address, use the ``get_ip()`` function

Example::
        >>> import connect_wifi
        >>> connect_wifi.init_wlan('Your Network Name',     \
                                   'Your Network Password' \
                                   max_retries=23)
        >>> connect_wifi.get_ip()

For information on MicroPython's WLAN built-in WiFi
    interfaces, see:
    docs.micropython.org/en/latest/library/network.WLAN.html
"""
import network
from time import sleep


# Network error messages
NETWORK_CONNECTION_ERROR = "Network connection failed"
SSID_ERROR = "Failed to obtain IP address"

# Create a WLAN network interface object in Station (STA) mode
wlan = network.WLAN(network.STA_IF)
```

```
def init_wlan(ssid, password, max_retries=10):
    """Initiate a wireless LAN connnection

    :param ssid: wireless network name
    :param password: wireless network password
    :param max_retries: number of connection attempts before
        giving up

    :raise RuntimeError: If the network connection failed

    :return: True (successful connection);
             False (unsuccessful connection)
    :rtype: bool
    """

    # Activate network interface
    wlan.active(True)

    # Connect to the specified wireless network, using the
    #   wireless network name and password
    wlan.connect(ssid, password)

    # Print a message to the console saying that the device
    #   is trying to connect
    print('Waiting for connection...')

    # Continue to loop as long as there are connection attempts
    while max_retries > 0:
        # wlan.status() < 0: connection failure
        # wlan.status() >= 3: connection successful
        #   or has a valid IP address
        if wlan.status() < 0 or wlan.status() >= 3:
            break
        print(max_retries, '.', sep='', end='', )
        max_retries -= 1
        sleep(1)  # delay before retrying

    # Check if the connection was unsuccessful
    if wlan.status() != network.STAT_GOT_IP:
        raise RuntimeError(NETWORK_CONNECTION_ERROR)
        return False  # unsuccessful connection

    # Connection was successful and an IP address was obtained
    else:
        # Get the IP address
        ip = wlan.ifconfig()[0]

        # Print a confirmation message to console
        print( 'Connected: ip = {}'.format(ip))
        return True  # successful connection

def get_ip():
```

```
    """Get the IP address if WiFi is connected

    :raise RuntimeError: If not connected

    :return: IP Address (successful connection);
             SSID_ERROR (unsuccessful connection)
    :rtype: bool
    """
    if wlan.isconnected():
        return wlan.ifconfig()[0]
    else:
        print('\nNot connected')
        raise RuntimeError(SSID_ERROR)
        return None
```

Fig 5-x. connect_wifi.py

Code Explanation

Note: For more information on MicroPython's WLAN built-in WiFi interfaces, see https://docs.micropython.org/en/latest/library/network.WLAN.html.

Let's look at how the code works.

- The network module is used for configuring and controlling WiFi connectivity on the Pico.
  The sleep() module function is needed to introduce delays in the code execution.

```
import network
from time import sleep
```

- Define network error messages that are printed to the console if a Runtime Error is raised.
  NETWORK_CONNECTION_ERROR: Unsuccessful network connection.
  SSID_ERROR: Unable to obtain an IP address because there is not a network connection.

```
NETWORK_CONNECTION_ERROR = "Network connection failed"
SSID_ERROR = "Failed to obtain IP address"
```

- Create a WLAN network interface object in "Station" (STA) mode to connect to an existing WiFi access point (like a home router).

```
wlan = network.WLAN(network.STA_IF)
```

- Define a function init_wlan() to initiate a wireless LAN connection that returns True if the network connection is successful.
  If the network connection is not successful, init_wlan() raises a Runtime Error, printing the NETWORK_CONNECTION_ERROR message and returns False.

  The init_wlan() function takes three arguments:

- ssid: wireless network name
- password: wireless network password
- max_retries: number of connection attempts before giving up

```
def init_wlan(ssid, password, max_retries=10):
    ...
```

- wlan.active(True) activates the network interface.

```
wlan.active(True)
```

- wlan.connect(ssid, password) connects to the specified wireless network, using the wireless network name ssid and password.

```
wlan.connect(ssid, password)
```

- A message is printed to the console saying that the device is attempting to connect.

```
print('Waiting for connection...')
```

- As long as there are connection attempts as specified by the max_retries argument, init_wlan() continues to loop, printing a dot ('.') to the console showing progress and delaying for a second between each retry attempt.
  The loop breaks if the there is a connection failure (wlan.status() < 0); it also breaks if successfully connected or it obtains a valid IP address (wlan.status() >= 3):

```
while max_retries > 0:
    if wlan.status() < 0 or wlan.status() >= 3:
        break
    print(max_retries, '.', sep='', end='', )
    max_retries -= 1
    sleep(1)  # delay before retrying
```

- If the connection was unsuccessful, a RuntimeError with the NETWORK_CONNECTION_ERROR error message is raised and init_wlan() returns False (unsuccessful connection).

```
if wlan.status() != network.STAT_GOT_IP:
    raise RuntimeError(NETWORK_CONNECTION_ERROR)
    return False
```

- However, if the connection was successful and an IP address was obtained, the ip addressed is printed to the console and init_wlan() returns True (successful connection):

```
else:
    ip = wlan.ifconfig()[0]

    print( 'Connected: ip = {}'.format(ip))
    return True
```

- The module function get_ip() returns the IP address if connected to the WiFi network. If not connected to the WiFi network, the function raises a Runtime Error, printing the SSID_ERROR message to the console.

  Note that the ifconfig() method returns a 4-tuple (IP address, subnet mask, gateway, DNS server), and that ifconfig()[0] accesses the IP address.

```
def get_ip():
    if wlan.isconnected():
        return wlan.ifconfig()[0]
    else:
        print('\nNot connected')
        raise RuntimeError(SSID_ERROR)
        return None
```

pico_event.py

The following module obtains a unique event header and hardware parameters for the Pico.

Notes

Event Time A call to time.time() returns the number of *seconds* since the Unix Epoch.

If you require more precision, however, you can use the time.time_ns() function which returns the number of *nanoseconds* since the Unix Epoch. But when you do, remember that the localtime() function takes seconds, not nanoseconds. Hence, time_local would have to be adjusted accordingly:

```
# get the time for this event in nanoseconds
time_unix  = time.time_ns()
time_local = "%4d/%02d/%02d %02d:%02d:%02d" %
time.localtime(time_unix) // 1_000_000_000)[:6]
```

Hardware Parameters Especially when you're developing a Pico-based system, it's often useful to know hardware parameters such as free memory and space as well as the CPU core temperature of the Pico when debugging it. This information can be included in the Event header or body as needed.

```
"""
pico_event.py
--------
To obtain a unique event header for the Pico,
  use the ``header()`` function
To obtain hardware parameters for the Pico,
  use the ``hardware_parameters()`` function

Examples::
        >>> import pico_event
        >>> pico_event.header()
        >>> pico_event.hardware_parameters()
"""
import gc
from machine import unique_id, ADC
from os import urandom, statvfs
from time import time, localtime
```

```
# Get the serial number of the Pico's flash
machine_unique_id = unique_id().hex()

# Define the version of this event
EVENT_VERSION = "1.0.0"

def header():
    """Get event header

    :return: event header for the Pico
    :rtype: dictionary
    """
    # Get a unique id for this event
    event_id = uuid4()

    # Get the time for this event
    time_unix  = time() # Unix epoch time
    time_local = "%4d/%02d/%02d %02d:%02d:%02d" \
                 % localtime(time_unix)[:6]

    # Define the event header
    event_header = {
                       "machine_unique_id": machine_unique_id,
                       "time_unix":         time_unix,
                       "time_local":        time_local,
                       "event_id":          event_id,
                       "event_version":     EVENT_VERSION,
                   }

    return event_header

"""Generate a version 4 UUID compliant to RFC 4122"""
def uuid4():
    random_x = bytearray(urandom(16))
    random_x[6] = (random_x[6] & 0x0F) | 0x40
    random_x[8] = (random_x[8] & 0x3F) | 0x80
    h = random_x.hex()
    return str('-'.join((h[0:8], h[8:12], \
                         h[12:16], h[16:20], h[20:32])))

# Set up ADC internal temperature reading
temperature_sensor = ADC(ADC.CORE_TEMP)
conversion_factor = 3.3 / (65535)

def hardware_parameters():
    """Get hardware parameters for the Pico

    :return: hardware info about the Pico
    :rtype: dictionary
    """
    # Get the core temperature of the microcontroller
    temp_reading = temperature_sensor.read_u16() \
```

```
                  * conversion_factor
    temp_celsius = 27 - (temp_reading - 0.706)/0.001721
    temp_celsius = "{:,.1f} C".format(temp_celsius)

    # Get flash memory size and storage consumption
    flash_status = statvfs("/")
    flash_size = flash_status[1] * flash_status[2]
    flash_free = flash_status[0] * flash_status[3]
    flash_used = flash_size - flash_free

    # Get the number of bytes of available heap RAM
    gc.collect()
    free_memory = gc.mem_free()

    hw_params = {
          "temp_celsius": temp_celsius,
          "flash_size":   flash_size,
          "flash_used":   flash_used,
          "flash_free":   flash_free,
          "free_memory":  free_memory
      }

    return hw_params
```

Fig 5-x. pico_event.py

Code Explanation

Let's look at how the code works.

- The gc module provides an interface to the garbage collector.
  The unique_id module function returns a unique identifier for the Pico.
  The ADC module provides an interface to the Analog-to-Digital Converter (ADC) on the Pico.
  The urandom() module function generates a string of random bytes suitable for creating unique identifiers.
  The statvfs() module function retrieves information about the file system.
  The time() module function returns the current time in seconds since the Epoch.
  The localtime() module function converts the time in seconds since the Epoch into a human-readable date and time format.

```
import gc
from machine import unique_id, ADC
from os import urandom, statvfs
from time import time, localtime
```

- The unique_id().hex() function gets the serial number of the Pico's flash.

```
machine_unique_id = unique_id().hex()
```

- The version of the event is defined by EVENT_VERSION.

```
EVENT_VERSION = "1.0.0"
```

- The header() function gets the Event header that should be included with all Events.

```
def header():

    # Get a unique id for this event
    event_id = uuid4()

    # Get the time for this event
    time_unix  = time() # Unix epoch time
    time_local = "%4d/%02d/%02d %02d:%02d:%02d" \
                % localtime(time_unix)[:6]

    # Define the event header
    event_header = {
                    "machine_unique_id": machine_unique_id,
                    "time_unix":         time_unix,
                    "time_local":        time_local,
                    "event_id":          event_id,
                    "event_version":     EVENT_VERSION,
                 }

    return event_header
```

- Get a unique id for this event.

```
event_id = uuid4()
```

- Get the unix time and the local time for this event.

```
time_unix  = time() # Unix epoch time
time_local = "%4d/%02d/%02d %02d:%02d:%02d" \
            % localtime(time_unix)[:6]
```

- The Event header is a MicroPython dictionary of the Pico's flash serial number (machine_unique_id), the unix time (as measured by the number of seconds since the Epoch, the local time, a unique id for this event, and the Event version. MicroPython will automatically convert this dictionary to JSON when it returns it as part of an HTTP response object.

```
event_header = {
                "machine_unique_id": machine_unique_id,
                "time_unix":         time_unix,
                "time_local":        time_local,
                "event_id":          event_id,
                "event_version":     EVENT_VERSION,
             }

return event_header
```

- The uuid4() function returns a version 4 UUID compliant to RFC 4122.
  This UUID uniquely identifies an Event.

```
def uuid4():
    ...
```

- random_x = bytearray(). This line gets 16 high-quality, cryptographically secure random bytes.

  ```
  random_x = bytearray(urandom(16))
  ```

- random_x[6] = () and random_x[8] = (). These lines set the "version" and "variant" bits per RFC 4122.

  ```
  random_x[6] = (random_x[6] & 0x0F) | 0x40
  random_x[8] = (random_x[8] & 0x3F) | 0x80
  ```

- h = random_x.hex() generates a 32-character hexadecimal string from the byte array.

  ```
  h = random_x.hex()
  ```

- return str(). This line returns the UUID string correctly formatted with hyphens.

  ```
  return str('-'.join((h[0:8], h[8:12], \
                       h[12:16], h[16:20], h[20:32])))
  ```

- The internal temperature is read using the Pico's built-in Analog-to-Digital Converter (ADC).

```
temperature_sensor = ADC(ADC.CORE_TEMP)
conversion_factor = 3.3 / (65535)
```

- The hardware_parameters() function returns hardware information about the Pico, specifically the core temperature of its microcontroller, amount of flash available and used, and the amount of free memory available. This information answers two basic questions about the operating conditions of the Pico that can affect its performance and longevity: How hot is it running at? How much memory (both flash and RAM) is available?

```
def hardware_parameters():

    # Get the core temperature of the microcontroller
    temp_reading = temperature_sensor.read_u16() \
                   * conversion_factor
    temp_celsius = 27 - (temp_reading - 0.706)/0.001721
    temp_celsius = "{:,.1f} C".format(temp_celsius)

    # Get flash memory size and storage consumption
    flash_status = statvfs("/")
    flash_size = flash_status[1] * flash_status[2]
    flash_free = flash_status[0] * flash_status[3]
    flash_used = flash_size - flash_free

    # Get the number of bytes of available heap RAM
    gc.collect()
    free_memory = gc.mem_free()
```

```
    hw_params = {
        "temp_celsius": temp_celsius,
        "flash_size":   flash_size,
        "flash_used":   flash_used,
        "flash_free":   flash_free,
        "free_memory":  free_memory
    }

    return hw_params
```

- Getting the core temperature of the microcontroller. You can use the Pico's ADC to determine this temperature by reading the Pico's internal temperature sensor and converting that digital value to a temperature.

```
temp_reading = temperature_sensor.read_u16() \
               * conversion_factor
temp_celsius = 27 - (temp_reading - 0.706)/0.001721
temp_celsius = "{:,.1f} C".format(temp_celsius)
```

- The statvfs() module function tells you the flash memory size (flash_size = fragment size * size of fs in f_frsize units) and storage consumption (flash_free = file system block size * number of free blocks) on the Pico.

```
flash_status = statvfs("/")
flash_size = flash_status[1] * flash_status[2]
flash_free = flash_status[0] * flash_status[3]
flash_used = flash_size - flash_free
```

- Getting an accurate number of bytes of available heap RAM requires first using MicroPython's garbage collector to reclaim memory from objects that are no longer actively used by the MicroPython program. This is followed by the garbage collector's mem_free() function.

```
gc.collect()
free_memory = gc.mem_free()
```

- The hardware_parameters() function returns the hw_params = {...} dictionary of the Pico's core temperature, amount of flash used and available, and the amount of free memory available. MicroPython will automatically convert this dictionary to JSON when it returns it as part of an HTTP response object.

```
hw_params = {
        "temp_celsius": temp_celsius,
        "flash_size":   flash_size,
        "flash_used":   flash_used,
        "flash_free":   flash_free,
        "free_memory":  free_memory
    }

return hw_params
```

Introducing Microdot

The 'Hello, world!' Microdot web server in this section uses various view functions to handle HTTP requests for different web routes that have a matching URL. In Microdot, a web route is a decorated view function defined with the keyword 'async' that handles an application URL. Example:

```
@app.get('/')
async def index(request):
    return 'Hello'
```

If you navigate to http://[the ip address of your Pico]/ (which matches the URL '/'), Microdot responds with the plain text string 'Hello'.

Like Flask, Microdot automatically converts Python dictionaries and lists to JSON objects when returning them as HTTP responses. Here's the barebones MicroPython code for a simple "Hello, world!" web application:

```
from microdot import Microdot

app = Microdot()

@app.get('/')
async def index(request):
    return {'Hello': 'world!'}

app.run(debug=True)
```

Fig 5-x. Barebones "Hello, world!" Microdot example

In the above, Microdot's @app.get() decorator defines an HTTP GET request handler for the index() view function, mapping the top level root URL of the website ('/') to the index() function. Specifically, when Microdot receives a GET request for the root URL from a client, it converts the {'hello': 'world'} dictionary into a JSON object that it returns to the client as a JSON response.

For example, a Microdot web application responding with {"Hello": "world!"} to an HTTP GET request from a browser will render that dictionary as a JSON object

```
{
    "Hello": "world!"
}
```

Fig 5-x. "Hello, world!" as a returned JSON object

To see how decorated view functions work in Microdot, we'll write microdot_HelloWorld.py which uses various view functions to handle web requests and return web responses for different URL routes.

Code

Using Thonny (File > Save as), copy and save the Python module below to your target Pico microcontroller.

microdot_HelloWorld.py

The following program uses the Microdot web server with various view functions to handle web requests and return web responses for different URL routes.

```
"""
microdot_HelloWorld.py
--------
Microdot webserver for greeting the world

"""
import asyncio, sys
from microdot import Microdot
import connect_wifi

# Add my_secrets.py to the .gitignore file to make sure
#   that my_secrets.py is never checked into GitHub
import my_secrets
ssid = my_secrets.SSID          # Your SSID (Network Name)
password = my_secrets.PASSWORD  # Your Wi-Fi PASSWORD

# Initialize the WiFi Interface
if not connect_wifi.init_wlan(ssid, password, max_retries=10):
    print('WiFi authentication error: {}'\
          .format(connect_wifi.SSID_ERROR))
    print('Exiting program')
    sys.exit(0)
else:
    ip_address = connect_wifi.get_ip()

# Instantiate a Microdot webserver
app = Microdot()

# Microdot communications interface

# Plain text response
@app.get('/')
async def index(request):
    return 'Hello'
```

```
# http://[the ip address of your Pico]/
# returns: 'Hello'

# Dictionary response
@app.get('/hello')
async def hello(request):
    return {'Hello': 'world!'}
# http://[the ip address of your Pico]/hello
# returns: {'Hello': 'world!'}

# List response
@app.get('/people')
async def people(request):
    return ["John", "Anna", "Peter"]
# http://[the ip address of your Pico]/people
# returns: ["John","Anna","Peter"]

# Dictionary / List response
@app.get('/hello/people')
async def people(request):
    people_list = ["John", "Anna", "Peter"]
    return {'Hello': people_list}
# http://[the ip address of your Pico]/hello/people
# returns: {"Hello":["John","Anna","Peter"]}

# Main entry point for the event loop
async def main():
    print("Starting async task ...")
    await app.start_server(host=ip_address, port=80, debug=True)

# Start the event loop
if __name__ == '__main__':

    try:
        # Run the Microdot webserver
        print("Starting Microdot server ...")
        main_task=asyncio.run(main())

    # Keyboard interrupt caught
    except KeyboardInterrupt:
        print("\nUser interrupted the program")

    # Unexpected error
    except Exception as e:
        print(f"An unexpected error occurred: {e}")

    # End the program gracefully
    finally:
        app.shutdown()
        print("\nMicrodot server stopped.")
```

Fig 5-x. microdot_HelloWorld.py

Code Explanation

Let's look at how the code works.

- The asyncio library allows you to write concurrent code using MicroPython's asynchronous programming functionality. The sys module is used to stop the execution of the current program if the WiFi network is unavailable.
  The microdot module is the Microdot webserver.
  The connect_wifi module uses its init_wlan() function to connect to a wireless network and its get_ip() function to obtain an IP address for your Pico.

```
import asyncio, sys
from microdot import Microdot
import connect_wifi
```

- The my_secrets module contains the name of your network (SSID) and your network password.

```
import my_secrets
ssid = my_secrets.SSID            # Your SSID (Network Name)
password = my_secrets.PASSWORD    # Your Wi-Fi PASSWORD
```

You should add my_secrets.py to your .gitignore file to make sure that my_secrets.py is never checked into a GitHub code repository.

```
# Add my_secrets.py to the .gitignore file to make sure
#   that my_secrets.py is never checked into GitHub
SSID      = 'MyNetwork'         # YOUR SSID (Network Name)
PASSWORD = 'MyPassword'         # YOUR WiFi PASSWORD
```

- To initialize the WiFi interface, use the connect_wifi.init_wlan() and connect_wifi.get_ip() module functions.

```
# Initialize the WiFi Interface
if not connect_wifi.init_wlan(ssid, password, max_retries=10):
    print('WiFi authentication error: {}'\
          .format(connect_wifi.SSID_ERROR))
    print('Exiting program')
    sys.exit(0)
else:
    ip_address = connect_wifi.get_ip()
```

- Instantiating the Microdot class creates a Microdot webserver.

```
app = Microdot()
```

- The Microdot communications interface consists of a get(url_pattern) decorator that is used to register a function as a GET request handler for a given URL.

- The @app.get('/') decorator registers the async index(request) function as a GET request handler. The index() function returns "Hello" as a plain text response.

```
@app.get('/')
async def index(request):
    return 'Hello'
```

- The @app.get('/hello') decorator registers the async hello(request) function as a GET request handler. The hello() function returns the MicroPython dictionary {'Hello': 'world!'} as a JSON object.

```
@app.get('/hello')
async def hello(request):
    return {'Hello': 'world!'}
```

- The @app.get('/people') decorator registers the async people(request) function as a GET request handler. The people() function returns the MicroPython list ["John","Anna","Peter"] as a JSON object.

```
@app.get('/people')
async def people(request):
    return ["John", "Anna", "Peter"]
```

- The @app.get('/hello/people') decorator registers the async people(request) function as a GET request handler. The people() function returns {"Hello":["John","Anna","Peter"]}, a MicroPython dictionary with 'Hello' as a Key with the corresponding list ["John","Anna","Peter"] as a Value. MicroPython automatically converts this dictionary to a JSON response object.

```
@app.get('/hello/people')
async def people(request):
    people_list = ["John", "Anna", "Peter"]
    return {'Hello': people_list}
```

- The main entry point for the event loop is async main() which schedules the Microdot server to be run asynchronously.

```
async def main():
    print("Starting async task ...")
    await app.start_server(host=ip_address, port=80, debug=True)
```

- The try-except block runs the main() asynchronous task but catches a user interrupt (e.g. Ctrl-C) to stop the program and prints the message "Microdot server stopped." to the console when the program finishes.

```
try:
    # Run the Microdot webserver
    print("Starting Microdot server ...")
    main_task=asyncio.run(main())

# Keyboard interrupt caught
except KeyboardInterrupt:
    print("\nUser interrupted the program")

# Unexpected error
except Exception as e:
    print(f"An unexpected error occurred: {e}")

# End the program gracefully
```

```
    finally:
        app.shutdown()
        print("\nMicrodot server stopped.")
```

Procedure / Steps

> ⚠ **Warning:** Do not connect your host or your Pico to the internet on an insecure network!!!

Run the MicroPython code on your target Pico.

microdot_HelloWorld.py

1. Using Thonny (File > Open), select microdot_HelloWorld.py
2. Go to the Run menu
   Select "Run current script"

Tests and Results

If you open a browser to http://[the ip address of your Pico], while running microdot_HelloWorld.py, you should see something like:

```
Hello
```

If you open a browser to http://[the ip address of your Pico]/hello, while running microdot_HelloWorld.py, you should see something like:

```
{
  "Hello": "world!"
}
```

If you open a browser to http://[the ip address of your Pico]/people, while running, microdot_HelloWorld.py you should see something like:

```
[
  "John",
  "Anna",
  "Peter"
]
```

If you open a browser to http://[the ip address of your Pico]/hello/people, while running, microdot_HelloWorld.py you should see something like:

```
{
  "Hello": [
    "John",
    "Anna",
    "Peter"
  ]
}
```

Note that in the main entry point for the event loop, async def main(), Microdot defaults to starting a web server on port 5000 which you can override to port=80, the default port for web servers that use HTTP. By setting the parameter debug=True when you start the server, Microdot will let you know its ip address and port. You should see something like:

```
Starting async server on 192.168.0.100:80...
```

If debug=True, Microdot will also let you know the HTTP header it sends in response to HTTP GET requests for the {"Hello": "world!"} page. Try refreshing the {"Hello": "world!"} page several times. In the Python Shell of Thonny, you should see:

```
GET /hello 200
GET /hello 200
GET /hello 200
...
```

The GET /hello 200 statements are HTTP OK responses indicating that your browser's GET requests succeeded.

Congratulations—you've just created your first web API using Microdot for your Pico!

Parsing Route (URL) Converters and Query Parameters

Microdot provides a straightforward way to parse URL parameters in two primary ways: Route (URL) Converters or Query Parameters. In this section, your microdot_HelloName.py program will illustrate both types of parsing.

Route Converters in Microdot

In Microdot, URL parameters can be parsed using Route Parameters which convert variable components of the URL path itself that are defined as arguments using angle brackets ('< >') within the route decorator. (See https://microdot.readthedocs.io/en/latest/intro.html#including-dynamic-components-in-the-url-path.)

Types of Route Parameters in Microdot

Microdot supports the following route converter types:

- **string**: string (default type)
- **int**: integer (must be a valid integer or the route won't match)
- **re**: regular expression (must be valid or the route won't match)
- **path**: remainder of the URL as a path

Example:

```
@app.get('/hello/<string:name>')
async def hello(request, name):
    return {'Hello': '{}!'.format(name)}
```

If you navigate to

```
http://[the ip address of your Pico]/hello/Anna
```

the decorated view function above returns

```
{
  "Hello": "Anna!"
}
```

Route Converters can combine multiple dynamic components. Example:

```
@app.get('/user/<string:first_name>/<string:last_name>/<int:id>')
async def get_user(request, first_name, last_name, id):
    person = {
                "First Name": first_name,
                "Last Name": last_name,
                "ID": id
            }
    return person
```

If you navigate to

```
http://[the ip address of your Pico]/user/Peter/Jones/3
```

the decorated view function above returns

```
{"Last Name": "Jones", "ID": 3, "First Name": "Peter"}
```

(Disclaimer: The name “Peter Jones” used in this book is fictional and any resemblance to a real person living or dead is purely coincidental.)

Query Parameters

Query Parameters are appended to a URL after a question mark (?). They consist of param-value (key-value) pairs separated by ampersands (&). You can extract data from a query string with the request.args attribute and incorporate that data into your Microdot web applications.

Individual Query Parameters use a different name for each parameter. You access the parameter value by name with request.args.get() which may optionally include a default value. Example:

```
@app.get('/greet')
async def greet_person(request):
  # Get query parameters from the request object

  name = request.args.get('name', 'world!')       # Get 'name' or
default to 'world!'

  message = request.args.get('message', 'Hello') # Get 'message'
or default to 'Hello'
```

If you navigate to

```
http://[the ip address of your Pico]/greet?name=Peter&message=Hi
```

the decorated view function above returns

```
{"message": "Hi", "name": "Peter"}
```

MultiDict Query Parameters for Multiple Values list all values associated with a given parameter name. You access this list by the specific parameter name with request.args.getlist().

Individual and MultiDict Query Parameters can be combined. Example:

```
@app.get('/greet/people')
async def greet_people(request):
    # Get all values for the parameter 'name'
    peoples_names = request.args.getlist('name')

    message = request.args.get('message', 'Hello') # Get
'message' or default to 'Hello'
```

If you navigate to

```
http://[the ip address of your
Pico]/greet/people?message=Welcome&name=John&name=Anna&name=Peter
```

the decorated view function above returns

```
{"message": "Welcome", "people": ["John", "Anna", "Peter"]}
```

Code

Using Thonny (File > Save as), copy and save the Python module below to your target Pico microcontroller.

microdot_HelloName.py

The following program demonstrates parsing URL parameters with Route (URL) Converters and with Query Parameters.

```
"""
microdot_HelloName.py
--------
Microdot webserver for greeting people by name

"""
import asyncio, sys
from microdot import Microdot
import connect_wifi

# Add my_secrets.py to the .gitignore file to make sure
#   that my_secrets.py is never checked into GitHub
import my_secrets
ssid = my_secrets.SSID          # Your SSID (Network Name)
password = my_secrets.PASSWORD  # Your Wi-Fi PASSWORD

# Initialize the WiFi Interface
if not connect_wifi.init_wlan(ssid, password, max_retries=10):
    print('WiFi authentication error: {}'.\
```

```
        format(connect_wifi.SSID_ERROR))
    print('Exiting program')
    sys.exit(0)
else:
    ip_address = connect_wifi.get_ip()

# Instantiate a Microdot webserver
app = Microdot()

# Microdot communications interface
@app.get('/')
async def index(request):
    return 'Hello'
# http://[the ip address of your Pico]
# returns: "Hello"

@app.get('/hello')
async def hello(request):
    return {'Hello': 'world!'}
# http://[the ip address of your Pico]/hello
# returns: {"Hello": "world!"}

# List response
@app.get('/people')
async def people(request):
    return ["John", "Anna", "Peter"]
# http://[the ip address of your Pico]/people
# returns: ["John", "Anna", "Peter"]

# Route Parameters
# ----------------
# string (default type): string
@app.get('/hello/<string:name>')
async def hello(request, name):
    return {'Hello': '{}!'.format(name)}
# http://[the ip address of your Pico]/hello/Anna
# returns: {"Hello": "Anna!"}

# re: regular expression (must be valid or the route won't match)
@app.get('/user/<re:[a-zA-Z0-9]*:username>')
async def get_user(request, username):
    return {'User': username}
# http://[the ip address of your Pico]/user/AnnaSmith2
# returns: {"User": "AnnaSmith2"}

# path: remainder of the URL as a path
@app.get('/syslogs/<path:log_path>')
async def get_syslogs(request, log_path):
    return {'syslogs path': log_path}
# http://[the ip address of your Pico]/syslogs//var/log
# returns: {"syslogs path": "/var/log"}

# Parameter combinations
```

```
#   int: integer (must be a valid integer
#        or the route won't match)
@app.get('/user/<string:first_name>/<string:last_name>/<int:id>')
async def get_user(request, first_name, last_name, id):
    person = {
                "First Name": first_name,
                "Last Name": last_name,
                "ID": id
            }
    return person
# http://[the ip address of your Pico]/user/Peter/Jones/3
# returns: {"Last Name": "Jones", "ID": 3, "First Name": "Peter"}

# Query parameters
# ----------------
# Individual Query Parameters:
#   param-value pairs separated by ampersands (&)
#   /my_endpoint?param1=value1&param2=value2
@app.get('/greet')
async def greet_person(request):
  # Get query parameters from the request object
  # Get 'name' or default to 'world!'
  name = request.args.get('name', 'world!')

  # Get 'message' or default to 'Hello'
  message = request.args.get('message', 'Hello')

  return {'message': message, 'name': name}
# http://[the ip address of your Pico]/greet?name=Anna
#   returns: {"message": "Hello", "name": "Anna"}

#http://[the ip address of your Pico]/greet?name=Peter&message=Hi
#   returns: {"message": "Hi", "name": "Peter"}
# http://[the ip address of your Pico]/greet
#   returns: {"message": "Hello", "name": "world!"}

# MultiDict Query Parameters for Multiple Values
#   list of all values associated with a specific parameter
#   /my_endpoint?param=value1&param=value2
@app.get('/greet/people')
async def greet_people(request):
    # Get all values for the parameter 'name'
    peoples_names = request.args.getlist('name')

    # Get 'message' or default to 'Hello'
    message = request.args.get('message', 'Hello')

    return {'message': message, 'people': peoples_names}
# http://[the ip address of your Pico]
# /greet/people?name=John&name=Anna&name=Peter
#   returns: {"message": "Hello",
#             "people": ["John", "Anna", "Peter"]}
# http://[the ip address of your Pico]
```

```
# /greet/people?message=Welcome&name=John&name=Anna&name=Peter
#   returns: {"message": "Welcome",
#             "people": ["John", "Anna", "Peter"]}
# Main entry point for the event loop
async def main():
    print("Starting async task ...")
    await app.start_server(host=ip_address, port=80, debug=True)

if __name__ == '__main__':

    # Start event loop
    try:
        # Run the Microdot webserver
        print("Starting Microdot server ...")
        main_task=asyncio.run(main())

    # Keyboard interrupt caught
    except KeyboardInterrupt:
        print("\nUser interrupted the program")

    # Unexpected error
    except Exception as e:
        print(f"An unexpected error occurred: {e}")

    # End the program gracefully
    finally:
        app.shutdown()
        print("\nMicrodot server stopped.")
```

Fig 5-x. microdot_HelloName.py

Code Explanation

Let's look at how the code works.

- The asyncio library allows you to write concurrent code using MicroPython's asynchronous programming functionality. The sys module is used to stop the execution of the current program if the WiFi network is unavailable.
  The microdot module is the Microdot webserver.
  The connect_wifi module uses its init_wlan() function to connect to a wireless network and its get_ip() function to obtain an IP address for your Pico.

```
import asyncio, sys
from microdot import Microdot
import connect_wifi
```

- The my_secrets module contains the name of your network (SSID) and your network password.

```
import my_secrets
ssid = my_secrets.SSID          # Your SSID (Network Name)
password = my_secrets.PASSWORD  # Your Wi-Fi PASSWORD
```

You should add my_secrets.py to your .gitignore file to make sure that my_secrets.py is never checked into a GitHub code repository.

```
# Add my_secrets.py to the .gitignore file to make sure
#   that my_secrets.py is never checked into GitHub
SSID     = 'MyNetwork'         # YOUR SSID (Network Name)
PASSWORD = 'MyPassword'        # YOUR WiFi PASSWORD
```

- To initialize the WiFi interface, use the connect_wifi.init_wlan() and connect_wifi.get_ip() module functions.

```
# Initialize the WiFi Interface
if not connect_wifi.init_wlan(ssid, password, max_retries=10):
    print('WiFi authentication error: {}'.\
          format(connect_wifi.SSID_ERROR))
    print('Exiting program')
    sys.exit(0)
else:
    ip_address = connect_wifi.get_ip()
```

- Instantiating the Microdot class creates a Microdot webserver.

```
app = Microdot()
```

- The Microdot communications interface consists of a get(url_pattern) decorator that is used to register a function as a GET request handler for a given URL.

- The @app.get('/') decorator registers the async index(request) function as a GET request handler. The index() function returns "Hello" as a plain text response.

```
@app.get('/')
async def index(request):
    return 'Hello'
```

- The @app.get('/hello') decorator registers the async hello(request) function as a GET request handler. The hello() function returns the MicroPython dictionary {'Hello': 'world!'} as a JSON object.

```
@app.get('/hello')
async def hello(request):
    return {'Hello': 'world!'}
```

- The @app.get('/people') decorator registers the async people(request) function as a GET request handler. The people() function returns the MicroPython list ["John","Anna","Peter"] as a JSON object.

```
@app.get('/people')
async def people(request):
    return ["John", "Anna", "Peter"]
```

- The @app.get('/hello/<string:name>') decorator registers the async people(request) function as a GET request handler. When a string name is provided as route parameter, the view function returns a dictionary with 'Hello' as a Key and that name as its corresponding Value. MicroPython automatically converts this dictionary to a JSON response object.

```
@app.get('/hello/<string:name>')
async def hello(request, name):
    return {'Hello': '{}!'.format(name)}
```

- The @app.get('/user/<re:[a-zA-Z0-9]*:username>') decorator registers the async get_user(request) function as a GET request handler. When a username is a valid match for the regular expression, the view function returns a dictionary with 'User' as a Key and that username as its corresponding Value. MicroPython automatically converts this dictionary to a JSON response object.

```
@app.get('/user/<re:[a-zA-Z0-9]*:username>')
async def get_user(request, username):
    return {'User': username}
```

- The @app.get('/syslogs/<path:log_path>') decorator registers the async get_syslogs(request) function as a GET request handler. The view function converts the remainder of the URL, the route parameter, to a path which it returns as the Value to a 'syslogs path' Key in a JSON response object.

```
@app.get('/syslogs/<path:log_path>')
async def get_syslogs(request, log_path):
    return {'syslogs path': log_path}
```

- Route Parameters can be combined.
  The
  @app.get('/user/<string:first_name>/<string:last_name>/<int:id>') decorator registers the async get_user(request) function as a GET request handler. When a string first_name, string last_name and an int id are provided as route parameters, the view function returns a dictionary with all three as Values corresponding to each of these Keys. MicroPython automatically converts this dictionary to a JSON response object.

```
@app.get('/user/<string:first_name>/<string:last_name>/<int:id>')
async def get_user(request, first_name, last_name, id):
    person = {
                "First Name": first_name,
                "Last Name": last_name,
                "ID": id
            }
    return person
```

- Individual Query Parameters are param-value pairs separated by ampersands.
  The @app.get('/greet') decorator registers the async greet_person(request) function as a GET request handler. When a URL of query parameters are provided as a route parameter, the view function uses `request.args.get()` to access each parameter-value pair with a default value. MicroPython automatically converts the returned dictionary to a JSON response object.

```
@app.get('/greet')
async def greet_person(request):
  # Get query parameters from the request object

  # Get 'name' or default to 'world!'
```

```
    name = request.args.get('name', 'world!')

    # Get 'message' or default to 'Hello'
    message = request.args.get('message', 'Hello')

    return {'message': message, 'name': name}
```

- MultiDict Query Parameters for Multiple Values parses the URL for a list of all values associated with a specific parameter. The @app.get('/greet/people') decorator registers the async greet_people(request) function as a GET request handler. When a URL of query parameters are provided as a route parameter, the view function uses request.args.getlist() to access a list of all values associated with a specific parameter. The greet_people() view function combines MultiDict Query Parameters with Individual Query Parameters in its JSON response object.

```
@app.get('/greet/people')
async def greet_people(request):
    # Get all values for the parameter 'name'
    peoples_names = request.args.getlist('name')

    # Get 'message' or default to 'Hello'
    message = request.args.get('message', 'Hello')

    return {'message': message, 'people': peoples_names}
```

- The main entry point for the event loop is async main() which schedules the Microdot server to be run asynchronously.

```
async def main():
    print("Starting async task ...")
    await app.start_server(host=ip_address, port=80, debug=True)
```

- The try-except block runs the main() asynchronous task but catches a user interrupt (e.g. Ctrl-C) to stop the program and prints the message "Microdot server stopped." to the console when the program finishes.

```
try:
    # Run the Microdot webserver
    print("Starting Microdot server ...")
    main_task=asyncio.run(main())

# Keyboard interrupt caught
except KeyboardInterrupt:
    print("\nUser interrupted the program")

# Unexpected error
except Exception as e:
    print(f"An unexpected error occurred: {e}")

# End the program gracefully
finally:
    app.shutdown()
    print("\nMicrodot server stopped.")
```

Procedure / Steps

> ⚠ **Warning:** Do not connect your host or your Pico to the internet on an insecure network!!!

Run the MicroPython code on your target Pico.

microdot_HelloName.py

1. Using Thonny (File > Open), select microdot_HelloName.py
2. Go to the Run menu
   Select "Run current script"

Tests and Results

While running microdot_HelloName.py, open a web browser to each of the URLs listed below. Do you get the corresponding HTTP responses from Microdot?

```
URL: http://[the ip address of your Pico]
HTTP response: "Hello!"

URL: http://[the ip address of your Pico]/hello
HTTP response: {"Hello": "world!"}

URL: http://[the ip address of your Pico]/people
HTTP response: ["John", "Anna", "Peter"]

URL: http://[the ip address of your Pico]/hello/Anna
HTTP response: {"Hello": "Anna!"}

URL: http://[the ip address of your Pico]/user/AnnaSmith2
HTTP response: {"User": "AnnaSmith2"}

URL: http://[the ip address of your Pico]/syslogs//var/log
HTTP response: {"syslogs path": "/var/log"}

URL: http://[the ip address of your Pico]/user/Peter/Jones/3
HTTP response: {"Last Name": "Jones", "ID": 3, "First Name":
"Peter"}

URL: http://[the ip address of your Pico]/greet?name=Anna
HTTP response: {"message": "Hello", "name": "Anna"})

URL: http://[the ip address of your
Pico]/greet?name=Peter&message=Hi
HTTP response: {"message": "Hi", "name": "Peter"})

URL: http://[the ip address of your Pico]/greet
```

```
HTTP response: {"message": "Hello", "name": "world!"})

URL: http://[the ip address of your
Pico]/greet/people?name=John&name=Anna&name=Peter
HTTP response: {"message": "Hello", "people": ["John", "Anna",
"Peter"]}

URL: http://[the ip address of your
Pico]/greet/people?message=Welcome&name=John&name=Anna&name=Peter
HTTP response: {"message": "Welcome", "people": ["John", "Anna",
"Peter"]}
```

Congratulations—you've shown how to parse URL Parameters in Microdot using Route Converters and Query Parameters!

Performing actions via a RESTful API

The REST architectural style organizes the design of a RESTful API around uniquely defined resources. Using REST over HTTP as an application protocol does not tie a web API to any particular implementation but takes advantage of open standards allowing for a uniform interface for flexible API and client application development. When exchanging representations of resources via a RESTful interface, machine-to-machine (M2M)data interactions typically employ a wide HTTP vocabulary. For the most part, URIs (Uniform Resource Identifiers) represent resources (nouns); HTTP methods (like GET, POST, PUT, PATCH and DELETE) represent actions (verbs) performed on those resources. GET and POST are the HTTP verbs (methods) most frequently used by browsers on the internet.

In this section, your 'Hello, Blinky!' program combines the HTTP GET and PUT verbs in a decorated view function to handle an HTML form with buttons that turn an external LED on and off. For machine-to-machine data interchanges, a view function in Microdot can provide a means for obtaining sensory information about the physical world—the core temperature of the microcontroller chip on the Pico, for instance—as well as information about actions that were performed—such as blinking an external LED. As your example program shows, this event information can then be displayed on an HTML form.

By using a RESTful API, however, Microdot can also perform actions in view functions that return JSON objects. For example, you can use a view function to turn the external LED attached to your Pico on and off via a URL path.

How? By defining the HTTP endpoints '/light/on' and '/light/off' or by using URL or Query Parameters and adding the relevant view function to each route:

```
@app.get('/light/on')
async def index(request):
    led.value(1)
    return {"led_state": "ON"}

@app.get('/light/off')
async def light_off(request):
    led.value(0)
    return {"led_state": "OFF"}

# Route Parameter: LED state must be an integer
@app.get('/api/v0.1/light/<int:state>')
async def light_state(request, state):
    if state != 0:  # turn LED ON for non-zero state
```

```
        led_state = "ON"
        led.value(1)
    else:
        led_state = "OFF"
        led.value(0)
    return {"led_state": led_state}

# Query Parameter: LED state must be either "ON" or "OFF"
@app.get('/api/v0.1/light')
async def light_state(request):
    # Get query parameters from the request object
    led_state = request.args.get('state', 'Unknown')
    if (state != 'ON') and (state != 'OFF'):
        raise ValueError(f"led_state = {led_state} "\
                         f"(must be 'ON' or 'OFF')")

    if led_state == 'ON':
        led.value(1)
    else:
        led.value(0)
    return {"led_state": led_state}
```

Fig 5-x. Example of defining the HTTP endpoints for turning LED on and off

API Versioning

Finally, your program will introduce API versioning into its web routes.

A web API is a kind of contract between your web server and its data clients. Adding a version to the URLs of a Microdot web server is a simple way to indicate the web services the server application exposes. New clients can use new features and resources while the web server application supports older clients (although, as always, there can be trade-offs depending on the context of use).

URI versioning (inserting a "/v1/" in the URL, for instance) is not uncommon on private internal networks or even on public networks like the Internet. It's pragmatic (though offensive to purists and not without reason). For large server applications that change around a lot, URI versioning can become cumbersome to manage. But for smaller, purpose-built applications like your embedded Pico system that are specifically designed to do one thing well, URI versioning is a simple, straightforward mechanism that is easy to use and understand. No versioning at all, however, works only if the web API will never change or never introduce a breaking change (like unrecognized fields) that a client data consumer can't ignore.

Code

Using Thonny (File > Save as), copy and save the Python module below to your target Pico microcontroller.

microdot_HelloBlinky.py

This program uses the HTTP verbs GET and POST in the methods argument of the @app.route() route decorator to handle an HTML form with buttons that turn an external LED on and off. But it will also blink the LED by defining the HTTP endpoints '/light/on' and '/light/off' as well as by using URL parameters and adding the relevant view function for each route decorator.

```
"""
microdot_HelloBlinky.py
--------
Microdot webserver for turning an LED ON and OFF

"""
import gc
from machine import Pin, ADC
import asyncio, sys
from microdot import Microdot, Response
from time import time, localtime
import connect_wifi

# Add my_secrets.py to the .gitignore file to make sure
#   that my_secrets.py is never checked into GitHub
import my_secrets
ssid = my_secrets.SSID          # Your SSID (Network Name)
password = my_secrets.PASSWORD  # Your WiFi PASSWORD

# Set up external LED
led = Pin(16, Pin.OUT)  # GPIO16

# Set up ADC internal temperature reading
temperature_sensor = ADC(ADC.CORE_TEMP)
conversion_factor = 3.3 / (65535)

# Initialize the WiFi Interface
if not connect_wifi.init_wlan(ssid, password, max_retries=10):
    print('WiFi authentication error: {}'.\
          format(connect_wifi.SSID_ERROR))
    print('Exiting program')
    sys.exit(0)
else:
    ip_address = connect_wifi.get_ip()

# Instantiate a Microdot webserver
app = Microdot()
```

```
# Microdot communications interface
@app.get('/')
async def index(request):
    return 'Hello'

led_state = "OFF"
def webpage(time_local, temp_celsius, free_memory, led_state):
    # Template HTML
    html = f"""
    <!doctype html>
    <html>
        <head><title>Hello, Blinky!</title></head>
        <body>
            <h1>Hello, Blinky!</h1>
            <form method="POST">
                <button type="submit" name="led_on">\
                    Turn LED on</button><br/>
                <button type="submit" name="led_off">\
                    Turn LED off</button>
            </form>

            <p>LED is {led_state}</p>
            <p>Local Date/Time: {time_local}</p>
            <p>Temperature: {temp_celsius}</p>
            <p>Memory Available: {free_memory}</p>
        </body>
    </html>
    """
    return str(html)

@app.route('/api/v0.1/light_switch', methods=['GET', 'POST'])
async def light_switch(request):
    # Initialize the LED light to off
    led.value(0)
    led_state = "OFF"

    # Turn LED light on if the client sent a POST request to turn
    #   on the LED
    if request.method == 'POST':
        if 'led_on' in request.form:
            led.value(1)
            led_state = "ON"

    # Get the Unix epoch time as well as the local time
    time_unix  = time()  # Unix epoch time
    time_local = "%4d/%02d/%02d %02d:%02d:%02d" \
                 % localtime(time_unix)[:6]

    # Get the core temperature of the microcontroller
    temp_reading = temperature_sensor.read_u16() \
                   * conversion_factor
    temp_celsius = 27 - (temp_reading - 0.706)/0.001721
    temp_celsius = "{:,.1f} C".format(temp_celsius)
```

```
    # Check the number of bytes of available heap RAM
    KB = 1024
    gc.collect()
    free_memory = gc.mem_free()
    free_memory = "{:,.1f} KB".format(free_memory/KB)

    # Generate the HTML form
    html =  webpage(time_local, \
                    temp_celsius, \
                    free_memory, \
                    led_state)

    # Respond to the HTTP request with the HTML form
    #   HTTP status code: 200 for OK
    #   Content is an HTML markup document
    return Response(html, status_code=200, \
                    headers={'Content-Type': 'text/html'})

@app.get('/api/v0.1/light/on')
async def light_on(request):
    led.value(1)
    return {"led_state": "ON"}
# http://[the ip address of your Pico]/api/v0.1/light/on
#   returns: {"led_state": "ON"}

@app.get('/api/v0.1/light/off')
async def light_off(request):
    led.value(0)
    return {"led_state": "OFF"}
# http://[the ip address of your Pico]/api/v0.1/light/off
#   returns: {"led_state": "OFF"}

# Route Parameter: LED state must be an integer
@app.get('/api/v0.1/light/<int:state>')
async def light_state(request, state):
    if state != 0:  # turn LED ON for non-zero state
        led_state = "ON"
        led.value(1)
    else:
        led_state = "OFF"
        led.value(0)
    return {"led_state": led_state}
# http://[the ip address of your Pico]/api/v0.1/light/1
#   returns: {"led_state": "ON"}
# http://[the ip address of your Pico]/api/v0.1/light/0
#   returns: {"led_state": "OFF"}

# Query Parameter: LED state must be either "ON" or "OFF"
@app.get('/api/v0.1/light')
async def light_state(request):
    # Get query parameters from the request object
    # Get 'state' or default to 'Unknown'
```

```
    led_state = request.args.get('state', 'Unknown')
    if (led_state != 'ON') and (led_state != 'OFF'):
        raise ValueError(\
            f"led_state = {led_state} (must be 'ON' or 'OFF')")

    if led_state == 'ON':
        led.value(1)
    else:
        led.value(0)
    return {"led_state": led_state}
# http://[the ip address of your Pico]/api/v0.1/light?state=ON
#    returns: {"led_state": ON"}
# http://[the ip address of your Pico]/api/v0.1/light?state=OFF
#    returns: {"led_state": OFF"}

# Main entry point for the event loop
async def main():
    print("Starting async task ...")
    await app.start_server(host=ip_address, port=80, debug=True)

# Start the event loop
if __name__ == '__main__':

    try:
        # Run the Microdot webserver
        print("Starting Microdot server ...")
        main_task=asyncio.run(main())

    # Keyboard interrupt caught
    except KeyboardInterrupt:
        print("\nUser interrupted the program")

    # Unexpected error
    except Exception as e:
        print(f"An unexpected error occurred: {e}")

    # End the program gracefully
    finally:
        # Turn off LED
        led.value(0)
        app.shutdown()
        print("\nMicrodot server stopped.")
```

Fig 5-x. microdot_HelloBlinky.py

Code Explanation

Let's look at how the code works.

- The gc module provides an interface to the garbage collector. The Pin module allows you to configure and control GPIO pins on the Pico.

The ADC module provides an interface to the Analog-to-Digital Converter (ADC) on the Pico.
The asyncio library allows you to write concurrent code using MicroPython's asynchronous programming functionality. The sys module is used to stop the execution of the current program if the WiFi network is unavailable.
The microdot module is the Microdot webserver.
The Response object allows you to create a custom HTTP response with explicit control over the body, status code, and headers directly within your route functions.
The time() module function returns the current time in seconds since the Epoch.
The localtime() module function converts the time in seconds since the Epoch into a human-readable date and time format.
The connect_wifi module uses its init_wlan() function to connect to a wireless network and its get_ip() function to obtain an IP address for your Pico.

```
import gc
from machine import Pin, ADC
import asyncio, sys
from microdot import Microdot, Response
from time import time, localtime
import connect_wifi
```

- The my_secrets module contains the name of your network (SSID) and your network password.

```
import my_secrets
ssid = my_secrets.SSID           # Your SSID (Network Name)
password = my_secrets.PASSWORD   # Your WiFi PASSWORD
```

You should add my_secrets.py to your .gitignore file to make sure that my_secrets.py is never checked into a GitHub code repository.

```
# Add my_secrets.py to the .gitignore file to make sure
#   that my_secrets.py is never checked into GitHub
SSID     = 'MyNetwork'        # YOUR SSID (Network Name)
PASSWORD = 'MyPassword'       # YOUR WiFi PASSWORD
```

- led = Pin(...) sets up the LED on the designated GPIO pin.

```
led = Pin(16, Pin.OUT)  # GPIO16
```

- To initialize the WiFi interface, use the connect_wifi.init_wlan() and connect_wifi.get_ip() module functions.

```
# Initialize the WiFi Interface
if not connect_wifi.init_wlan(ssid, password, max_retries=10):
    print('WiFi authentication error: {}'.\
          format(connect_wifi.SSID_ERROR))
    print('Exiting program')
    sys.exit(0)
else:
    ip_address = connect_wifi.get_ip()
```

- Instantiating the Microdot class creates a Microdot webserver.

```
app = Microdot()
```

- The Microdot communications interface consists of a get(url_pattern) decorator that is used to register a function as a GET request handler for a given URL.

- The @app.get('/') decorator registers the async index(request) function as a GET request handler. The index() function returns "Hello" as a plain text response.

```
@app.get('/')
async def index(request):
    return 'Hello'
```

- Initialize the LED state.

```
led_state = "OFF"
```

- The webpage(...) function returns an HTML form template with the following arguments inserted into the form body.
    - time_local: The local time
    - temp_celsius: The core temperature of the microcontroller in degrees Celsius
    - free_memory: The amount of available RAM
    - led_state: Whether the attached LED is ON or OFF

```
def webpage(time_local, temp_celsius, free_memory, led_state):
    #Template HTML
    html = f"""
    <!doctype html>
    <html>
        <head><title>Hello, Blinky!</title></head>
        <body>
            <h1>Hello, Blinky!</h1>
            <form method="POST">
                <button type="submit" name="led_on">\
                    Turn LED on</button><br/>
                <button type="submit" name="led_off">\
                    Turn LED off</button>
            </form>

            <p>LED is {led_state}</p>
            <p>Local Date/Time: {time_local}</p>
            <p>Temperature: {temp_celsius}</p>
            <p>Memory Available: {free_memory}</p>
        </body>
    </html>
    """
    return str(html)
```

- The @app.route() decorator registers the async light_switch(request) function as a request handler that handles both HTTP GET and POST requests from a client. It returns an HTML form in response to either type of request.

```
@app.route('/api/v0.1/light_switch', methods=['GET', 'POST']
async def light_switch(request):
    # Initialize the LED light to off
```

```
led.value(0)
led_state = "OFF"

if request.method == 'POST':
    if 'led_on' in request.form:
        led.value(1)  # Turn LED light on
        led_state = "ON"

# get the time
time_unix  = time() # Unix epoch time
time_local = "%4d/%02d/%02d %02d:%02d:%02d" \
             % localtime(time_unix)[:6]

# get the core temperature of the RP2040
temp_reading = temperature_sensor.read_u16() \
               * conversion_factor
temp_celsius = 27 - (temp_reading - 0.706)/0.001721
temp_celsius = "{:,.1f} C".format(temp_celsius)

# Check the number of bytes of available heap RAM
KB = 1024
gc.collect()
free_memory = gc.mem_free()
free_memory = "{:,.1f} KB".format(free_memory/KB)

# Generate the HTML form
html =  webpage(time_local, \
                temp_celsius, \
                free_memory, \
                led_state)

# Respond to the HTTP request with the HTML form
#   HTTP status code: 200 for OK
#   Content is an HTML markup document
return Response(html, status_code=200, \
                headers={'Content-Type': 'text/html'})
```

- Initializing the LED to off puts the LED into a known state for the request handler.

```
led.value(0)
led_state = "OFF"
```

- If the client sent a POST request to turn the LED on via a form button, the LED is turned ON.

```
if request.method == 'POST':
    if 'led_on' in request.form:
        led.value(1)
        led_state = "ON"
```

- Getting the Unix epoch time as well as the local time, getting the core temperature of the microcontroller, and checking the number of bytes of available heap RAM form the basis of an Entity Event. The code for each of these actions is explained in the pico_event.py module presented at the beginning of this chapter.

- The @app.get('/api/v0.1/light/on') decorator registers the async light_on(request) function as a GET request handler that turns on the LED and returns the LED state as a MicroPython dictionary in the form of a JSON object.

```
@app.get('/api/v0.1/light/on')
async def light_on(request):
    led.value(1)
    return {"led_state": "ON"}
```

- The @app.get('/api/v0.1/light/off') decorator registers the async light_on(request) function as a GET request handler that turns off the LED and returns the LED state as a MicroPython dictionary in the form of a JSON object.

```
@app.get('/api/v0.1/light/off')
async def light_off(request):
    led.value(0)
    return {"led_state": "OFF"}
```

- You can use a Route Parameter to turn the LED on or off.
  The @app.get('/api/v0.1/light/<int:state>') decorator registers the async light_state(request, state) function as a GET request handler. When a non-zero integer is passed to the view function as `state`, the LED is turned on. If it is zero, the LED is turned off. The LED state is returned as a MicroPython dictionary that is automatically converted as a JSON response object.

```
@app.get('/api/v0.1/light/<int:state>')
async def light_state(request, state):
    if state != 0:  # turn LED ON for non-zero state
        led_state = "ON"
        led.value(1)
    else:
        led_state = "OFF"
        led.value(0)
    return {"led_state": led_state}
```

- Alternatively, you can use a Query Parameter to turn the LED on or off.
  The @app.get('/api/v0.1/light) decorator registers the async light_state(request) function as a GET request handler. The query parameter state must be either 'ON' or 'OFF'. Example: /api/v0.1/light?state=ON. The view function uses `request.args.get()` to access the parameter-value pair with a default value of 'Unknown' if the state is neither 'ON' nor 'OFF'.

```
@app.get('/api/v0.1/light')
async def light_state(request):
   # Get query parameters from the request object
    led_state = request.args.get('state', 'Unknown') # Get
'state' or default to 'Unknown'
    if (led_state != 'ON') and (led_state != 'OFF'):
        raise ValueError(\
            f"led_state = {led_state} (must be 'ON' or 'OFF')")
```

```
    if led_state == 'ON':
        led.value(1)
    else:
        led.value(0)
    return {"led_state": led_state}
```

- The main entry point for the event loop is async main() which schedules the Microdot server to be run asynchronously.

```
async def main():
    print("Starting async task ...")
    await app.start_server(host=ip_address, port=80, debug=True)
```

- The try-except block runs the main() asynchronous task but catches a user interrupt (e.g. Ctrl-C) to stop the program and prints the message "Microdot server stopped." to the console when the program finishes.

```
    try:
        # Run the Microdot webserver
        print("Starting Microdot server ...")
        main_task=asyncio.run(main())

    # Keyboard interrupt caught
    except KeyboardInterrupt:
        print("\nUser interrupted the program")

    # Unexpected error
    except Exception as e:
        print(f"An unexpected error occurred: {e}")

    # End the program gracefully
    finally:
        # Turn off LED
        led.value(0)
        app.shutdown()
        print("\nMicrodot server stopped.")
```

Procedure / Steps

> ⚠ **Warning:** Do not connect your host or your Pico to the internet on an insecure network!!!

Run the MicroPython code on your target Pico.

microdot_HelloBlinky.py

1. Using Thonny (File > Open), select microdot_HelloBlinky.py
2. Go to the Run menu
   Select "Run current script"

Tests and Results

While running microdot_HelloBlinky.py, open a web browser to each of the URLs listed below. Do you get the corresponding HTTP responses from Microdot?

```
URL: http://[the ip address of your Pico]
HTTP response: "Hello"

URL: http://[the ip address of your Pico]/api/v0.1/light/on
HTTP response: {"led_state": "ON"}

URL: http://[the ip address of your Pico]/api/v0.1/light/off
HTTP response: {"led_state": "OFF"}

URL: http://[the ip address of your Pico]/api/v0.1/light/1
HTTP response: {"led_state": "ON"}

URL: http://[the ip address of your Pico]/api/v0.1/light/0
HTTP response: {"led_state": "OFF"}

URL: http://[the ip address of your Pico]/api/v0.1/light?state=ON
HTTP response: {"led_state": ON"}

URL: http://[the ip address of your
Pico]/api/v0.1/light?state=OFF
HTTP response: {"led_state": OFF"}
```

Congratulations! You've shown how to combine HTTP verbs (GET and POST) in the general app.route() decorator to handle form data. You've also parsed Route Converters and Query Parameters to turn the external LED attached to your Pico on and off, showing that actions can be performed in view functions that return JSON objects.

Entity Event-Driven Embedded Pico Systems

At the beginning of this chapter you learned that, if a return value is a MicroPython dictionary, Microdot automatically converts the dictionary to a JSON object as its response. (Example: the dictionary {"Hello, world!"} becomes the JSON response object {"Hello": "world!"}.) By adding meta information to this dictionary in the form of an Event header with a unique identifier (e.g. a UUID), you can transform a Pico's HTTP response into a JSON object that a data consumer can easily read.

Events register occurrences that have *happened*. We can see the change in state of an LED light for ourselves just by looking at it but an Entity Event-Driven Embedded Pico System can communicate such occurrences as Events to other machines through its RESTful API interface. But you can also communicate sensing information about the physical world through that API interface at the same time. In the code below, pico_event.hardware_parameters() adds information to the Event about the temperature and available memory / file storage on the Pico:

```
@app.get('/api/v0.1/light/off')
async def light_off(request):
    led.value(0)
    event_header = pico_event.header()
    event_body   = {
                       'led_state': 'OFF'
                       'hardware_parameters': \
                       pico_event.hardware_parameters()
                   }
    return {"header": event_header, "body": event_body}
```

Fig 5-x. Example Microdot Entity-Event View Function

A data consumer in an Entity-Event driven architecture will generally *not* be a browser but a system that can make a request—for example via an HTTP request through a web API over a network—and get an HTTP response in a machine readable format that it can understand like JSON. Sometimes, as in the case of blinking an LED, the request itself can trigger an action that then becomes part of the Event!

Code

Using Thonny (File > Save as), copy and save the Python module below to your target Pico microcontroller.

microdot_HelloPico.py

This program adds event information to a Microdot web server's responses with minimal overhead. This allows the application to communicate events through its RESTful API as data that it senses from the physical world and as actions that it performs in it, transforming the embedded Pico system into an Entity-Event Driven one!

Since the program is based on the microdot_HelloBlinky.py example, only the primary differences with that example will be explained.

```
"""
microdot_HelloPico.py
---------
Microdot webserver for turning an LED ON and OFF
    + Event information

"""
import gc
from machine import Pin, ADC
import asyncio, sys
from microdot import Microdot, Response
from time import time, localtime
import connect_wifi, pico_event

# Add my_secrets.py to the .gitignore file to make sure
#   that my_secrets.py is never checked into GitHub
import my_secrets
ssid = my_secrets.SSID          # Your SSID (Network Name)
password = my_secrets.PASSWORD  # Your Wi-Fi PASSWORD

# Set up external LED
led = Pin(16, Pin.OUT)  # GPIO16

# Set up ADC internal temperature reading
temperature_sensor = ADC(ADC.CORE_TEMP)
conversion_factor = 3.3 / (65535)

# Initialize the WiFi Interface
if not connect_wifi.init_wlan(ssid, password, max_retries=10):
    print('WiFi authentication error: {}'\
          .format(connect_wifi.SSID_ERROR))
    print('Exiting program')
    sys.exit(0)
else:
    ip_address = connect_wifi.get_ip()

# Instantiate a Microdot webserver
app = Microdot()

# Microdot communications interface
@app.get('/')
```

```
async def index(request):
    return 'Hello'

led_state = "OFF"
def webpage(time_local, temp_celsius, free_memory, led_state):
    # Template HTML
    html = f"""
    <!doctype html>
    <html>
        <head><title>Hello, Pico!</title></head>
        <body>
            <h1>Hello, Pico!</h1>
            <form method="POST">
                <button type="submit" name="led_on">\
                    Turn LED on</button><br/>
                <button type="submit" name="led_off">\
                    Turn LED off</button>
            </form>

            <p>LED is {led_state}</p>
            <p>Local Date/Time: {time_local}</p>
            <p>Temperature: {temp_celsius}</p>
            <p>Memory Available: {free_memory}</p>
        </body>
    </html>
    """
    return str(html)

@app.route('/api/v0.1/light_switch', methods=['GET', 'POST'])
async def light_switch(request):
    # Initialize the LED light to off
    led.value(0)
    led_state = "OFF"

    # Turn LED light on if the client sent
    #    a POST request to turn on the LED
    if request.method == 'POST':
        if 'led_on' in request.form:
            led.value(1)
            led_state = "ON"

    # Get the Unix epoch time as well as the local time
    time_unix  = time()  # Unix epoch time
    time_local = "%4d/%02d/%02d %02d:%02d:%02d" \
                 % localtime(time_unix)[:6]

    # Get the core temperature of the microcontroller
    temp_reading = temperature_sensor.read_u16() \
                   * conversion_factor
    temp_celsius = 27 - (temp_reading - 0.706)/0.001721
    temp_celsius = "{:,.1f} C".format(temp_celsius)

    # Check the number of bytes of available heap RAM
```

```
    KB = 1024
    gc.collect()
    free_memory = gc.mem_free()
    free_memory = "{:,.1f} KB".format(free_memory/KB)

    # Generate the HTML form
    html =  webpage(time_local, \
                    temp_celsius, \
                    free_memory, \
                    led_state)

    # Respond to the HTTP request with the HTML form
    #   HTTP status code: 200 for OK
    #   Content is an HTML markup document
    return Response(html, status_code=200, \
                    headers={'Content-Type': 'text/html'})

@app.get('/api/v0.1/light/on')
async def light_on(request):
    led.value(1)
    event_header = pico_event.header()
    event_body   = {
                     'led_state': 'ON',
                     'hardware_parameters': \
                           pico_event.hardware_parameters()
                   }
    return {"header": event_header, "body": event_body}
# http://[the ip address of your Pico]/api/v0.1/light/on
#   returns: event header and body with led_state = ON

@app.get('/api/v0.1/light/off')
async def light_off(request):
    led.value(0)
    event_header = pico_event.header()
    event_body   = {
                     'led_state': 'OFF',
                     'hardware_parameters': \
                           pico_event.hardware_parameters()
                   }
    return {"header": event_header, "body": event_body}
# http://[the ip address of your Pico]/api/v0.1/light/off
#   returns: event header and body with led_state = OFF

# Route Parameter: LED state must be an integer
@app.get('/api/v0.1/light/<int:state>')
async def light_state(request, state):
    if state != 0:  # turn LED ON for non-zero state
        led_state = "ON"
        led.value(1)
    else:
        led_state = "OFF"
        led.value(0)
```

```
    event_header = pico_event.header()
    event_body   = {
                        'led_state': led_state,
                        'hardware_parameters': \
                            pico_event.hardware_parameters()
                    }
    return {"header": event_header, "body": event_body}
# http://[the ip address of your Pico]/api/v0.1/light/1
# http://[the ip address of your Pico]/api/v0.1/light/0
#   returns: event header and body with led_state = ON or OFF

# Query Parameter: LED state must be either "ON" or "OFF"
@app.get('/api/v0.1/light')
async def light_state(request):
    # Get query parameters from the request object

    # Get 'state' or default to 'Unknown'
    led_state = request.args.get('state', 'Unknown')
    if (led_state != 'ON') and (led_state != 'OFF'):
        raise ValueError(\
            f"led_state = {led_state} (must be 'ON' or 'OFF')")

    if led_state == 'ON':
        led.value(1)
    else:
        led.value(0)

    event_header = pico_event.header()
    event_body   = {
                        'led_state': led_state,
                        'hardware_parameters': \
                            pico_event.hardware_parameters()
                    }
    return {"header": event_header, "body": event_body}
# http://[the ip address of your Pico]/api/v0.1/light?state=ON
# http://[the ip address of your Pico]/api/v0.1/light?state=OFF
#   returns: event header and body with led_state = ON or OFF

# Main entry point for the event loop
async def main():
    print("Starting async task ...")
    await app.start_server(host=ip_address, port=80, debug=True)

# Start the event loop
if __name__ == '__main__':

    try:
        # Run the Microdot webserver
        print("Starting Microdot server ...")
        main_task=asyncio.run(main())

    # Keyboard interrupt caught
    except KeyboardInterrupt:
```

```
        print("\nUser interrupted the program")

    # Unexpected error
    except Exception as e:
        print(f"An unexpected error occurred: {e}")

    # End the program gracefully
    finally:
        # Turn off LED
        led.value(0)
        app.shutdown()
        print("\nMicrodot server stopped.")
```

Fig 5-x. microdot_HelloPico.py

Code Explanation

Let's look at how the code works. (Refer to the microdot_HelloBlinky.py example for the program that microdot_HelloPico.py is based on.)

- The connect_wifi module uses its init_wlan() function to connect to a wireless network and its get_ip() function to obtain an IP address for your Pico.
  The pico_event module obtains a unique event header for your Pico and obtains hardware parameters for it.

```
import connect_wifi, pico_event
```

- The @app.get('/api/v0.1/light/on') decorator registers the async light_on(request) function as a GET request handler that turns on the LED and returns an Event as a JSON response object that includes the LED state.
  The code for the pico_event.header() and pico_event.hardware_parameters() module functions is explained in the `pico_event.py` module presented at the beginning of this chapter.

```
@app.get('/api/v0.1/light/on')
async def light_on(request):
    led.value(1)
    event_header = pico_event.header()
    event_body   = {
                      'led_state': 'ON',
                      'hardware_parameters': \
                      pico_event.hardware_parameters()
                   }
    return {"header": event_header, "body": event_body}
```

- The @app.get('/api/v0.1/light/off') decorator registers the async light_off(request) function as a GET request handler that turns off the LED and returns an Event as a JSON response object that includes the LED state.
  The code for the pico_event.header() and pico_event.hardware_parameters() module functions is explained

in the pico_event.py module presented at the beginning of this chapter.

```
@app.get('/api/v0.1/light/off')
async def light_off(request):
    led.value(0)
    event_header = pico_event.header()
    event_body   = {
                    'led_state': 'OFF',
                    'hardware_parameters': \
                         pico_event.hardware_parameters()
                   }
    return {"header": event_header, "body": event_body}
```

- The @app.get('/api/v0.1/light/<int:state>') decorator registers the async light_state(request, state) function as a GET request handler that turns off the LED and returns an Event as a JSON response object that includes the LED state.
  When a non-zero integer is passed to the view function as state, the LED is turned on. If it is zero, the LED is turned off.
  The code for the pico_event.header() and pico_event.hardware_parameters() module functions is explained in the pico_event.py module presented at the beginning of this chapter.

```
@app.get('/api/v0.1/light/<int:state>')
async def light_state(request, state):
    if state != 0:  # turn LED ON for non-zero state
        led_state = "ON"
        led.value(1)
    else:
        led_state = "OFF"
        led.value(0)

    event_header = pico_event.header()
    event_body   = {
                    'led_state': led_state,
                    'hardware_parameters': \
                        pico_event.hardware_parameters()
                   }
    return {"header": event_header, "body": event_body}
```

- The @app.get('/api/v0.1/light') decorator registers the async light_state(request) function as a GET request handler that turns off the LED and returns an Event as a JSON response object that includes the LED state.
  The query parameter state must be either 'ON' or 'OFF'. Example: /api/v0.1/light?state=ON. The view function uses request.args.get() to access the parameter-value pair with a default value of 'Unknown' if the state is neither 'ON' nor 'OFF'. The code for the pico_event.header() and pico_event.hardware_parameters() module functions is explained in the pico_event.py module presented at the beginning of this chapter.

```
@app.get('/api/v0.1/light')
async def light_state(request):
```

```
    # Get query parameters from the request object

    # Get 'state' or default to 'Unknown'
    led_state = request.args.get('state', 'Unknown')
    if (led_state != 'ON') and (led_state != 'OFF'):
        raise ValueError(\
            f"led_state = {led_state} (must be 'ON' or 'OFF')")

    if led_state == 'ON':
        led.value(1)
    else:
        led.value(0)

    event_header = pico_event.header()
    event_body   = {
                    'led_state': led_state,
                    'hardware_parameters': \
                        pico_event.hardware_parameters()
                 }
    return {"header": event_header, "body": event_body}
```

- The main entry point for the event loop is async main() which schedules the Microdot server to be run asynchronously.

```
async def main():
    print("Starting async task ...")
    await app.start_server(host=ip_address, port=80, debug=True)
```

- The try-except block runs the main() asynchronous task but catches a user interrupt (e.g. Ctrl-C) to stop the program and prints the message "Microdot server stopped." to the console when the program finishes.

```
    try:
        # Run the Microdot webserver
        print("Starting Microdot server ...")
        main_task=asyncio.run(main())

    # Keyboard interrupt caught
    except KeyboardInterrupt:
        print("\nUser interrupted the program")

    # Unexpected error
    except Exception as e:
        print(f"An unexpected error occurred: {e}")

    # End the program gracefully
    finally:
        # Turn off LED
        led.value(0)
        app.shutdown()
        print("\nMicrodot server stopped.")
```

Procedure / Steps

> ⚠ **Warning:** Do not connect your host or your Pico to the internet on an insecure network!!!

Run the MicroPython code on your target Pico.

microdot_HelloPico.py

1. Using Thonny (File > Open), select microdot_HelloPico.py
2. Go to the Run menu
   Select "Run current script"

Tests and Results

Open your browser to the ip address with the API endpoint set to "on" (example: http://[the ip address of your Pico]/api/v0.1/light/on). The external LED turns on (if it wasn't already on!) and you should see something like the following which uniquely identifies the change in state and records it as an event, along with other relevant information about the event:


```
{
  "header": {
    "event_id": "3e93b24c-6345-4009-af70-a1ac3548e2fb",
    "time_local": "2025/07/09 16:46:01",
    "time_unix": 1752079561,
    "event_version": "1.0.0",
    "machine_unique_id": "31415926535897932384 6zza"
  },
  "body": {
    "led_state": "ON",
    "hardware_parameters": {
      "free_memory": 168352,
      "temp_celsius": "33.6 C",
      "flash_size": 868352,
      "flash_used": 548864,
      "flash_free": 319488
    }
  }
}
```


If you now navigate to http://[the ip address of your Pico]/api/v0.1/light/off, the external LED turns off (if it wasn't already off!) and you should see something like the following which uniquely identifies the change in state and records it as an event, along with other relevant information about the event:

```
{
  "header": {
    "event_id": "7f133422-fe26-4056-aa3d-d127da6342ce",
    "time_local": "2025/07/09 16:47:17",
    "time_unix": 1752079637,
    "event_version": "1.0.0",
    "machine_unique_id": "314159265358979323846zza"
  },
  "body": {
    "led_state": "OFF",
    "hardware_parameters": {
      "free_memory": 168640,
      "temp_celsius": "34.1 C",
      "flash_size": 868352,
      "flash_used": 548864,
      "flash_free": 319488
    }
  }
}
```


Note that the response contains the status of the LED light that was triggered by an HTTP GET request. Put differently, when you navigated to the "light/on" API endpoint in your browser, your Pico turned on the external LED light attached to it and responded with an Event that then reported the ON/OFF status of that light!

While running microdot_HelloPico.py, open a web browser to each of the URLs listed below. Do you get HTTP responses from Microdot with event information containing the ON or OFF state of the LED?

```
URL: http://[the ip address of your Pico]/api/v0.1/light/1

URL: http://[the ip address of your Pico]/api/v0.1/light/0

URL: http://[the ip address of your Pico]/api/v0.1/light?state=ON

URL: http://[the ip address of your
Pico]/api/v0.1/light?state=OFF
```

Congratulations—you've shown how to initiate actions on your Pico (e.g. blinking an LED) and you've shown how to include event information in the HTTP responses to requests from data consumers on the same network, thereby transforming your Pico into an Entity Event-Driven Embedded System!

References and Further Exploration

Microdot

- https://microdot.readthedocs.io/en/latest/
- https://blog.miguelgrinberg.com/post/microdot-yet-another-python-web-framework
- https://github.com/miguelgrinberg/microdot
- https://microdot.readthedocs.io/en/stable/freezing.html

Flask

- https://pypi.org/project/Flask/
- *Flask Web Development* 2nd ed. by Miguel Grinberg (O'Reilly: 2018, ISBN-13: 978-1491991732)
- https://courses.miguelgrinberg.com/p/flask-mega-tutorial

cloc utility

- https://github.com/AlDanial/cloc

Peter Hinch tutorial on using asyncio in MicroPython

- https://github.com/peterhinch/micropython-async/blob/master/v3/docs/TUTORIAL.md

HTTP Request Methods

- https://www.w3schools.com/tags/ref_httpmethods.asp

Chapter 6

1. Chapter Introduction
2. Programming Environment and Setup
    a. Introduction
    b. Equipment and Components
    c. Setup and Construction
    d. Code
3. A very simple LED traffic light
    a. Introduction
    b. Code
    c. Procedure / Steps
    d. Tests and Results
4. Using an ISR to check for a button press
    a. Introduction
    b. Code
    c. Procedure / Steps
    d. Tests and Results
5. Using asyncio with an ISR
    a. Introduction
    b. Code
    c. Procedure / Steps
    d. Tests and Results
6. Integrating an asyncio application with Microdot
    a. Introduction
    b. Code
    c. Procedure / Steps
    d. Tests and Results
7. References and Further Exploration

Pelican Crossing using asyncio and Microdot

Implement concurrency on your Entity Event-Driven Embedded Pico Systems using asyncio's and Microdot's cooperative multitasking approach, improving responsiveness and efficient resource usage

The Entity Events in this book have been limited thus far to reading information contained on the Pico itself (like its core temperature) or determining whether a button has been pressed. To show that your Pico is capable of acting on the world in a controlled way, you've connected an external LED to the Pico and blinked it. Blinking an LED is a very basic action that is an important first step in showing that you can connect electromechanical components to your Pico's microcontroller via its GPIO pins. You then conveyed those Entity Events through the Pico's external communications interface over a wireless network, first with sockets, then with Microdot.

As we have seen, an Entity Event-Driven Embedded Pico System can both *sense* the world and *act* on it. Between *sensing* and *acting*, however, the microcontroller on your Pico is capable of *thinking* in the sense of making logical decisions based on sensory input and acting on those decisions. Programmable logic makes embedded systems, even very simple ones, a useful part of our daily lives. A traffic light controller, for instance, which changes lights on a timer and can monitor if a pedestrian wishes to cross a street is essential for regulating the flow of traffic, keeping accidents from happening.

Pelican (Pedestrian Light Controlled) Crossing Traffic Lights

Traffic lights manage traffic flow, often communicating with other systems while doing so. They are an everyday real-world application of embedded systems. Like most embedded systems, they are designed to perform a specific purpose. Traffic lights combine hardware such as lights and sensors with software that controls timing and sequences.

In this chapter, you'll use *cooperative multitasking* in MicroPython to simulate a traffic light system known as a *Pelican Crossing* (*PELICON* is a portmanteau of *pe*destrian *li*ght *con*trolled—like motel from 'motor' / 'hotel' or brunch from 'breakfast' / 'lunch'). A Pelican Crossing is a type of pedestrian crossing system with traffic signals that was introduced into the United Kingdom, its Crown Dependencies and British Overseas Territories in 1969 (https://en.wikipedia.org/wiki/Pelican_crossing).

In addition to a traffic light, the Pelican system has a button for pedestrians to push when they wish to cross the street. If they press the button, the light turns red, stopping traffic for a short period of time, during which the system produces an audible beep to assist visually impaired pedestrians as they cross. Afterwards, the light resumes its usual sequence of light changes.

For a Pelican Crossing traffic light system using LEDs, a button press is an event that your Pico senses concurrently during this usual sequence of light changes. It then processes this information, slowing and stopping traffic long enough for pedestrians to get across the street.

One possible way to implement the concurrency requirement is to use MicroPython's _thread library on the Pico. While a main thread on core 0 handles the sequencing of lights, a second, additional thread on core 1 runs in an infinite loop, constantly monitoring for a button press. When a button is pressed, the button reader thread on core 1 sets a global button_pressed variable to True if it's false.

The main thread on core 0 keeps checking this shared memory variable in its own infinite while loop, turning the traffic light to red and making an audible beeping sound when the button has been pressed which allows pedestrians to cross the street. The main thread then resets the button_pressed flag back to False before proceeding with the normal traffic light sequence until the thread running on Core 1 signals that the button has been pressed again.

Cooperative Multitasking with MicroPython's asyncio Library

Although this possible solution effectively demonstrates threading on the Pico, it should be pointed out that—at the time of this writing—threading in MicroPython is still considered experimental. The threading API is in flux and it is not yet officially documented on the MicroPython.org website (https://docs.MicroPython.org/en/latest/library/_thread.html).

Aside from these concerns about using MicroPython threading, for all but the simplest of applications, threading bugs are notoriously subtle and hard to detect for developers. Threading bugs can cause an application to behave erratically and unpredictably. They can cause an application to freeze, getting stuck in deadlocks waiting for other threads to release resources. They can lead to race conditions that result in inconsistent or corrupted data. In short, while threads offer benefits such as improved responsiveness and performance, they likewise introduce significant complexities in managing and orchestrating concurrency in an application.

But by using cooperative multitasking with MicroPython's asyncio library, your Pelican Crossing traffic light system can run concurrent tasks asynchronously without the need to import the _thread library. Cooperative multitasking is widely used in memory-constrained embedded systems where the efficient use of resources is critical. (Not surprisingly, early memory-constrained Unix-based systems and personal computers employed cooperative multitasking as their main scheduling scheme.)

Cooperative multitasking with the asyncio library is comparatively simpler and easier to implement than truly parallel systems utilizing multithreaded programming. MicroPython's asyncio library is a style of concurrent programming that utilizes a single-threaded, single-process design. It gives the *appearance* of parallelism without the pitfalls associated with multiple threads running on multiple processors.

In cooperative multitasking, well-behaved processes cooperate with each other by voluntarily yielding control when logically blocked or are otherwise idle. Notably, the RAM footprint of the MicroPython asyncio library is small. And there is minimal overhead in switching contexts between processes. Cooperative multitasking with MicroPython asyncio is both fast and efficient.

MicroPython's asyncio library helps you write robust code for applications that involve a lot of waiting for external resources. With just a few keyword combinations (e.g. async def) and expressions (e.g. await asyncio.sleep_ms()) you can write clean, efficient, scalable code for concurrent applications bottlenecked by I/O. Examples: button presses, network requests, file operations and database interactions.

Cooperative multitasking works well for embedded applications running under tight memory constraints. Since it excels at handling I/O bound tasks, it can be an ideal choice for your Entity Event-Driven Embedded Pico Systems applications. Cooperative multitasking with MicroPython asyncio on your Pico also happens to dovetail nicely and in a straightforward way with the Microdot webserver framework which was designed to be fully asynchronous and uses MicroPython's asyncio library for its asynchronous operation.

In this chapter, you'll first construct a barebones LED traffic light system without a button or a buzzer for a crosswalk. A basic traffic light follows a defined transition of light changes (red, yellow, green) that shows how loops and delays combine to manage sequences of events.

In the second section, you'll check that an Active Piezo buzzer is making an audible sound before attaching it to your traffic light system along with a button. Then you'll add a button using an interrupt service routine (ISR) to check if it's been pressed, much like you did in the section on debouncing buttons in the "Hello, Blinky! chapter.

Together, the buzzer and button will interact with the traffic light and alter the logical flow of light changes. When a button is pressed, the light turns red, a buzzer sounds, a pedestrian can cross the road. Just like a real Pelican Traffic Light system, the red light remains ON even after the buzzer has stopped making an audible sound. A pedestrian already in the crosswalk while the buzzer was going can reach the other side of the road before the light turns green again.

In the third section, you'll write a traffic light program that uses *cooperative multitasking* in your MicroPython program to watch for button press events while the traffic light goes through its normal sequence of light changes. Since an ISR can disrupt the asyncio event loop, you'll write an asyncio button function that interfaces with the ISR-context code of the button interrupt while maintaining the integrity of the loop. This function includes a button debounce algorithm which sets a button press *asyncio event* that can be handled by the traffic lights for a pedestrian crossing.

Finally, you'll use cooperative multitasking to communicate events (such as whether a crosswalk button has been pressed and how many times it was pressed) with microservices and other data consumers / AI agents over a WiFi network via Microdot, completing your Pelican Crossing traffic light system and transforming it into an Entity Event-Driven Embedded Pico System!

Programming Environment and Setup

For the examples in this chapter, you'll need the following.

Programming Environment
Host computer running either:
- Windows
- Raspberry Pi OS or Linux
- macOS
Host computer with the following installed:
- Python 3.10 or above
- Thonny (thonny.org)
Target microcontroller:
- Pico with MicroPython installed
micro USB cable

Equipment and Components

Components used in this chapter (see fritzing.org for components created with Fritzing):

Description	Image
Male-to-male jumper wires	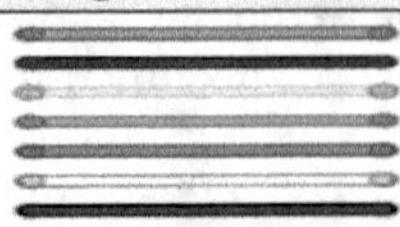
Full-sized Breadboard	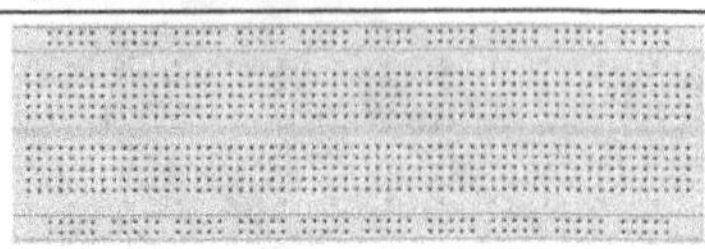
330 Ohm resistors (orange, orange, and brown stripes)	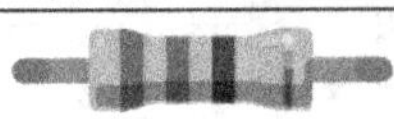

Description	Image
Active Piezo Buzzer	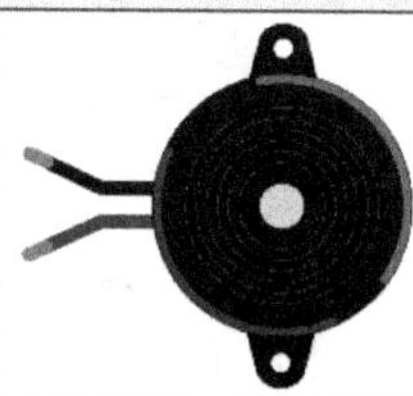
Push button switch	
Red LED - the cathode (- negative) lead is the shorter lead - the anode (+ positive) lead is the longer lead	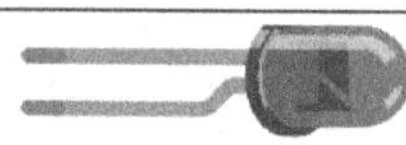
Yellow LED - the cathode (- negative) lead is the shorter lead - the anode (+ positive) lead is the longer lead	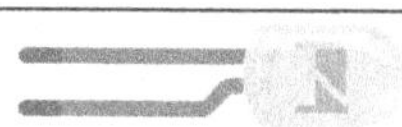
Green LED - the cathode (- negative) lead is the shorter lead - the anode (+ positive) lead is the longer lead	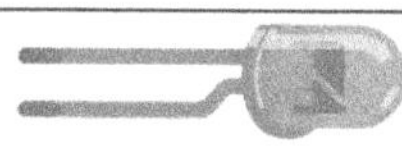

Fig 6-x. Components used in this chapter

Setup and Construction

Refer to Appendix A for a pinout guide to the Raspberry Pi Pico W.
Refer to Appendix C for a pinout guide to the Raspberry Pi Pico 2W.

Before you begin constructing the circuit, make sure your Pico is unplugged from your host computer.

1. Connect one end of a 330 Ohm resistor to the same column as the Pico's GPIO16 pin (this should be column 20 on a numbered breadboard with the Pico's GP01 pin aligned to column 1). Connect the other end to column 24.

2. Connect the anode (the longer leg) of the red LED to column 24 (the same column as the end of the resistor).
3. Connect the cathode (the shorter leg) of the red LED to the ground rail on the breadboard.
4. Connect one end of a jumper wire to GPIO17 and the other to column 29.
5. Connect one end of a 330 Ohm resistor to column 29. Connect the other end to column 33.
6. Connect the anode (the longer leg) of the yellow LED to column 33.
7. Connect the cathode (the shorter leg) of the yellow LED to the ground rail on the breadboard.
8. Connect one end of a jumper wire to GPIO18 and the other to column 37.
9. Connect one end of a 330 Ohm resistor to column 37. Connect the other end to column 41.
10. Connect the anode (the longer leg) of the green LED to column 41.
11. Connect the cathode (the shorter leg) of the green LED to the ground rail on the breadboard.
12. Add a push button switch so that it straddles the center divide. Connect one leg to pin GPIO15 and the other leg to a GND pin (Pin 18).
13. Connect one end of a jumper wire to GP14 and the other to column 48.
14. Add a Piezo button so that it straddles the center divide. Connect the anode (+ positive) to column 48 on the same side as the jumper wire. Connect the cathode to column 48 on the side with the 3 LEDs and resistors.
15. Connect one end of a jumper wire to column 48 and the other to the ground rail on the breadboard.
16. Finally, connect a GND pin (Pin 38) on the Pico with a jumper in column 3 to the ground rail on the breadboard.
17. Your finished circuit should resemble Figure 6-x:

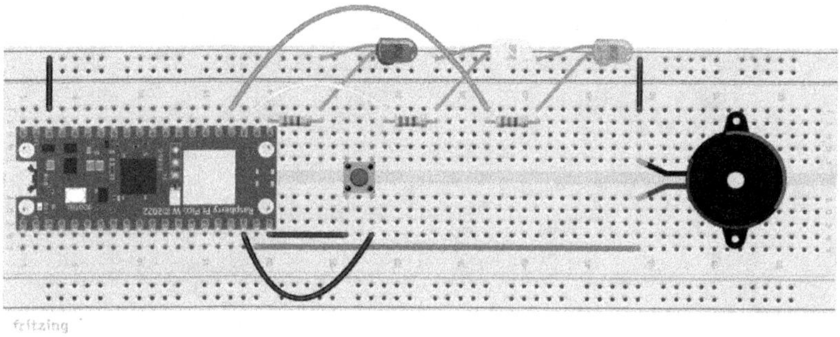

Fig 6-x. Red, Yellow and Green LEDs connected to the Pico with a Push Button and Piezo Buzzer

Now plug your Pico back into your host computer with a micro USB cable.

Installing Microdot

To install Microdot on your Pico using Thonny, select "Manage packages..." from the Tools menu:

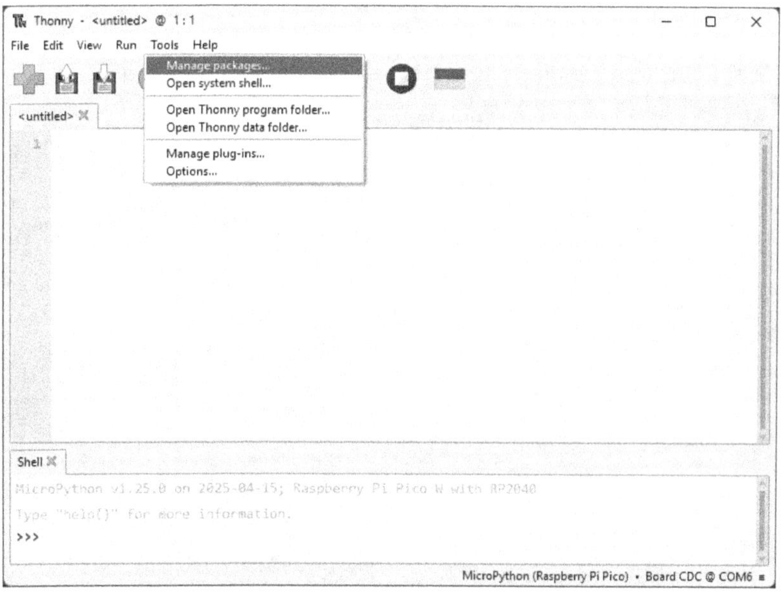

Fig 6-x. Thonny's Package Manager

Search for "microdot" and install the latest stable version of the package:

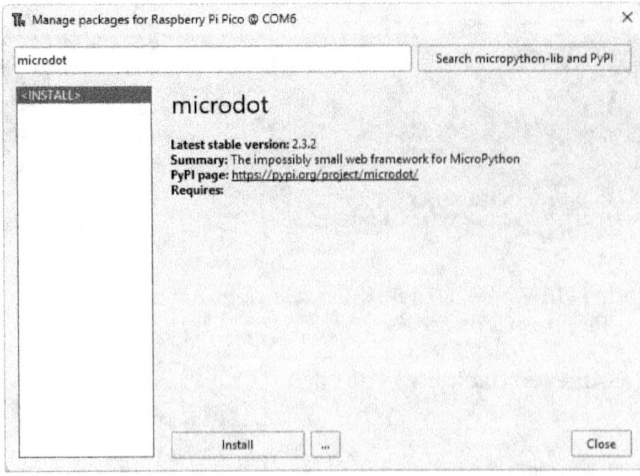

Fig 6-x. Installing Microdot with Thonny

Synchronizing the Pico's Real Time Clock using Thonny

To synchronize the Pico's Real Time Clock using Thonny, select "Options..." from the Tools menu:

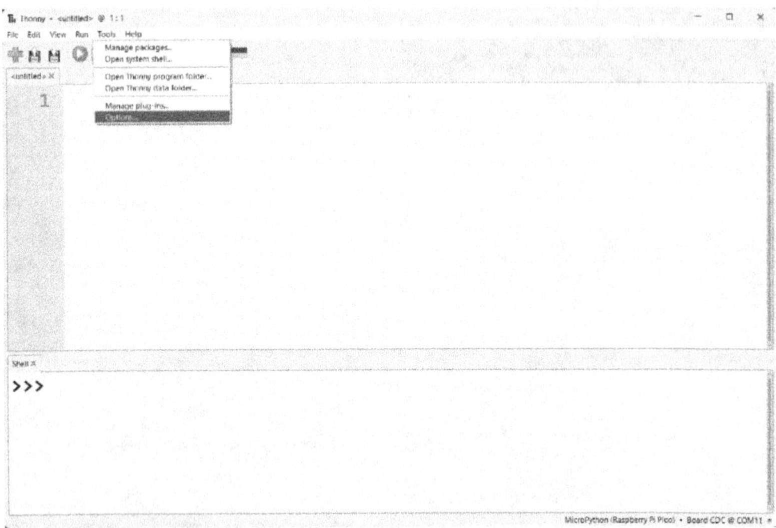

Fig 6-x. Thonny's Tools Options Menu

Choose the Interpreter tab and check the box labeled "Synchronize device's real time clock" to enable this feature.

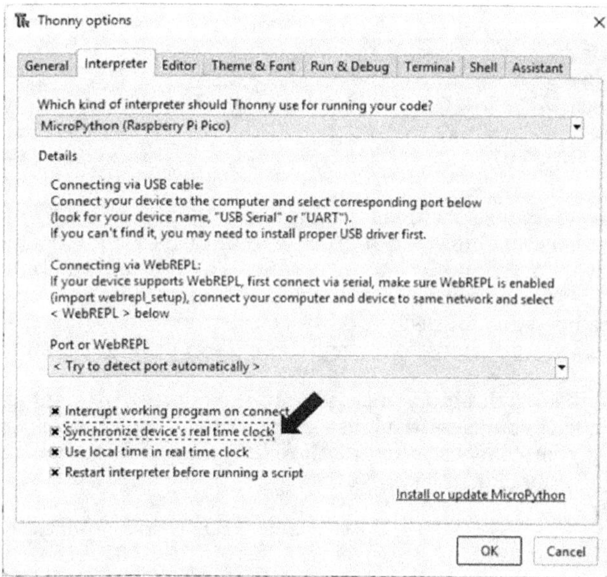

Fig 6-x. Synchronizing the Pico's RTC using Thonny

Code

Using Thonny (File > Save as), copy and save the Python modules below to your target Pico microcontroller.

config.py

The config module stores event information about the Pelican Crossing Traffic Light System.

```
button_pressed = False
button_counter = 0
```

Fig 6-x. config.py

Code Explanation

Let's look at how the code works.

- The microdot_TrafficLights application updates the following event information in the config module about the Pelican Crossing Traffic Light System which can then be communicated to data consumers through the Microdot webserver communications interface.

```
button_pressed = False
button_counter = 0
```

my_secrets.py

This code separates sensitive information such as your WiFi credentials and other sensitive information from your application logic which helps prevent accidentally exposing sensitive information if you share your MicroPython code with others. It also makes your code more reusable since you can easily modify your authentication credentials in one place without having to change the Python programs that import it.

Keep this file in a directory accessible to the MicroPython interpreter's import path. If you use GitHub as a source code repository, make sure to add my_secrets.py to your .gitignore file so that my_secrets.py is not accidentally checked into GitHub.

```
# Add my_secrets.py to the .gitignore file to make sure
#   that my_secrets.py is never checked into GitHub
SSID     = 'MyNetwork'          # YOUR SSID (Network Name)
PASSWORD = 'MyPassword'         # YOUR WiFi PASSWORD
```

Fig 6-x. my_secrets_EXAMPLE.py

Code Explanation

Let's look at how to use the my_secrets.py module in your MicroPython code.

- The my_secrets module contains sensitive information such as your WiFi network's SSID and password. After importing it, you can access variables within the this module and assign their values to local variables.

```
import my_secrets
ssid = my_secrets.SSID          # Your SSID (Network Name)
password = my_secrets.PASSWORD  # Your WiFi PASSWORD
```

connect_wifi.py

You'll have to initiate a WiFi connection every time you use your Pico on a WiFi network. This module displays connection progress and handles connection failures. You can increase the max_retries variable if your Pico requires more time to establish a connection to your particular network.

⚠ **Warning: DO NOT connect your Pico to an insecure network!!!**

```
"""
connect_wifi.py
-----------
To connect to a wireless network,
    use the ``init_wlan()`` function
To obtain the IP address, use the ``get_ip()`` function

Example::
        >>> import connect_wifi
        >>> connect_wifi.init_wlan('Your Network Name',        \
                                   'Your Network Password' \
                                   max_retries=23)
        >>> connect_wifi.get_ip()

For information on MicroPython's WLAN built-in WiFi
    interfaces, see:
    docs.micropython.org/en/latest/library/network.WLAN.html
"""
import network
from time import sleep


# Network error messages
NETWORK_CONNECTION_ERROR = "Network connection failed"
SSID_ERROR = "Failed to obtain IP address"

# Create a WLAN network interface object in Station (STA) mode
wlan = network.WLAN(network.STA_IF)

def init_wlan(ssid, password, max_retries=10):
    """Initiate a wireless LAN connnection

    :param ssid: wireless network name
    :param password: wireless network password
    :param max_retries: number of connection attempts before
        giving up

    :raise RuntimeError: If the network connection failed

    :return: True (successful connection);
             False (unsuccessful connection)
    :rtype: bool
    """

    # Activate network interface
    wlan.active(True)

    # Connect to the specified wireless network, using the
    #   wireless network name and password
    wlan.connect(ssid, password)
```

```
    # Print a message to the console saying that the device
    #   is trying to connect
    print('Waiting for connection...')

    # Continue to loop as long as there are connection attempts
    while max_retries > 0:
        # wlan.status() < 0: connection failure
        # wlan.status() >= 3: connection successful
        #   or has a valid IP address
        if wlan.status() < 0 or wlan.status() >= 3:
            break
        print(max_retries, '.', sep='', end='', )
        max_retries -= 1
        sleep(1)  # delay before retrying

    # Check if the connection was unsuccessful
    if wlan.status() != network.STAT_GOT_IP:
        raise RuntimeError(NETWORK_CONNECTION_ERROR)
        return False  # unsuccessful connection

    # Connection was successful and an IP address was obtained
    else:
        # Get the IP address
        ip = wlan.ifconfig()[0]

        # Print a confirmation message to console
        print( 'Connected: ip = {}'.format(ip))
        return True  # successful connection

def get_ip():
    """Get the IP address if WiFi is connected

    :raise RuntimeError: If not connected

    :return: IP Address (successful connection);
             SSID_ERROR (unsuccessful connection)
    :rtype: bool
    """
    if wlan.isconnected():
        return wlan.ifconfig()[0]
    else:
        print('\nNot connected')
        raise RuntimeError(SSID_ERROR)
        return None
```

Fig 6-x. connect_wifi.py

Code Explanation

Note: For more information on MicroPython's WLAN built-in WiFi interfaces, see https://docs.micropython.org/en/latest/library/network.WLAN.html.

Let's look at how the code works.

- The network module is used for configuring and controlling WiFi connectivity on the Pico.
  The sleep() module function is needed to introduce delays in the code execution.

```
import network
from time import sleep
```

- Define network error messages that are printed to the console if a Runtime Error is raised.
  NETWORK_CONNECTION_ERROR: Unsuccessful network connection.
  SSID_ERROR: Unable to obtain an IP address because there is not a network connection.

```
NETWORK_CONNECTION_ERROR = "Network connection failed"
SSID_ERROR = "Failed to obtain IP address"
```

- Create a WLAN network interface object in "Station" (STA) mode to connect to an existing WiFi access point (like a home router).

```
wlan = network.WLAN(network.STA_IF)
```

- Define a function init_wlan() to initiate a wireless LAN connection that returns True if the network connection is successful.
  If the network connection is not successful, init_wlan() raises a Runtime Error, printing the NETWORK_CONNECTION_ERROR message and returns False.

  The init_wlan() function takes three arguments:
  - ssid: wireless network name
  - password: wireless network password
  - max_retries: number of connection attempts before giving up

```
def init_wlan(ssid, password, max_retries=10):
    ...
```

- wlan.active(True) activates the network interface.
  ```
  wlan.active(True)
  ```
- wlan.connect(ssid, password) connects to the specified wireless network, using the wireless network name ssid and password.
  ```
  wlan.connect(ssid, password)
  ```
- A message is printed to the console saying that the device is attempting to connect.
  ```
  print('Waiting for connection...')
  ```
- As long as there are connection attempts as specified by the max_retries argument, init_wlan() continues to loop, printing a dot ('.') to the console showing progress and delaying for a second between each retry attempt.
  The loop breaks if the there is a connection failure (wlan.status() < 0); it also breaks if successfully connected or it obtains a valid IP address (wlan.status() >= 3):

```
    while max_retries > 0:
        if wlan.status() < 0 or wlan.status() >= 3:
            break
        print(max_retries, '.', sep='', end='', )
        max_retries -= 1
        sleep(1)  # delay before retrying
```

- If the connection was unsuccessful, a RuntimeError with the NETWORK_CONNECTION_ERROR error message is raised and init_wlan() returns False (unsuccessful connection).

```
    if wlan.status() != network.STAT_GOT_IP:
        raise RuntimeError(NETWORK_CONNECTION_ERROR)
        return False
```

- However, if the connection was successful and an IP address was obtained, the ip addressed is printed to the console and init_wlan() returns True (successful connection):

```
    else:
        ip = wlan.ifconfig()[0]

        print( 'Connected: ip = {}'.format(ip))
        return True
```

- The module function get_ip() returns the IP address if connected to the WiFi network. If not connected to the WiFi network, the function raises a Runtime Error, printing the SSID_ERROR message to the console.

  Note that the ifconfig() method returns a 4-tuple (IP address, subnet mask, gateway, DNS server), and that ifconfig()[0] accesses the IP address.

```
def get_ip():
    if wlan.isconnected():
        return wlan.ifconfig()[0]
    else:
        print('\nNot connected')
        raise RuntimeError(SSID_ERROR)
        return None
```

pico_event.py

The following module obtains a unique event header and hardware parameters for the Pico.

Notes

Event Time A call to time.time() returns the number of *seconds* since the Unix Epoch.

If you require more precision, however, you can use the time.time_ns() function which returns the number of *nanoseconds* since the Unix Epoch. But when you do, remember that the localtime() function takes seconds, not nanoseconds. Hence, time_local would have to be adjusted accordingly:

```
# get the time for this event in nanoseconds
time_unix  = time.time_ns()
time_local = "%4d/%02d/%02d %02d:%02d:%02d" %
time.localtime(time_unix) // 1_000_000_000)[:6]
```

Hardware Parameters Especially when you're developing a Pico-based system, it's often useful to know hardware parameters such as free memory and space as well as the CPU core temperature of the Pico when debugging it. This information can be included in the Event header or body as needed.

```
"""
pico_event.py
---------
To obtain a unique event header for the Pico,
  use the ``header()`` function
To obtain hardware parameters for the Pico,
  use the ``hardware_parameters()`` function

Examples::
        >>> import pico_event
        >>> pico_event.header()
        >>> pico_event.hardware_parameters()
"""
import gc
from machine import unique_id, ADC
from os import urandom, statvfs
from time import time, localtime

# Get the serial number of the Pico's flash
machine_unique_id = unique_id().hex()

# Define the version of this event
EVENT_VERSION = "1.0.0"

def header():
    """Get event header

    :return: event header for the Pico
    :rtype: dictionary
    """
    # Get a unique id for this event
    event_id = uuid4()

    # Get the time for this event
    time_unix  = time() # Unix epoch time
    time_local = "%4d/%02d/%02d %02d:%02d:%02d" \
                 % localtime(time_unix)[:6]

    # Define the event header
```

```
    event_header = {
                      "machine_unique_id": machine_unique_id,
                      "time_unix":         time_unix,
                      "time_local":        time_local,
                      "event_id":          event_id,
                      "event_version":     EVENT_VERSION,
                  }

    return event_header

"""Generate a version 4 UUID compliant to RFC 4122"""
def uuid4():
    random_x = bytearray(urandom(16))
    random_x[6] = (random_x[6] & 0x0F) | 0x40
    random_x[8] = (random_x[8] & 0x3F) | 0x80
    h = random_x.hex()
    return str('-'.join((h[0:8], h[8:12], \
                         h[12:16], h[16:20], h[20:32])))

# Set up ADC internal temperature reading
temperature_sensor = ADC(ADC.CORE_TEMP)
conversion_factor = 3.3 / (65535)

def hardware_parameters():
    """Get hardware parameters for the Pico

    :return: hardware info about the Pico
    :rtype: dictionary
    """
    # Get the core temperature of the microcontroller
    temp_reading = temperature_sensor.read_u16() \
                   * conversion_factor
    temp_celsius = 27 - (temp_reading - 0.706)/0.001721
    temp_celsius = "{:,.1f} C".format(temp_celsius)

    # Get flash memory size and storage consumption
    flash_status = statvfs("/")
    flash_size = flash_status[1] * flash_status[2]
    flash_free = flash_status[0] * flash_status[3]
    flash_used = flash_size - flash_free

    # Get the number of bytes of available heap RAM
    gc.collect()
    free_memory = gc.mem_free()

    hw_params = {
          "temp_celsius": temp_celsius,
          "flash_size":   flash_size,
          "flash_used":   flash_used,
          "flash_free":   flash_free,
          "free_memory":  free_memory
        }
```

```
    return hw_params
```

Fig 6-x. pico_event.py

Code Explanation

Let's look at how the code works.

- The gc module provides an interface to the garbage collector.
  The unique_id module function returns a unique identifier for the Pico.
  The ADC module provides an interface to the Analog-to-Digital Converter (ADC) on the Pico.
  The urandom() module function generates a string of random bytes suitable for creating unique identifiers.
  The statvfs() module function retrieves information about the file system.
  The time() module function returns the current time in seconds since the Epoch.
  The localtime() module function converts the time in seconds since the Epoch into a human-readable date and time format.

```
import gc
from machine import unique_id, ADC
from os import urandom, statvfs
from time import time, localtime
```

- The unique_id().hex() function gets the serial number of the Pico's flash.

```
machine_unique_id = unique_id().hex()
```

- The version of the event is defined by EVENT_VERSION.

```
EVENT_VERSION = "1.0.0"
```

- The header() function gets the Event header that should be included with all Events.

```
def header():

    # Get a unique id for this event
    event_id = uuid4()

    # Get the time for this event
    time_unix  = time() # Unix epoch time
    time_local = "%4d/%02d/%02d %02d:%02d:%02d" \
                 % localtime(time_unix)[:6]

    # Define the event header
    event_header = {
                     "machine_unique_id": machine_unique_id,
                     "time_unix":         time_unix,
                     "time_local":        time_local,
                     "event_id":          event_id,
                     "event_version":     EVENT_VERSION,
```

```
                    }

    return event_header
```

- Get a unique id for this event.

```
event_id = uuid4()
```

- Get the unix time and the local time for this event.

```
time_unix  = time() # Unix epoch time
time_local = "%4d/%02d/%02d %02d:%02d:%02d" \
             % localtime(time_unix)[:6]
```

- The Event header is a MicroPython dictionary of the Pico's flash serial number (machine_unique_id), the unix time (as measured by the number of seconds since the Epoch, the local time, a unique id for this event, and the Event version. MicroPython will automatically convert this dictionary to JSON when it returns it as part of an HTTP response object.

```
event_header = {
                   "machine_unique_id": machine_unique_id,
                   "time_unix":         time_unix,
                   "time_local":        time_local,
                   "event_id":          event_id,
                   "event_version":     EVENT_VERSION,
               }

return event_header
```

- The uuid4() function returns a version 4 UUID compliant to RFC 4122.
  This UUID uniquely identifies an Event.

```
def uuid4():
    ...
```

- random_x = bytearray(). This line gets 16 high-quality, cryptographically secure random bytes.

```
random_x = bytearray(urandom(16))
```

- random_x[6] = () and random_x[8] = (). These lines set the "version" and "variant" bits per RFC 4122.

```
random_x[6] = (random_x[6] & 0x0F) | 0x40
random_x[8] = (random_x[8] & 0x3F) | 0x80
```

- h = random_x.hex() generates a 32-character hexadecimal string from the byte array.

```
h = random_x.hex()
```

- return str(). This line returns the UUID string correctly formatted with hyphens.

```
return str('-'.join((h[0:8], h[8:12], \
                     h[12:16], h[16:20], h[20:32])))
```

- The internal temperature is read using the Pico's built-in Analog-to-Digital Converter (ADC).

```
temperature_sensor = ADC(ADC.CORE_TEMP)
conversion_factor = 3.3 / (65535)
```

- The hardware_parameters() function returns hardware information about the Pico, specifically the core temperature of its microcontroller, amount of flash available and used, and the amount of free memory available. This information answers two basic questions about the operating conditions of the Pico that can affect its performance and longevity: How hot is it running at? How much memory (both flash and RAM) is available?

```
def hardware_parameters():

    # Get the core temperature of the microcontroller
    temp_reading = temperature_sensor.read_u16() \
                   * conversion_factor
    temp_celsius = 27 - (temp_reading - 0.706)/0.001721
    temp_celsius = "{:,.1f} C".format(temp_celsius)

    # Get flash memory size and storage consumption
    flash_status = statvfs("/")
    flash_size = flash_status[1] * flash_status[2]
    flash_free = flash_status[0] * flash_status[3]
    flash_used = flash_size - flash_free

    # Get the number of bytes of available heap RAM
    gc.collect()
    free_memory = gc.mem_free()

    hw_params = {
          "temp_celsius": temp_celsius,
          "flash_size":   flash_size,
          "flash_used":   flash_used,
          "flash_free":   flash_free,
          "free_memory":  free_memory
    }

    return hw_params
```

- Getting the core temperature of the microcontroller. You can use the Pico's ADC to determine this temperature by reading the Pico's internal temperature sensor and converting that digital value to a temperature.

```
temp_reading = temperature_sensor.read_u16() \
               * conversion_factor
temp_celsius = 27 - (temp_reading - 0.706)/0.001721
temp_celsius = "{:,.1f} C".format(temp_celsius)
```

- The statvfs() module function tells you the flash memory size (flash_size = fragment size * size of fs in f_frsize units) and storage consumption (flash_free = file system block size * number of free blocks) on the Pico.

```
flash_status = statvfs("/")
flash_size = flash_status[1] * flash_status[2]
flash_free = flash_status[0] * flash_status[3]
flash_used = flash_size - flash_free
```

- Getting an accurate number of bytes of available heap RAM requires first using MicroPython's garbage collector to reclaim memory from objects that are no longer actively used by the MicroPython program. This is followed by the garbage collector's mem_free() function.

```
gc.collect()
free_memory = gc.mem_free()
```

- The hardware_parameters() function returns the hw_params = {...} dictionary of the Pico's core temperature, amount of flash used and available, and the amount of free memory available. MicroPython will automatically convert this dictionary to JSON when it returns it as part of an HTTP response object.

```
hw_params = {
        "temp_celsius": temp_celsius,
        "flash_size":   flash_size,
        "flash_used":   flash_used,
        "flash_free":   flash_free,
        "free_memory":  free_memory
    }

return hw_params
```

A very simple LED traffic light

You can build a very simple LED traffic light by attaching red, yellow and green LEDs to your Pico—plus resistors for each LED to limit the current going to them so that they don't burn out (or worse, damage your Pico!).

At a high level, your simple traffic light will change lights using various timings for each of the LEDs:

1. Turn on the red LED for a certain amount of time (light_duration); then turn it off
2. Turn on the yellow LED for half the time (light_duration // 2) of the red LED; then turn it off
3. Turn on the green LED for a certain amount of time (light_duration); then turn it off

You'll see how easy it is to set different timings for each of the traffic lights.

Of course, an actual traffic management system will likely handle multiple traffic signals and set their timings to different values to maximize traffic flow depending on the time of day and other information about the overall traffic network. But this very basic LED traffic light simulator illustrates how the logical sequence of events in an embedded control system can interact with the external world in managing traffic.

Code

Using Thonny (File > Save as), copy and save the Python module below to your target Pico microcontroller.

simple_TrafficLights.py

Running the code below will simulate a simple traffic light.

```
"""
simple_TrafficLights.py
--------
Simple LED Traffic Lights, no crosswalk

Traffic Light Logic Flow::
    Red -> Green, Green -> Yellow -> Red
```

```
"""
from machine import Pin
from time import sleep

# Set up LED traffic lights
led_RED    = Pin(16, Pin.OUT)  # GPIO16
led_YELLOW = Pin(17, Pin.OUT)
led_GREEN  = Pin(18, Pin.OUT)

# LED Traffic Controller
light_duration = 4  # seconds
while True:
    # Red light
    led_RED.value(1)
    sleep(light_duration)
    led_RED.value(0)

    # Green light
    led_GREEN.value(1)
    sleep(light_duration)
    led_GREEN.value(0)

    # Yellow light
    led_YELLOW.value(1)
    sleep(light_duration // 2)
    led_YELLOW.value(0)
```

Fig 6-x. simple_TrafficLights.py

Code Explanation

- The Pin module allows you to configure and control GPIO pins on the Pico.
  The sleep() module function is needed to introduce delays in the code execution.

```
from machine import Pin
from time import sleep
```

- led_COLOR = Pin(...) sets up the LED traffic light on the designated GPIO pin.

```
led_RED    = Pin(16, Pin.OUT)  # GPIO16
led_YELLOW = Pin(17, Pin.OUT)
led_GREEN  = Pin(18, Pin.OUT)
```

- Define the traffic light duration in seconds.

```
light_duration = 4  # seconds
```

- The while True loop controls the traffic light, turning on and off each LED in turn.

```
while True:
    # Red light
    led_RED.value(1)
    sleep(light_duration)
```

```
    led_RED.value(0)

    # Green Light
    led_GREEN.value(1)
    sleep(light_duration)
    led_GREEN.value(0)

    # Yellow Light
    led_YELLOW.value(1)
    sleep(light_duration // 2)
    led_YELLOW.value(0)
```

Procedure / Steps

Run the MicroPython code on your target Pico.

1. Using Thonny (File > Open), select simple_TrafficLights.py
2. Go to the Run menu
   Select "Run current script"

Tests and Results

When you run simple_TrafficLights.py on your Pico, the Red, Yellow and Green external LEDs will simulate an actual traffic light by turning on and off each LED in sequence according to the light durations you specified in the program. The pattern of lights repeats indefinitely until you stop the program (e.g. Ctrl-C).

Using an ISR to check for a button press

Now let's add a push button and a buzzer to your LED traffic light.

First you'll write a test program to make sure the Piezo Buzzer is making a sound.

Next you'll write a traffic light program that uses an ISR to check if the crosswalk button has been pressed. (Recall that you wrote a button press program using ISRs in the section on debouncing buttons in Chapter 3—you'll debounce the crosswalk button in the same way.) If an interrupt flag indicates that the button has been pressed, the traffic light turns the red LED on and the Piezo Buzzer sounds while a pedestrian crosses the street. As before, you'll set the various timings for each of the traffic lights.

Code

Using Thonny (File > Save as), copy and save the Python modules below to your target Pico microcontroller.

test_PiezoBuzzer.py

The following code checks that the Active Piezo Buzzer makes an audible sound.

```
"""
test_PiezoBuzzer.py
--------
Check that Active Piezo Buzzer makes a sound

"""
from machine import Pin
from time import sleep

# Set up active Piezo buzzer
buzzer = Pin(14, Pin.OUT)  # GPIO14

for i in range(10):
    buzzer.value(1)
    sleep(0.2)
    buzzer.value(0)
    sleep(0.2)
```

Fig 6-x. test_PiezoBuzzer.py

- The Pin module allows you to configure and control GPIO pins on the Pico.
  The sleep() module function is needed to introduce delays in the code execution.

```
from machine import Pin
from time import sleep
```

- buzzer = Pin(...) sets up an active Piezo buzzer on the designated GPIO pin.

```
buzzer = Pin(14, Pin.OUT)  # GPIO14
```

- The for loop turns the buzzer on and off 10 times.

```
for i in range(10):
    buzzer.value(1)
    sleep(0.2)
    buzzer.value(0)
    sleep(0.2)
```

ISR_TrafficLights.py

The following code is for an LED Traffic Light with an active Piezo crosswalk buzzer. It uses interrupts to monitor when a pedestrian wishes to cross by pressing a button.

```
"""
ISR_TrafficLights.py
--------
Simple LED Traffic Light with active Piezo crosswalk buzzer using
    button interrupts

Traffic Light Logic Flow::
  No Pedestrian:
      Red -> Green, Green -> Yellow -> Red
  Pedestrian Crossing:
      Setting the interrupt_flag variable = 1 indicates that
          the crosswalk button was pressed
      On next Red, buzz for 5 seconds allowing pedestrian to
          cross then set interrupt_flag = 0 and proceed to
          No Pedestrian sequence

"""
from machine import Pin
from time import sleep, ticks_ms, ticks_diff

# Set up LED traffic lights
led_RED    = Pin(16, Pin.OUT)  # GPIO16
led_YELLOW = Pin(17, Pin.OUT)
led_GREEN  = Pin(18, Pin.OUT)

# Set up GPIO pins connected to the crosswalk buzzer and button
buzzer = Pin(14, Pin.OUT)              # GPIO14
button = Pin(15, Pin.IN, Pin.PULL_UP)  # GPIO15
```

```
# Define an ISR callback function for a crosswalk button press
interrupt_flag = 0
last_debounce_time = 0
def button_isr(pin):
    global interrupt_flag, last_debounce_time
    current_time = ticks_ms()  # get current time in milliseconds

    # Debounce: Has the button been held down for at least 50ms?
    if ticks_diff(current_time, last_debounce_time) > 50:
        interrupt_flag = 1  # set interrupt flag
        last_debounce_time = current_time

# Initialize the IRQ
button.irq(trigger = Pin.IRQ_FALLING, handler = button_isr)

# LED Traffic Light Controller
def main_program(light_duration = 4):
    global interrupt_flag

    button_counter = 0  # the button has not yet been pressed
    while True:
        # Crosswalk button pressed?
        if interrupt_flag == 1:
            # Clear the interrupt flag for the next button press
            interrupt_flag = 0

            # Increment crosswalk button counter
            button_counter = button_counter + 1
            print(f"Crosswalk button counter = {button_counter}")

            # Turn red light on for the pedestrians to cross
            led_RED.value(1)

            # Make buzzing sound for 5 seconds
            #     while the pedestrians cross
            for i in range(10):
                buzzer.value(1)
                sleep(0.2)
                buzzer.value(0)
                sleep(0.2)

        # Red light
        led_RED.value(1)
        sleep(light_duration)
        led_RED.value(0)

        # Green light
        led_GREEN.value(1)
        sleep(light_duration)
        led_GREEN.value(0)

        # Yellow light
        led_YELLOW.value(1)
```

```
        sleep(light_duration // 2)
        led_YELLOW.value(0)

if __name__ == '__main__':
    try:
        # Start main program
        main_program(light_duration = 4)

    # Keyboard interrupt caught
    except KeyboardInterrupt:
        print("\nUser interrupted the program.")

    # Unexpected error
    except Exception as e:
        print(f"An unexpected error occurred: {e}")

    # End the program gracefully
    finally:
        # Turn off traffic light LEDs
        led_RED.off()
        led_YELLOW.off()
        led_GREEN.off()

        print("\nISR Pelican Traffic Light"
              " Controller program ended.")
```

Fig 6-x. ISR_TrafficLights.py

- The Pin module allows you to configure and control GPIO pins on the Pico.
  The sleep() module function is needed to introduce delays in the code execution.

```
from machine import Pin
from time import sleep, ticks_ms, ticks_diff
```

- led_COLOR = Pin(...) sets up the LED traffic lights on the designated GPIO pins.

```
led_RED    = Pin(16, Pin.OUT)  # GPIO16
led_YELLOW = Pin(17, Pin.OUT)
led_GREEN  = Pin(18, Pin.OUT)
```

- buzzer = Pin(...) sets up an active Piezo buzzer on the designated GPIO pin.

```
buzzer = Pin(14, Pin.OUT)  # GPIO14
```

- button = Pin(...) initializes the push button connected to GPIO15 as an input pin with a pull-up resistor enabled that reads HIGH when the button is not pressed.

```
button = Pin(15, Pin.IN, Pin.PULL_UP)  # GPIO15
```

- The button_pressed variable indicates that a pedestrian has pushed the crosswalk button and is intialized to False.

```
button_pressed = False
```

```
* button_isr() is an ISR callback function that executes when the
interrupt is triggered by a button press.
The pin argument is the specific pin that triggered the
interrupt.
```python
def button_isr(pin):
    ...
```

- The global interrupt_flag is a boolean flag signaling to the main program that a pedestrian has pushed the crosswalk button. The global last_debounce_time saves the time of the last valid button event. This timestamp is used to determine whether the button has been held down for at least 50ms.

```
global interrupt_flag, last_debounce_time
```

- When the button interrupt is triggered, the time in milliseconds (ms) is captured.

```
current_time = ticks_ms()
```

- **Debounce.** Check if the time elapsed since the previous valid button event (last_debounce_time) is greater than 50 milliseconds. This logic helps prevent multiple triggers when a mechanical button "bounces" (makes and breaks contact multiple times rapidly) before settling into a stable state during a single button press. If a stable button press has been detected–the debounce condition is met–the interrupt flag is set to 1 indicating to the main program that a valid button press has occurred. A new reference point for debouncing the next button press event is then established by updating the last_debounce_time to the current_time.

```
if ticks_diff(current_time, last_debounce_time) > 50:
    interrupt_flag = 1  # set interrupt flag
    last_debounce_time = current_time
```

- button.irq() attaches an interrupt to the crosswalk button pin.
  - trigger=Pin.IRQ_FALLING specifies that the interrupt should be triggered when the button is released, going from HIGH to LOW (i.e. on a falling edge).
  - handler = button_isr: The associated ISR callback function when the interrupt is triggered.

```
button.irq(trigger = Pin.IRQ_FALLING, handler = button_isr)
```

- The main_program() controls the traffic light, turning on and off each LED traffic light in turn until it detects that the interrupt flag has been set to 1 indicating that the crosswalk button has been pressed. When it has, the traffic lights controller sets the interrupt flag to 0 for the next button press, increments a button counter and toggles the red led light ON while making a buzzing sound for 5 seconds, allowing pedestrians to proceed through the crosswalk.

```
def main_program(light_duration = 4):
    global interrupt_flag

    button_counter = 0  # the button has not yet been pressed
    while True:
```
```

```
# Crosswalk button pressed?
if interrupt_flag == 1:
    # Clear the interrupt flag for the next button press
    interrupt_flag = 0

    # Increment crosswalk button counter
    button_counter = button_counter + 1
    print(f"Crosswalk button counter = {button_counter}")

    # Turn red light on for the pedestrians to cross
    led_RED.value(1)

    # Make buzzing sound for 5 seconds
    #     while the pedestrians cross
    for i in range(10):
        buzzer.value(1)
        sleep(0.2)
        buzzer.value(0)
        sleep(0.2)
...
```

- The traffic lights controller then proceeds with the normal flow of traffic light changes until the next time that the crosswalk button has been pressed.

```
# Red light
led_RED.value(1)
await asyncio.sleep(light_duration)
led_RED.value(0)

# Green light
led_GREEN.value(1)
await asyncio.sleep(light_duration)
led_GREEN.value(0)

# Yellow light
led_YELLOW.value(1)
await asyncio.sleep(light_duration // 2)
led_YELLOW.value(0)
```

- The try-except block runs the main_program() task but catches a user interrupt (e.g. Ctrl-C) and any unexpected errors, and finally turns off the LED traffic lights when the program finishes.

```
try:
    # Start main program
    main_program(light_duration = 4)

# Keyboard interrupt caught
except KeyboardInterrupt:
    print("\nUser interrupted the program.")

# Unexpected error
except Exception as e:
    print(f"An unexpected error occurred: {e}")
```

```
    # End the program gracefully
    finally:
        # Turn off traffic light LEDs
        led_RED.off()
        led_YELLOW.off()
        led_GREEN.off()

        print("\nISR Pelican Traffic Light"
              " Controller program ended.")
```

Procedure / Steps

Run the MicoPython code on your target Pico.

test_PiezoBuzzer.py

1. Using Thonny (File > Open), select test_PiezoBuzzer.py
2. Go to the Run menu
   Select "Run current script"

ISR_TrafficLights.py

1. Using Thonny (File > Open), select ISR_TrafficLights.py
2. Go to the Run menu
   Select "Run current script"

Tests and Results

test_PiezoBuzzer.py

When you run test_PiezoBuzzer.py on your Pico, the Piezo buzzer will make a buzzing sound by turning on for 0.2 seconds and off for 0.2 seconds for a total of 10 times. This simple test makes sure that you have connected the Active Piezo buzzer to your Pico and that it is working properly.

ISR_TrafficLights.py

When you run ISR_TrafficLights.py on your Pico, the Red, Yellow and Green external LEDs will turn on and off in sequence simulating an actual traffic light-until you press the push button to indicate that a pedestrian wishes to cross the road. Then the button handler (the button_isr()) is triggered.

If the push button has been pressed for more than 50ms, a button counter is incremented and the traffic light finishes its current sequence and traffic is stopped (the RED led turns on).

An audible signal (the Piezo Buzzer) then indicates that it's safe for a pedestrian to cross the street. Subsequently, the traffic light resumes its normal sequence of light changes.

As you press the button to stop traffic, you should see something like the following in the Thonny Python Shell windows:

```
Crosswalk button counter = 1
Crosswalk button counter = 2
```

Congratulations! Using ISRs, you've put together a Pelican crossing using LEDs, a push button and a buzzer!

Using asyncio with an ISR

Now you'll write a traffic light program that uses asyncio with a button interrupt to check if the crosswalk button has been pressed, changing the lights and making an audible sound while pedestrians cross the street.

An ISR, however, can preempt the asyncio scheduler, disrupting its operation. When combining ISRs with asyncio, there are some important considerations which are illustrated in the example in this section.

What is an asyncio coroutine?

In MicroPython's asyncio library, a *coroutine function* is a special type of function defined with the keyword combination "async def" that is designed specifically for cooperative multitasking. Calling this coroutine function returns a *coroutine object* ("coro" for short) which is an instance representing the asynchronous logic defined in the function. Example:

```
# Define coroutine function
async def my_coroutine_function():
    print("Hello, world!")
    await asyncio.sleep(1)
    return "How about a nice game of chess?"

# Create a coroutine object by calling the coroutine function
coro_object = my_coroutine_function()
```

To execute the above print() statement, you need to await the coro or schedule it as an asyncio task for an asyncio event loop to begin executing it concurrently. The event loop can then pause and resume this task at specific points—defined within the coroutine function using the await keyword—typically when the coro is awaiting the results of an I/O bound or another asynchronous operation.

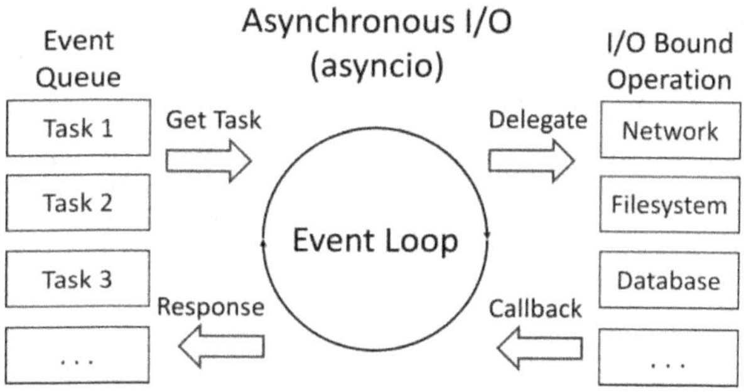

Fig 6-x. MicroPython asyncio event loop

When the awaited operation completes, the asyncio event loop resumes running the suspended coroutine from where it left off until the next await point pauses its execution or until the coroutine completes its execution. This is how coroutines enable non-blocking I/O operations and concurrency within a single thread on a single CPU core.

A real-world analogy

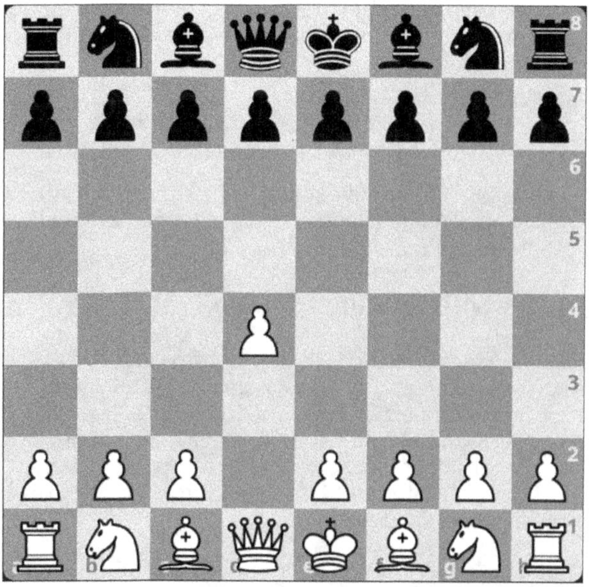

Fig 6-x. Image Source: Lichess.org / Queen's Pawn Opening (1. d4)

How do asyncio coroutines facilitate concurrent code using a single thread on a single CPU core?

In his PyCon 2017 talk "Asynchronous Python for the Complete Beginner" (https://www.youtube.com/watch?v=iG6fr81xHKA), Miguel Grinberg draws an analogy between asyncio and chess Grandmaster Judit Polgár (https://en.wikipedia.org/wiki/Judit_Polgár) playing 24 amateur players during a chess exhibition tournament. If a game averages 30 pair-moves and Judit Polgár makes a chess move every 5 seconds while her opponent takes 55 seconds to make their countermove, a single game takes approximately 30 minutes to complete.

$$\begin{aligned} one\ game &= 30\ moves \times \frac{5\ seconds}{champion\ move} + 30\ moves \times \frac{55\ seconds}{countermove} \\ &= 30\ minutes \end{aligned}$$

If she played 24 opponents *synchronously* one game at a time, the entire chess exhibition would take about 12 hours—most of her time would be spent waiting on her opponents to play.

$$\begin{aligned} tournament\ time &= 24\ games \times \frac{30\ minutes}{game} \\ &= 12\ hours \end{aligned}$$

On the other hand, if she were to move *asynchronously* between tables making just one move at a table in 5 seconds before moving to the next opponent, the entire exhibition would take only about 1 hour.

$$\begin{aligned} tournament\ time &= \left[\frac{5\ seconds}{champion\ move} \times \frac{30\ moves}{game}\right] \times 24\ games \\ &= 1\ hour \end{aligned}$$

One Judit Polgár, one thread of execution (her playing during the tournament), 24 opponents (asyncio tasks) that don't block her time while the others are taking theirs!

Using an ISR with asyncio code

Safely interfacing between the ISR code context and the asyncio code context involves implementing an asyncio coroutine with synchronization performed by asyncio.ThreadSafeFlag. This flag, as its name suggests, is a thread safe flag that is designed for cross-context signaling. It is an efficient means by which a coroutine can act as an intermediary that translates an ISR's signal into an asyncio event that maintains the integrity of the scheduler.

Since only one task may wait on an asyncio.ThreadSafeFlag, a common and recommended pattern is to have a dedicated asyncio bridging task wait for the ISR to set this flag and call asyncio_event.set() when it is which notifies the asyncio event loop, thereby ensuring proper synchronization. Other asyncio functions can then process the event within the context of the asyncio event loop.

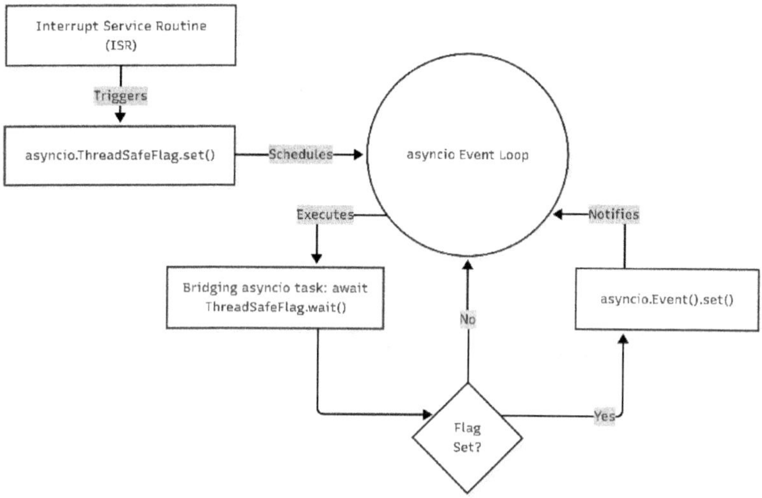

Fig 6-x. Cross-context signaling with asyncio bridging function

In this section, you'll write an ISR interrupt handler that sets an asyncio.ThreadSafeFlag when a button is pressed. In conjunction with this ISR, you'll write a dedicated coroutine, handle_button_press(), that waits for this flag to be set. Unlike the program in the previous section where the debouncing logic was implemented in the ISR code, the *coroutine* debounces the button to prevent multiple triggers from a single press. When the button signal has settled, the coroutine sets an asyncio.Event() flag, button_pressed_event.

If the traffic lights controller (the traffic_lights() coroutine) determines that a button press event has occurred—i.e. the asyncio.Event().is_set()—it immediately clears the event for the next button press, updates a button counter, turns the LED light red and makes an audible buzzing sound for pedestrians to cross the road. After the pedestrians have safely crossed, the traffic lights are turned on and off in a normal light sequence until the next button press event appears in the asyncio event loop.

ISRs provide your MicroPython applications quick reactions to events by temporarily halting the main program. Implementing the approach here allows running a dedicated coroutine alongside other asyncio tasks without blocking the entire application, effectively translating asynchronous signals like button presses into events in the asyncio event loop context. As we'll see in the next section, this can be essential for integrating your applications into asyncio web frameworks like Microdot.

Code

Using Thonny (File > Save as), copy and save the Python modules below to your target Pico microcontroller.

asyncioISR_TrafficLights.py

The following code is for an LED Traffic Light with an active Piezo buzzer. It uses an interrupt and asyncio to monitor when a pedestrian wishes to cross by pressing a button.

```
"""
asyncioISR_TrafficLights.py
--------
Pelican LED Traffic Lights with active Piezo crosswalk buzzer and
    push button using ISR and asyncio

Traffic Light Logic Flow::
  No Pedestrian:
      Red -> Green, Green -> Yellow -> Red
  Pedestrian Crossing:
      Setting the flag variable button_pressed = True indicates
          that the crosswalk button was pressed
      On next Red, buzz for 5 seconds allowing pedestrian to
          cross then set button_pressed = False and proceed to
          No Pedestrian sequence
"""
from machine import Pin
from time import sleep
import asyncio

# Set up LED traffic lights
led_RED    = Pin(16, Pin.OUT)  # GPIO16
led_YELLOW = Pin(17, Pin.OUT)
led_GREEN  = Pin(18, Pin.OUT)

# Set up GPIO pins connected to the crosswalk buzzer and button
crosswalk_buzzer = Pin(14, Pin.OUT)  # GPIO14
crosswalk_button = Pin(15, Pin.IN, Pin.PULL_UP)  # GPIO15

# Turn off LEDs
def turn_off_lights():
    print("Turning off lights")
    led_RED.value(0)      # Red light    OFF
    led_GREEN.value(0)    # Green light  OFF
    led_YELLOW.value(0)  # Yellow light OFF

# Asyncio flags to signal button press from ISR to asyncio task
button_pressed_flag = asyncio.ThreadSafeFlag()
button_pressed_event = asyncio.Event()

# Interrupt Service Routine (ISR) that sets the flag to signal
```

```
#     the handle_button_press() coroutine
def button_isr(pin):
    button_pressed_flag.set()

# Bridging ISR to asyncio event loop
async def handle_button_press():
    while True:
        # Wait for the button pressed flag to be set by the ISR
        await button_pressed_flag.wait()

        # Debounce the button for at least 50 ms to prevent
        #   multiple triggers from a single press
        await asyncio.sleep_ms(50)

        # Check button state again after debouncing the buttton
        if crosswalk_button.value() == 0:
            print("Button pressed!")
            button_pressed_event.set()


# LED Traffic Lights Controller
async def traffic_lights(light_duration = 4):
    """Simulate a traffic light using asyncio"""

    button_counter = 0  # the button has not yet been pressed
    while True:
        # If crosswalk button is pressed, clear
        #   the event for the next button press
        if button_pressed_event.is_set():
            button_pressed_event.clear()

            # Increment button counter
            button_counter = button_counter + 1
            print(f"Crosswalk button counter = {button_counter}")
            led_RED.value(1)

            # Make buzzing sound for 5 seconds
            #     while the pedestrians cross
            for i in range(10):
                crosswalk_buzzer.value(1)
                sleep(0.2)
                crosswalk_buzzer.value(0)
                sleep(0.2)
                await asyncio.sleep_ms(100)

        # Red light
        led_RED.value(1)
        await asyncio.sleep(light_duration)
        led_RED.value(0)

        # Green light
        led_GREEN.value(1)
        await asyncio.sleep(light_duration)
        led_GREEN.value(0)
```

```
        # Yellow Light
        led_YELLOW.value(1)
        await asyncio.sleep(light_duration // 2)
        led_YELLOW.value(0)

async def main():
    print("Starting async tasks ...")

    # Attach the interrupt handler to the button pin
    crosswalk_button.irq(trigger=Pin.IRQ_FALLING, \
                         handler=button_isr)

    # Create the button handling task
    button_task = \
            asyncio.create_task(handle_button_press())

    # Create traffic lights task
    traffic_controller_task = \
        asyncio.create_task(traffic_lights(light_duration = 4))

    # Schedule asyncio tasks to be run concurrently as a group
    await asyncio.gather(button_task, traffic_controller_task)

if __name__ == "__main__":

    # Start event loop
    try:
        main_task=asyncio.run(main())

    # Keyboard interrupt caught
    except KeyboardInterrupt:
        print("Traffic lights interrupted by user.")

    # Unexpected error
    except Exception as e:
        print(f"An unexpected error occurred: {e}")

    # Turn off LEDs
    finally:
        # Turn off the traffic lights
        turn_off_lights()

        # Cleanup (e.g., disable IRQ) if necessary
        crosswalk_button.irq(handler=None)  # Disable interrupt

        print("\nAsyncio Pelican Traffic Light Controller "
              "program ended.")
```

Fig 6-x. asyncioISR_TrafficLights.py

Code Explanation

- The Pin module allows you to configure and control GPIO pins on the Pico.
  The sleep() module function is needed to introduce delays in the code execution.
  The asyncio library allows you to write concurrent code using MicroPython's asynchronous programming functionality.

```
from machine import Pin
from time import sleep
import asyncio
```

- led_COLOR = Pin(...) sets up the LED traffic light on the designated GPIO pins.

```
led_RED    = Pin(16, Pin.OUT)  # GPIO16
led_YELLOW = Pin(17, Pin.OUT)
led_GREEN  = Pin(18, Pin.OUT)
```

- crosswalk_buzzer = Pin(...) sets up an active Piezo buzzer on the designated GPIO pin. crosswalk_button = Pin(...) sets up a crosswalk button on the designated GPIO pin.

```
crosswalk_buzzer = Pin(14, Pin.OUT)  # GPIO14
crosswalk_button = Pin(15, Pin.IN, Pin.PULL_UP)  # GPIO15
```

- Setting the GPIO pins to 0 turns off the LEDs.

```
def turn_off_lights():
    print ("Turning off lights")
    led_RED.value(0)      # Red Light    OFF
    led_GREEN.value(0)    # Green Light  OFF
    led_YELLOW.value(0)   # Yellow Light OFF
```

- Define the asyncio flags used to translate a button press signal from an ISR to a dedicated asyncio task.

```
button_pressed_flag = asyncio.ThreadSafeFlag()
button_pressed_event = asyncio.Event()
```

- The button_isr() ISR sets the flag that signals the asyncio handle_button_press() task that a button has been pressed.

```
def button_isr(pin):
    button_pressed_flag.set()
```

- The handle_button_press() coroutine bridges the ISR-context to the asyncio event loop.

```
async def handle_button_press():
    while True:
        ...
```

- It is a dedicated task waiting for the button pressed flag to be set by the ISR and debounces the button signal for at least 50ms to prevent multiple triggers from a single press.

```
        await button_pressed_flag.wait()
        await asyncio.sleep_ms(50)
```

- The button state is checked after debouncing the button. If the signal settles to a pressed state, the button pressed event is set (button_pressed_event.set()). Note that the crosswalk button value() will be low due since the GPIO Pin to which it is attached was defined as an input pin with a pull-up resistor enabled that reads HIGH when the button is not pressed.

```
    if crosswalk_button.value() == 0:
        print("Button pressed!")
        button_pressed_event.set()
```

- Define the traffic lights controller as an asyncio function with a default light duration in seconds. This coroutine controls the traffic light, turning on and off each LED traffic light in turn until it detects that the button pressed event has been set (button_pressed_event.is_set()) indicating that the crosswalk button has been pressed. When it has, the coroutine clears the event for the next button press, increments a button counter and toggles the red led light ON while making a buzzing sound for 5 seconds, allowing pedestrians to proceed through the crosswalk.

```
async def traffic_lights(light_duration = 4):

    button_counter = 0  # the button has not yet been pressed
    while True:
        # If crosswalk button is pressed, clear
        #    the event for the next button press
        if button_pressed_event.is_set():
            button_pressed_event.clear()

            # Increment button counter
            button_counter = button_counter + 1
            print(f"Crosswalk button counter = {button_counter}")
            led_RED.value(1)

            # Make buzzing sound for 5 seconds
            #      while the pedestrians cross
            for i in range(10):
                crosswalk_buzzer.value(1)
                sleep(0.2)
                crosswalk_buzzer.value(0)
                sleep(0.2)
                await asyncio.sleep_ms(100)
        ...
```

- The traffic lights controller then proceeds with the normal flow of traffic light changes until the next time that the crosswalk button has been pressed.

```
        # Red Light
        led_RED.value(1)
        await asyncio.sleep(light_duration)
        led_RED.value(0)

        # Green Light
        led_GREEN.value(1)
        await asyncio.sleep(light_duration)
        led_GREEN.value(0)
```

```
    # Yellow light
    led_YELLOW.value(1)
    await asyncio.sleep(light_duration // 2)
    led_YELLOW.value(0)
```

- The main() coroutine first attaches an interrupt handler to the crosswalk button pin and then creates the button and traffic controller asynchronous tasks scheduling those tasks to be run concurrently on the asyncio event loop as a group.

```
print("Starting async tasks ...")

# Attach the interrupt handler to the button pin
crosswalk_button.irq(trigger=Pin.IRQ_FALLING, \
                     handler=button_isr)

# Create the button handling task
button_task = \
         asyncio.create_task(handle_button_press())

# Create traffic lights task
traffic_controller_task = \
    asyncio.create_task(traffic_lights(light_duration = 4))

# Schedule asyncio tasks to be run concurrently as a group
await asyncio.gather(button_task, traffic_controller_task)
```

- the try-except block runs the main() asynchronous task but catches a user interrupt (e.g. Ctrl-C) to stop the program, finally turning off the LEDs and disabling the crosswalk button IRQ when the program finishes.

```
# Start event loop
try:
    main_task=asyncio.run(main())

# Keyboard interrupt caught
except KeyboardInterrupt:
    print("Traffic lights interrupted by user.")

# Unexpected error
except Exception as e:
    print(f"An unexpected error occurred: {e}")

# Turn off LEDs
finally:
    # Turn off the traffic lights
    turn_off_lights()

    # Cleanup (e.g., disable IRQ) if necessary
    crosswalk_button.irq(handler=None)  # Disable interrupt

    print("\nAsyncio Pelican Traffic Light Controller "
          "program ended.")
```

Procedure / Steps

Run the MicroPython code on your target Pico.

asyncioISR_TrafficLights.py

1. Using Thonny (File > Open), select asyncioISR_TrafficLights.py
2. Go to the Run menu
   Select "Run current script"

Tests and Results

asyncioISR_TrafficLights.py

When you run asyncioISR_TrafficLights.py on your Pico, the Red, Yellow and Green external LEDs will turn on and off in sequence simulating an actual traffic light—until you press the push button to indicate that a pedestrian wishes to cross the road. Then the handle_button_press() coroutine function (the function defined with async def) kicks in, debouncing the button and then sets button_pressed_event which lets the traffic lights controller (the traffic_lights() coroutine) know that the crosswalk button has been pressed.

If the push button has been pressed, traffic_lights() increments a button counter, stops traffic (the RED led turns on). An audible signal (the Piezo Buzzer) then indicates that it's safe for a pedestrian to cross the street. Subsequently, the traffic light resumes its normal sequence of light changes until the crosswalk button has been pushed again.

As you press the button to stop traffic, you should see something like the following in the Thonny Python Shell windows:

```
Starting async tasks ...
Button pressed!
Crosswalk button counter = 1
Button pressed!
Crosswalk button counter = 2
```

Congratulations! Using asyncio and ISRs, you've put together a Pelican crossing using LEDs, a push button and a buzzer!

Integrating an asyncio application with Microdot

In the previous chapter, we saw that Microdot uses asyncio. In this section, you'll see how straightforward it can be to use cooperative multitasking with Microdot. Simply by inserting await asyncio.sleep() and await asyncio.sleep_ms() expressions into your traffic light program, your code will yield control to the event loop for the duration specified in the sleep() and sleep_ms() functions. In a cooperative multitasking system, pausing execution allows the event loop to execute other tasks such as communicating Entity Events over a wireless network via Microdot.

You'll use asyncio to integrate your Pelican Crossing application with Microdot, transforming your traffic light controller into an Entity Event-Driven Embedded Pico System. Just like a "real" traffic system, your traffic light application will thus be able to communicate entity events like button presses and the number of times a button has been pressed to a microservice or other data consumer / AI agent on the same wireless network that your Pico is on.

Note that this example separates the concerns of your particular application from the communications interface that the Microdot webserver framework provides. While microdot_TrafficLights.py contains your application's core functionality and logic, webserver_TrafficLights.py uses decorators to register async coroutines (functions defined with async def) as request handlers for the various types of HTTP requests:

- get(url_pattern)
- post(url_pattern)
- put(url_pattern)
- patch(url_pattern)
- delete(url_pattern)

(For more information on these request handlers, see https://microdot.readthedocs.io/en/latest/api.html.)

Code

Using Thonny (File > Save as), copy and save the Python modules below to your target Pico microcontroller.

microdot_TrafficLights.py

The following code is a Pelican LED Traffic Light system with active Piezo crosswalk buzzer and push button using an interrupt and asyncio. The Microdot webserver provides data consumers with event details.

```
"""
microdot_TrafficLights.py
--------
Pelican LED Traffic Lights with active Piezo crosswalk buzzer
    and push button using ISR

Traffic Light Logic Flow::
  No Pedestrian:
    Red -> Green, Green -> Yellow -> Red
  Pedestrian Crossing:
    Pressing the crosswalk button (config.button_pressed = True)
        indicates that a pedestrian wishes to cross
    On next Red, buzz for 5 seconds allowing pedestrian to cross
        then set config.button_pressed = False and proceed to
        No Pedestrian sequence

Use a Microdot webserver to provide data consumers with
  event details

"""
from machine import Pin
from time import sleep
import asyncio, webserver_TrafficLights, config

# Set up LED traffic lights
led_RED    = Pin(16, Pin.OUT)  # GPIO16
led_YELLOW = Pin(17, Pin.OUT)
led_GREEN  = Pin(18, Pin.OUT)

# Set up GPIO pins connected to the crosswalk buzzer and button
crosswalk_buzzer = Pin(14, Pin.OUT)                # GPIO14
crosswalk_button = Pin(15, Pin.IN, Pin.PULL_UP)  # GPIO15

# Turn off LEDs
def turn_off_lights():
    print("Turning off lights")
    led_RED.value(0)     # Red light    OFF
    led_GREEN.value(0)   # Green light  OFF
    led_YELLOW.value(0)  # Yellow light OFF

# Asyncio flags to signal button press from ISR to asyncio task
button_pressed_flag = asyncio.ThreadSafeFlag()
button_pressed_event = asyncio.Event()

# Interrupt Service Routine (ISR) that sets the flag to signal
#     the handle_button_press() coroutine
def button_isr(pin):
```

```
    button_pressed_flag.set()

# Bridging ISR to asyncio event loop
async def handle_button_press():
    while True:
        # Wait for the button pressed flag to be set by the ISR
        await button_pressed_flag.wait()

        # Debounce the button for at least 50 ms to prevent
        #   multiple triggers from a single press
        await asyncio.sleep_ms(50)

        # Check button state again after debouncing the buttton
        if crosswalk_button.value() == 0:
            print("Button pressed!")
            button_pressed_event.set()

# LED Traffic Lights Controller
async def traffic_lights(light_duration = 4):
    """Simulate a Pelican traffic light using asyncio"""

    config.button_counter = 0
    while True:
        # If crosswalk button is pressed, clear
        #   the event for the next button press
        if button_pressed_event.is_set():
            button_pressed_event.clear()

            # Pedestrians are in crosswalk
            config.button_pressed = True

            # Increment button counter
            config.button_counter = config.button_counter + 1
            print(f"Crosswalk button counter = "
                  f"{config.button_counter}")
            led_RED.value(1)

            # Make buzzing sound for 5 seconds
            #     while the pedestrians cross
            for i in range(10):
                crosswalk_buzzer.value(1)
                sleep(0.2)
                crosswalk_buzzer.value(0)
                sleep(0.2)
                await asyncio.sleep_ms(100)

            # Pedestrians have crossed the road
            config.button_pressed = False

        # Red Light
        led_RED.value(1)
        await asyncio.sleep(light_duration)
        led_RED.value(0)
```

```
        # Green Light
        led_GREEN.value(1)
        await asyncio.sleep(light_duration)
        led_GREEN.value(0)

        # Yellow Light
        led_YELLOW.value(1)
        await asyncio.sleep(light_duration // 2)
        led_YELLOW.value(0)

# Main entry point for the event loop
async def main():
    print("Starting async tasks ...")

    # Attach the interrupt handler to the button pin
    crosswalk_button.irq(trigger=Pin.IRQ_FALLING, \
                         handler=button_isr)

    # Create the button handling task
    button_task = \
            asyncio.create_task(handle_button_press())

    # Create the web server handling task
    web_server = asyncio.create_task(\
        webserver_TrafficLights.start_server())

    # Create traffic lights task
    traffic_controller_task = \
        asyncio.create_task(traffic_lights(light_duration = 4))

    # Schedule asyncio tasks to be run concurrently as a group
    await asyncio.gather(button_task, \
                         traffic_controller_task, \
                         web_server)

if __name__ == "__main__":

    # Start event loop
    try:
        main_task=asyncio.run(main())

    # Keyboard interrupt caught
    except KeyboardInterrupt:
        print("Traffic lights interrupted by user.")

    # Unexpected error
    except Exception as e:
        print(f"An unexpected error occurred: {e}")

    # Turn off LEDs
    finally:
        # Turn off the traffic lights
        turn_off_lights()
```

```
    print("\nMicrodot Pelican Traffic Light Controller "
          "program ended.")
```

Fig 6-x. microdot_TrafficLights.py

Code Explanation

Let's look at how the code works.

- The Pin module allows you to configure and control GPIO pins on the Pico.
  The sleep() module function is needed to introduce delays in the code execution.
  The asyncio library allows you to write concurrent code using MicroPython's asynchronous programming functionality.
  The webserver_TrafficLights module is a Microdot webserver for showing whether a pedestrian has pushed the crosswalk button and the number of times that button has been pushed.
  The config module stores event information about the button.

```
from machine import Pin
from time import sleep
import asyncio, webserver_TrafficLights, config
```

- led_COLOR = Pin(...) sets up the LED traffic light on the designated GPIO pin.

```
led_RED    = Pin(16, Pin.OUT)  # GPIO16
led_YELLOW = Pin(17, Pin.OUT)
led_GREEN  = Pin(18, Pin.OUT)
```

- crosswalk_buzzer = Pin(...) sets up an active Piezo buzzer on the designated GPIO pin. crosswalk_button = Pin(...) sets up a crosswalk button on the designated GPIO pin.

```
crosswalk_buzzer = Pin(14, Pin.OUT)               # GPIO14
crosswalk_button = Pin(15, Pin.IN, Pin.PULL_UP)  # GPIO15
```

- Setting the GPIO pins to 0 turns off the LEDs.

```
def turn_off_lights():
    print ("Turning off lights")
    led_RED.value(0)     # Red Light    OFF
    led_GREEN.value(0)   # Green Light  OFF
    led_YELLOW.value(0)  # Yellow Light OFF
```

- Define the asyncio flags used to translate a button press signal from an ISR to a dedicated asyncio task.

```
button_pressed_flag = asyncio.ThreadSafeFlag()
button_pressed_event = asyncio.Event()
```

- The button_isr() ISR sets the flag that signals the asyncio handle_button_press() task that a button has been pressed.

```
def button_isr(pin):
    button_pressed_flag.set()
```

- The handle_button_press() coroutine bridges the ISR-context to the asyncio event loop.

```
async def handle_button_press():
    while True:
        ...
```

- It is a dedicated task waiting for the button pressed flag to be set by the ISR and debounces the button signal for at least 50ms to prevent multiple triggers from a single press.

```
        await button_pressed_flag.wait()
        await asyncio.sleep_ms(50)
```

- The button state is checked after debouncing the button. If the signal settles to a pressed state, the button pressed event is set (button_pressed_event.set()). Note that the crosswalk button value() will be low due since the GPIO Pin to which it is attached was defined as an input pin with a pull-up resistor enabled that reads HIGH when the button is not pressed.

```
        if crosswalk_button.value() == 0:
            print("Button pressed!")
            button_pressed_event.set()
```

- Define the traffic lights controller as an asyncio function with a default light duration in seconds. This coroutine controls the traffic light, turning on and off each LED traffic light in turn until it detects that the button pressed event has been set (button_pressed_event.is_set()) indicating that the crosswalk button has been pressed. When it has, the coroutine clears the event for the next button press, increments a button counter and toggles the red led light ON while making a buzzing sound for 5 seconds, allowing pedestrians to proceed through the crosswalk.

```
async def traffic_lights(light_duration = 4):

    config.button_counter = 0
    while True:
        # If crosswalk button is pressed, clear
        #   the event for the next button press
        if button_pressed_event.is_set():
            button_pressed_event.clear()

            # Pedestrians are in crosswalk
            config.button_pressed = True

            # Increment button counter
            config.button_counter = config.button_counter + 1
            print(f"Crosswalk button counter = "
                  "{config.button_counter}")
            led_RED.value(1)

            # Make buzzing sound for 5 seconds
            #     while the pedestrians cross
            for i in range(10):
                crosswalk_buzzer.value(1)
                sleep(0.2)
                crosswalk_buzzer.value(0)
                sleep(0.2)
```

```
            await asyncio.sleep_ms(100)

        # Pedestrians have crossed the road
        config.button_pressed = False
    ...
```

- The traffic lights controller then proceeds with the normal flow of traffic light changes until the next time that the crosswalk button has been pressed.

```
    # Red Light
    led_RED.value(1)
    await asyncio.sleep(light_duration)
    led_RED.value(0)

    # Green Light
    led_GREEN.value(1)
    await asyncio.sleep(light_duration)
    led_GREEN.value(0)

    # Yellow Light
    led_YELLOW.value(1)
    await asyncio.sleep(light_duration // 2)
    led_YELLOW.value(0)
```

- The main() coroutine first attaches an interrupt handler to the crosswalk button pin and then creates the button, web server, and Microdot traffic controller asynchronous tasks scheduling those tasks to be run concurrently on the asyncio event loop as a group.

```
print("Starting async tasks ...")

# Attach the interrupt handler to the button pin
crosswalk_button.irq(trigger=Pin.IRQ_FALLING, \
                     handler=button_isr)

# Create the button handling task
button_task = \
          asyncio.create_task(handle_button_press())

# Create the web server handling task
web_server = asyncio.create_task(\
    webserver_TrafficLights.start_server())

# Create traffic lights task
traffic_controller_task = \
    asyncio.create_task(traffic_lights(light_duration = 4))

# Schedule asyncio tasks to be run concurrently as a group
await asyncio.gather(button_task, \
                     traffic_controller_task, \
                     web_server)
```

- the try-except block runs the main() asynchronous task but catches a user interrupt (e.g. Ctrl-C) to stop the program, finally turning off the LEDs and disabling the crosswalk button IRQ when the program finishes.

```
# Start event loop
try:
    main_task=asyncio.run(main())

# Keyboard interrupt caught
except KeyboardInterrupt:
    print("Traffic lights interrupted by user.")

# Unexpected error
except Exception as e:
    print(f"An unexpected error occurred: {e}")

# Turn off LEDs
finally:
    # Turn off the traffic lights
    turn_off_lights()

    print("\nMicrodot Pelican Traffic Light Controller "
          "program ended.")
```

webserver_TrafficLights.py

The Microdot webserver can provide event information about the Pelican Crossing Traffic Lights to potential data consumers.

```
"""
webserver_TrafficLights.py
--------
Microdot webserver for querying status of Pelican Traffic Lights
  for an LED Traffic Light using asyncio

"""
import asyncio, sys
from microdot import Microdot
import config, connect_wifi, pico_event

# Add my_secrets.py to the .gitignore file to make sure
#   that my_secrets.py is never checked into GitHub
import my_secrets
ssid = my_secrets.SSID           # Your SSID (Network Name)
password = my_secrets.PASSWORD  # Your WiFi PASSWORD

# Initialize the WiFi Interface
if not connect_wifi.init_wlan(ssid, password, max_retries=10):
    print('WiFi authentication error: {}'\
          .format(connect_wifi.SSID_ERROR))
    print('Exiting program')
    sys.exit(0)
else:
    ip_address = connect_wifi.get_ip()
```

```
# Create microdot instance
app = Microdot()

# MicroDot communications interface
@app.get('/api/v0.1/hello')
async def hello(request):
    event_header = pico_event.header()
    event_body   = {'greeting': 'Hello, world!'}
    return {"header": event_header, "body": event_body}

@app.get('/api/v0.1/crosswalk')
async def crosswalk(request):
    event_header = pico_event.header()
    pelican_info = {
                    'pelican_button_pressed': \
                     config.button_pressed,
                    'button_counter': \
                     config.button_counter
                   }
    event_body   = {
                    'hardware_parameters': \
                     pico_event.hardware_parameters(),
                    'pelican_info': pelican_info
                   }
    return {"header": event_header, "body": event_body}

async def start_server():
    try:
        # Run the Microdot webserver
        print('Starting Microdot webserver ...')
        await app.start_server(host=ip_address, port=80,
                               debug=True)

    # Keyboard interrupt caught
    except KeyboardInterrupt:
        print("\nUser interrupted the program")

    # Unexpected error
    except Exception as e:
        print(f"An unexpected error occurred: {e}")

    # End the program gracefully
    finally:
        app.shutdown()
        print("\nMicrodot server stopped.")
```

Fig 6-x. webserver_TrafficLights.py

Code Explanation

Let's look at how the code works.

- The asyncio library allows you to write concurrent code using MicroPython's asynchronous programming functionality. The sys module is used to stop the execution of the current program if the WiFi network is unavailable.
  The microdot module is the Microdot webserver.
  The config module stores event information about the Pelican Crossing Traffic Light system. The connect_wifi module uses its init_wlan() function to connect to a wireless network and its get_ip() function to obtain an IP address for your Pico.
  The pico_event module obtains a unique event header for your Pico and obtains hardware parameters for it.

```
import asyncio, time, machine, sys
from microdot import Microdot
import config, connect_wifi, pico_event
```

- The my_secrets module contains the name of your network (SSID) and your network password.

```
import my_secrets
ssid = my_secrets.SSID          # Your SSID (Network Name)
password = my_secrets.PASSWORD  # Your WiFi PASSWORD
```

- To initialize the WiFi interface, use the connect_wifi.init_wlan() and connect_wifi.get_ip() module functions.

```
# Initialize the WiFi Interface
if not connect_wifi.init_wlan(ssid, password, max_retries=10):
    print('WiFi authentication error: {}'\
          .format(connect_wifi.SSID_ERROR))
    print('Exiting program')
    sys.exit(0)
else:
    ip_address = connect_wifi.get_ip()
```

- Instantiating the Microdot class creates a Microdot webserver.

```
app = Microdot()
```

- The Microdot communications interface consists of a get(url_pattern) decorator that is used to register a function as a GET request handler for a given URL.

- The @app.get('/api/v0.1/hello') decorator registers the async hello(request) function as a GET request handler. The hello() function returns a unique Pico event header along with a "Hello, world!" greeting.

```
@app.get('/api/v0.1/hello')
async def hello(request):
    event_header = pico_event.header()
    event_body   = {'greeting': 'Hello, world!'}
    return {"header": event_header, "body": event_body}
```

- The @app.get('/api/v0.1/crosswalk') decorator registers the async crosswalk() function as a GET request handler.

```
@app.get('/api/v0.1/crosswalk')
async def crosswalk(request):
    event_header = pico_event.header()
    pelican_info = {
                     'pelican_button_pressed': \
                      config.button_pressed,
                     'button_counter': \
                      config.button_counter
                   }
    event_body   = {
                     'hardware_parameters': \
                      pico_event.hardware_parameters(),
                     'pelican_info': pelican_info
                   }
    return {"header": event_header, "body": event_body}
```

- The async start_server() function tries to start Microdot with the ip address obtained when the WiFi interface was initialized. If it fails to do so, start_server() shuts down the Microdot webserver.

```
async def start_server():
    try:
        # Run the Microdot webserver
        print('Starting Microdot webserver ...')
        await app.start_server(host=ip_address, port=80,
                               debug=True)

    # Keyboard interrupt caught
    except KeyboardInterrupt:
        print("\nUser interrupted the program")

    # Unexpected error
    except Exception as e:
        print(f"An unexpected error occurred: {e}")

    # End the program gracefully
    finally:
        app.shutdown()
        print("\nMicrodot server stopped.")
```

Procedure / Steps

> ⚠ **Warning: DO NOT connect your Pico to an insecure network!!!**

Run the MicroPython code on your target Pico.

1. Using Thonny (File > Open), select microdot_TrafficLights.py
2. Go to the Run menu
   Select "Run current script"

Tests and Results

Open your browser to http://[the ip address of your Pico]/api/v0.1/hello. You should see something like:


```
{
  "header": {
    "event_id": "399f6213-53ec-431f-a538-f5fa78275aaf",
    "time_local": "2025/07/22 10:26:18",
    "time_unix": 1753179978,
    "event_version": "1.0.0",
    "machine_unique_id": "314159265358979323846zza"
  },
  "body": {
    "greeting": "Hello, world!"
  }
}
```


Open your browser to http://[the ip address of your Pico]/api/v0.1/crosswalk. You should see something like:


```
{
  "header": {
    "event_id": "399f6213-53ec-431f-a538-f5fa78275aaf",
    "time_local": "2025/07/22 10:22:48",
    "time_unix": 1753179768,
    "event_version": "1.0.0",
    "machine_unique_id": "314159265358979323846zza"
  },
  "body": {
    "hardware_parameters": {
      "free_memory": 155008,
      "temp_celsius": "34.1 C",
      "flash_size": 868352,
      "flash_used": 417792,
      "flash_free": 450560
    },
    "pelican_info": {
      "button_counter": 2,
      "pelican_button_pressed": true
    }
  }
}
```


When you navigate to the "crosswalk" API endpoint in your browser, your Pico reports the number of times the crosswalk button has been pressed since you started your application and if a pedestrian is currently in the crosswalk! Note that pelican_button_pressed changes to false once the traffic light returns to its normal sequence.

Congratulations! You've put together an Entity Event-Driven Embedded Pico System for a Pelican crossing using LEDs, a push button and a buzzer with cooperative multitasking!

References and Further Exploration

Pelican / Puffin Crossing

- https://en.wikipedia.org/wiki/Pelican_crossing
- https://en.wikipedia.org/wiki/Puffin_crossing
- Chapter 5 "Traffic light controller" of the Raspberry Pi Foundation's official Pico guide *Get Started with MicroPython on Raspberry Pi Pico*, 2nd ed by Gareth Halfacree and Ben Everard (Cambridge, UK: 2024, ISBN: 9781912047291)

Cooperative Multitasking and Asyncio

- https://en.wikipedia.org/wiki/Cooperative_multitasking).
- PyCon 2017: Asynchronous Python for the Complete Beginner by Miguel Grinberg
  https://www.youtube.com/watch?v=iG6fr81xHKA
  https://speakerdeck.com/pycon2017/miguel-grinberg-asynchronous-python-for-the-complete-beginner
- Peter Hinch's tutorial on using the MicroPython asyncio library
  https://github.com/peterhinch/MicroPython-async/blob/master/v3/docs/TUTORIAL.md
- Asyncio official documentation
  https://docs.micropython.org/en/latest/library/asyncio.html
  https://docs.python.org/3/library/asyncio.html
  https://docs.python.org/3/library/asyncio-task.html
- BBC Python Asyncio Series
  https://bbc.github.io/cloudfit-public-docs/
- Async IO in Python: A Complete Walkthrough
  https://realpython.com/async-io-python/
- Python Asyncio: The Complete Guide by Jason Brownlee
  https://superfastpython.com/python-asyncio/
- Getting Started with Asyncio in MicroPython (Raspberry Pi Pico)
  Digikey's Getting Started with Asyncio in MicroPython (Raspberry Pi Pico)

Microdot Request Handlers

- https://microdot.readthedocs.io/en/latest/api.html

Appendix A

Raspberry Pi Pico W pinout guide

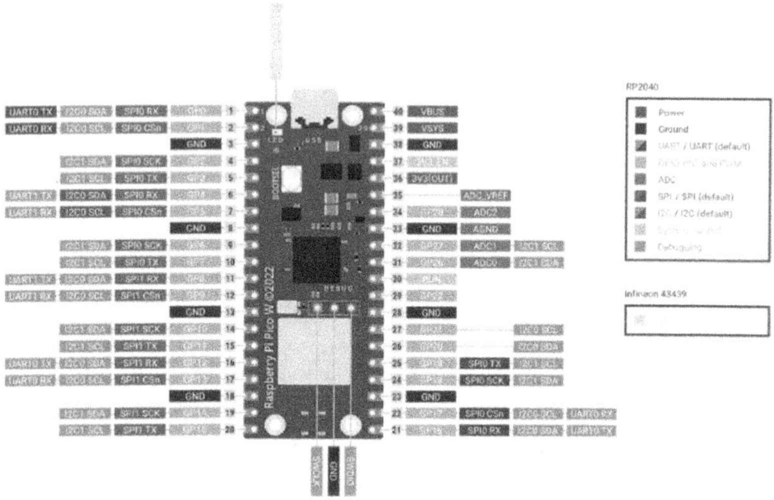

Image source: RaspberryPi.com (https://www.raspberrypi.com/)

Appendix B

Raspberry Pi Pico W Features

The Raspberry Pi Pico W is a low-cost, high-performance microcontroller board with flexible digital interfaces.

- Form factor: 21 mm × 51 mm × 1 mm
- Input power: 1.8–5.5V DC
- Operating temperature: -20°C to +70°C
- Dual-core Arm Cortex M0+ processor, flexible clock running up to 133 MHz
- 264KB of SRAM, and 2MB of on-board flash memory
- USB 1.1 with device and host support
- 26 × multi-function GPIO pins including 3 (GPIOs 26, 27, and 28) that can be used for ADC*
- 2 × SPI controllers
- 2 × I2C controllers
- 2 × UART
- 16 × controllable PWM channels
- 8 × Programmable I/O (PIO) state machines

The on-board 2.4GHz wireless interface has the following features:

- Wireless (802.11n), single-band (2.4 GHz)
- WPA3
- Soft access point supporting up to four clients
- Bluetooth 5.2
    - Support for Bluetooth LE Central and Peripheral roles
    - Support for Bluetooth Classic

* Note: GPIO29 can be configured to measure the input voltage that powers the board (VSYS) with ADC channel 3, but requires special handling to avoid conflicts since it is also shared with the WiFi's SPI clock pin.

Raspberry Pi Pico W Datasheets

- https://datasheets.raspberrypi.org/pico/pico_datasheet.pdf
- https://datasheets.raspberrypi.org/rp2040/rp2040_datasheet.pdf
- https://datasheets.raspberrypi.org/rp2040/hardware_design_with_rp2040.pdf
- https://datasheets.raspberrypi.com/picow/RPi-PicoW-PUBLIC-20220607.zip
- https://datasheets.raspberrypi.com/picow/PicoW-step.zip

Appendix C

Raspberry Pi Pico 2W pinout guide

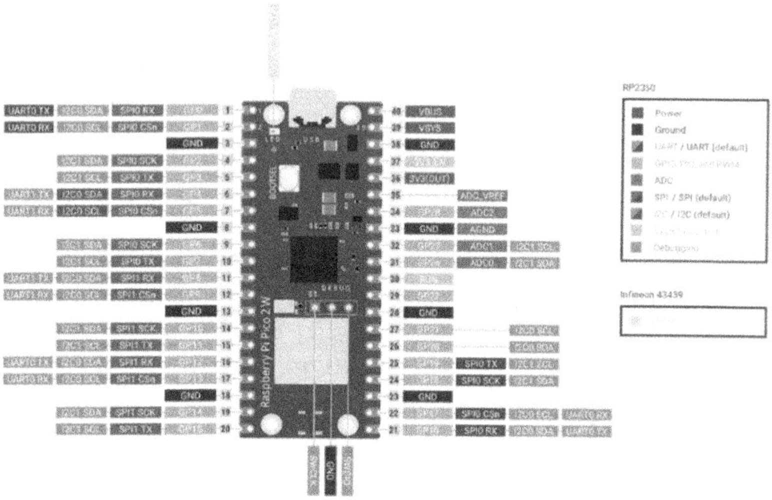

Image source: RaspberryPi.com (https://www.raspberrypi.com/)

Appendix D

Raspberry Pi Pico 2W Features

The Raspberry Pi Pico 2W is a low-cost, high-performance microcontroller board with flexible digital interfaces.

- Form factor: 21 mm × 51 mm × 1 mm
- Input power: 1.8–5.5V DC
- Operating temperature: -20°C to +70°C
- Dual Cortex-M33 or Hazard3 processors at up to 150MHz
- 520KB of SRAM, and 4MB of on-board flash memory
- 1 × USB 1.1 with host and device support
- 26 × multi-function GPIO pins including 3 (GPIOs 26, 27, and 28) that can be used for ADC*
- 2 × SPI controllers
- 2 × I2C controllers
- 2 × UART
- 24 × controllable PWM channels
- 12 × Programmable I/O (PIO) state machines

The on-board 2.4GHz wireless interface (802.11n) has the following features:

- Wireless (802.11n), single-band (2.4 GHz)
- WPA3
- Soft access point supporting up to four clients
- Bluetooth 5.2
    - Support for Bluetooth LE Central and Peripheral roles
    - Support for Bluetooth Classic

* Note: GPIO29 can be configured to measure the input voltage that powers the board (VSYS) with ADC channel 3, but requires special handling to avoid conflicts since it is also shared with the WiFi's SPI clock pin.

Raspberry Pi Pico 2W Datasheets

- http://datasheets.raspberrypi.com/picow/pico-2-w-datasheet.pdf
- https://datasheets.raspberrypi.com/rp2350/rp2350-datasheet.pdf
- https://datasheets.raspberrypi.com/rp2350/hardware-design-with-rp2350.pdf

Appendix E

Raspberry Pi fixes Erratum E9 bug affecting the Pico 2W

(Note: *stepping* is the IC term used to refer to a specific version or revision of an IC chip, analogous to software versioning.)

July 29th, 2025: Raspberry Pi has fixed the "Erratum E9" bug affecting the Pico 2W released in November 2024.

In August of 2024, Raspberry Pi launched the RP2350 A2 microcontroller that was on the original Pico 2W board. Shortly thereafter, the company confirmed a bug in the A2 stepping that became known as "Erratum E9" (see "RP2350-E9" on p.1357 of the RP2350 datasheet). This bug affected all GPIO pins–a GPIO pin configured as input using pull-down resistors will latch between 2.1-2.2V after its first use rather than be pulled back to ground.

The issue was "fixed through documentation" in the RP2350 datasheet, p.1359 by recommending that the input buffer should only be enabled immediately before reading, then disabling it again afterwards. Alternatively, the datasheet suggests connecting an external pull-down resistor of 8.2kΩ or less to the pin and ground.

The pull-up resistors on the the RP2350 A2 stepping, however, remain unaffected when configuring GPIO pins as input.

The easier fix, then, is to instead just use the internal pull-up resistors for your circuit, if you do not absolutely require the use of pull-down resistors. Pull-up resistors are commonly used to ensure a pin is pulled high to a default high (VCC) logic level when nothing else is actively driving it low. For instance, they are frequently used with switches, where the pull-up resistor keeps a pin high when the switch is open while pressing the switch connects the pin to ground.

On July 29th, 2025, Raspberry Pi announced the release of the A4 stepping for the RP2350 (see https://www.raspberrypi.com/news/rp2350-a4-rp2354-and-a-new-hacking-challenge/). The A4 stepping fixes Erratum E9–the pull resistors now work as they do in the RP2040 on the Pico W. It also fixes other bugs and security vulnerabilities discovered while developing the new stepping, and it improves functionality by supporting 5V tolerance on all GPIO pins. The company said in their announcement that eventually all Pico 2 products will use the A4 stepping but that it might be awhile.

In short, seeing “A4 stepping” in the context of the RP2350 microcontroller and the Pico 2W means that you're dealing with a new and improved version of the microcontroller that incorporates bug fixes and other enhancements to the previous A2 stepping.

Raspberry Pi announces the release of the A4 stepping for the RP2350
https://www.raspberrypi.com/news/rp2350-a4-rp2354-and-a-new-hacking-challenge/

RP2350 Datasheet
https://datasheets.raspberrypi.com/rp2350/rp2350-datasheet.pdf

Appendix F

Attributions and License Information

The "Babbling Sensor" illustration in this book

The "Babbling Sensor" illustration in this book is derived from the illustration placed into the public domain by Pearson Scott Foresman and donated to the Wikimedia Foundation:

- https://commons.wikimedia.org/wiki/File:Airplane_3_(PSF).png

Thonny IDE images and screenshots

Thonny (https://thonny.org) is a free, open-source Python IDE developed at the University of Tartu, Estonia, and distributed under the MIT license (Copyright © 2024 Aivar Annamaa):

Attribution Notice
Website images (https://thonny.org) and screenshots of the Thonny IDE programming environment used throughout this book are for illustrative purposes.

Breadboard diagrams and components created with Fritzing

Attribution Notice

Breadboard diagrams and components created with Fritzing (https://fritzing.org) are published under a Creative Commons Attribution-ShareAlike 3.0 license (creativecommons.org/licenses/by-sa/3.0/).

Use of NASA ISS silhouette icon in this book for the leaflet ISS location map

The NASA ISS silhouette icon in this book was created by NASA and put into the public domain by NASA in November 2015.

Attribution NASA, Public domain, via Wikimedia Commons:

- https://commons.wikimedia.org/wiki/File:International_Space_Station.svg

Use of leaflet map data in this book from OpenStreetMap(OSM)

Attribution Notice
Open Database License (ODbL) from OpenStreetMap for leaflet map data showing ISS location:

- https://www.openstreetmap.org/copyright
- https://osmfoundation.org/wiki/Licence

Use of NASA Photos in this book and data

The NASA photos used in this book were put into the public domain by NASA and adheres to NASA STI's notice of "Disclaimers, Copyright Notice, and Terms and Conditions of Use" per https://sti.nasa.gov/disclaimers/:

official duties) are not protected by copyright in the U.S. (17 U.S.C. §105) and may be used without obtaining permission from NASA. However, U.S. government works may contain privately created, copyrighted works (e.g., quote, photograph, chart, drawing, etc.) used under license or with permission of the copyright owner. Incorporation in a U.S. government work does not place the private work in the public domain.

Moreover, not all materials on or available through download from this Web site are U.S. government works. Some materials available from this Web site may be protected by copyrights owned by private individuals or organizations and may be subject to restrictions on use. For example, contractors and grantees are not considered Government employees; generally, they hold copyright to works they produce for the Government. Other materials may be the result of joint authorship due to collaboration between a Government employee and a private individual wherein the private individual will hold a copyright to the work jointly with U.S. Government. The Government is granted a worldwide license to use, modify, reproduce, release, perform, display, or disclose these works by or on behalf of the Government.

While NASA may publicly release copyrighted works in which it has government purpose licenses or specific permission to release, such licenses or permission do not necessarily transfer to others. Thus, such works are still protected by copyright, and recipients of the works must comply with the copyright law (Title 17 United States Code). Such copyrighted works may not be modified, reproduced, or redistributed without permission of the copyright owner.

If a recognizable person appears in a photograph or video recording, or the talent (such as a performance or narration) of a known individual is included in an audio or video recording, use for commercial purposes may infringe on a right of privacy or publicity. Permission should be obtained from the recognizable person or known individual. However, if the intended use of NASA material is primarily for educational or informational purposes (e.g., books, newspapers, and magazines reporting facts of historical significance), then such uses will generally not be considered an infringement of such personal rights.

Additional copyright information concerning copyright status is given in the metadata for the documents and other STI.

Documents
Documents available from this Web site are not protected by copyright unless noted. If not copyrighted, documents may be reproduced and distributed, without further permission from NASA. However, some documents or portions of documents available from this site may have been contributed by private individuals or organizations and may be copyrighted. If copyrighted, permission

should be obtained from the copyright owner prior to use (e.g., modification, reproduction, or redistribution).

Photography

Photographs available from this Web site are not protected by copyright unless noted. If not copyrighted, photographs may be reproduced and distributed without further permission from NASA. If copyrighted, permission should be obtained from the copyright owner prior to use. If a recognizable person appears in a photograph, use for commercial purposes may infringe a right of privacy or publicity and permission should be obtained from the recognizable person.

Audio Recordings

Audiotape recordings available from this Web site are not protected by copyright unless noted. If not copyrighted, audio recordings may be excerpted or reproduced and distributed, without further permission from NASA. If copyrighted, permission should be obtained from the copyright owner prior to use. Use for a commercial purpose of a portion or segment of an audio recording that incorporates the talent (such as narration or music) of a known individual, may infringe a right of publicity and permission should be obtained from the known individual.

Video Recordings

Video recordings (videotape and motion picture recordings) available from this Web site, including audio recordings therein, are not protected by copyright unless noted. If not copyrighted, video recordings may be reproduced and distributed, without further permission from NASA. If a video recording is copyrighted in its entirety or a portion of a recording contains copyrighted material, such as music or video footage, permission should be obtained from the copyright owner prior to use. Use for a commercial purpose of any portion or segment of a video recording that displays a recognizable person, or the talent (such as a performance or narration) of a known individual, may infringe on a right of privacy or publicity, and permission should be obtained from the recognizable person or known individual.

TERMS AND CONDITIONS OF USE

Unless additional terms and conditions are provided with specific materials, the following information specifies the terms and conditions under which the materials on or available from this Web site may be used.

NASA does not grant exclusive use rights with respect to NASA material.

NASA should be acknowledged as the source of its material.

It is unlawful to falsely claim copyright or other rights in NASA material.

```
Material available from this Web site may include visible NASA
identifiers (NASA name and initials, NASA Insignia, NASA
Logotype, NASA Seal, and NASA Program Identifiers). Use of such
material is generally non-objectionable, provided the NASA
identifiers appear in their factual context. Other uses of the
NASA Insignia, Seal, Logotype, or Program Identifiers require
approval under 14 C.F.R. Part 1221. Use of the NASA name and
initials is protected under 42 U.S.C. 2459b.

NASA material may not be used to state or imply the endorsement
by NASA or by any NASA employee of commercial products,
processes, or services, or used in any other manner that might
mislead.

Use of NASA identifiers which would express or imply such an
endorsement is strictly prohibited.

Use of the NASA name or initials as an identifying symbol by
organizations other than NASA is strictly prohibited.

NASA does not indemnify nor hold harmless users of NASA material,
nor release such users from copyright infringement.

NASA personnel are not authorized to sign indemnity or hold
harmless statements, releases from copyright infringement, or
documents granting exclusive use rights.
```

Use of JSON data in this book from Open-Notify.org

Attribution Notice
The JSON data in this book from the Open-Notify.org API is in the public domain and provided by NASA. The use of this data in this book adheres to NASA's "Images and Media Usage Guidelines":

- https://www.nasa.gov/nasa-brand-center/images-and-media/

See http://open-notify.org/Open-Notify-API/ for details.

Use of JSON data in this book from https://sunrise-sunset.org

Attribution Notice
Sunrise and sunset times in JSON format are from https://sunrise-sunset.org/api in adherence to its usage limits and attribution requirements.

"Queen's Pawn Opening" PNG chessboard

The "Queen's Pawn Opening" PNG image in this book was created by the author using the Lichess.org board editor (https://lichess.org/editor) under the website's commercial license:

- https://lichess.org/contact#help-authorize

Use of material under the MIT license by various copyright holders

Use of information in this book under the MIT license is per

- https://mit-license.org/

Attribution, Noncommercial, ShareAlike.

e. "Licensor" means the individual, individuals, entity or entities that offer(s) the Work under the terms of this License.

f. "Original Author" means, in the case of a literary or artistic work, the individual, individuals, entity or entities who created the Work or if no individual or entity can be identified, the publisher; and in addition (i) in the case of a performance the actors, singers, musicians, dancers, and other persons who act, sing, deliver, declaim, play in, interpret or otherwise perform literary or artistic works or expressions of folklore; (ii) in the case of a phonogram the producer being the person or legal entity who first fixes the sounds of a performance or other sounds; and, (iii) in the case of broadcasts, the organization that transmits the broadcast.

g. "Work" means the literary and/or artistic work offered under the terms of this License including without limitation any production in the literary, scientific and artistic domain, whatever may be the mode or form of its expression including digital form, such as a book, pamphlet and other writing; a lecture, address, sermon or other work of the same nature; a dramatic or dramatico-musical work; a choreographic work or entertainment in dumb show; a musical composition with or without words; a cinematographic work to which are assimilated works expressed by a process analogous to cinematography; a work of drawing, painting, architecture, sculpture, engraving or lithography; a photographic work to which are assimilated works expressed by a process analogous to photography; a work of applied art; an illustration, map, plan, sketch or three-dimensional work relative to geography, topography, architecture or science; a performance; a broadcast; a phonogram; a compilation of data to the extent it is protected as a copyrightable work; or a work performed by a variety or circus performer to the extent it is not otherwise considered a literary or artistic work.

h. "You" means an individual or entity exercising rights under this License who has not previously violated the terms of this License with respect to the Work, or who has received express permission from the Licensor to exercise rights under this License despite a previous violation.

i. "Publicly Perform" means to perform public recitations of the Work and to communicate to the public those public recitations, by any means or process, including by wire or wireless means or public digital performances; to make available to the public Works in such a way that members of the public may access these Works from a place and at a place individually chosen by them; to perform the Work to the public by any means or process and the communication to the public of the performances of the Work, including by public digital performance; to broadcast and rebroadcast the Work by any means including signs, sounds or images.

j. "Reproduce" means to make copies of the Work by any means including without limitation by sound or visual recordings and the right of fixation and reproducing fixations of the Work, including storage of a protected performance or phonogram in digital form or other electronic medium.

2. Fair Dealing Rights. Nothing in this License is intended to reduce, limit, or restrict any uses free from copyright or rights arising from limitations or exceptions that are provided for in connection with the copyright protection under copyright law or other applicable laws.

3. License Grant. Subject to the terms and conditions of this License, Licensor hereby grants You a worldwide, royalty-free, non-exclusive, perpetual (for the duration of the applicable copyright) license to exercise the rights in the Work as stated below:

a. to Reproduce the Work, to incorporate the Work into one or more Collections, and to Reproduce the Work as incorporated in the Collections;
b. to create and Reproduce Adaptations provided that any such Adaptation, including any translation in any medium, takes reasonable steps to clearly label, demarcate or otherwise identify that changes were made to the original Work. For example, a translation could be marked "The original work was translated from English to Spanish," or a modification could indicate "The original work has been modified.";
c. to Distribute and Publicly Perform the Work including as incorporated in Collections; and,
d. to Distribute and Publicly Perform Adaptations.

The above rights may be exercised in all media and formats whether now known or hereafter devised. The above rights include the right to make such modifications as are technically necessary to exercise the rights in other media and formats. Subject to Section 8(f), all rights not expressly granted by Licensor are hereby reserved, including but not limited to the rights described in Section 4(e).

4. Restrictions. The license granted in Section 3 above is expressly made subject to and limited by the following restrictions:

a. You may Distribute or Publicly Perform the Work only under the terms of this License. You must include a copy of, or the Uniform Resource Identifier (URI) for, this License with every copy of the Work You Distribute or Publicly Perform. You may not offer or impose any terms on the Work that restrict the terms of this License or the ability of the recipient of the Work to exercise the rights granted to that recipient under the terms of the License. You may not sublicense the Work. You must keep intact all notices that refer to this License and to the disclaimer of warranties with every copy of the Work You Distribute or Publicly Perform. When You Distribute or Publicly Perform the Work, You may not impose any effective technological measures on the Work that restrict the ability of a recipient of the Work from You to exercise the rights granted to that recipient under the terms of the License. This Section 4(a) applies to the Work as incorporated in a Collection, but this does not require the Collection apart from the Work itself to be made subject to the terms of this License. If You create a Collection, upon notice from any Licensor You must, to the extent practicable, remove from the Collection any credit as required by Section 4(d), as requested. If You create an Adaptation, upon notice from any Licensor You must, to the extent practicable, remove from the Adaptation any credit as required by Section 4(d), as requested.
b. You may Distribute or Publicly Perform an Adaptation only under: (i) the terms of this License; (ii) a later version of this License with the same License Elements as this License; (iii) a Creative Commons jurisdiction license (either this or a later license version) that contains the same License Elements as this License (e.g., Attribution-NonCommercial-ShareAlike 3.0 US) ("Applicable License"). You must include a copy of, or the URI, for Applicable License with every copy of each Adaptation You Distribute or Publicly Perform. You may not offer or impose any terms on the Adaptation that restrict the terms of the Applicable License or the ability of the recipient of the Adaptation to exercise the rights granted to that recipient under the terms of the Applicable License. You must keep intact all notices that refer to the Applicable License and to the disclaimer of warranties with every copy of the Work as included in the Adaptation You Distribute or Publicly Perform. When You Distribute or Publicly

Perform the Adaptation, You may not impose any effective technological measures on the Adaptation that restrict the ability of a recipient of the Adaptation from You to exercise the rights granted to that recipient under the terms of the Applicable License. This Section 4(b) applies to the Adaptation as incorporated in a Collection, but this does not require the Collection apart from the Adaptation itself to be made subject to the terms of the Applicable License.

c. You may not exercise any of the rights granted to You in Section 3 above in any manner that is primarily intended for or directed toward commercial advantage or private monetary compensation. The exchange of the Work for other copyrighted works by means of digital file-sharing or otherwise shall not be considered to be intended for or directed toward commercial advantage or private monetary compensation, provided there is no payment of any monetary compensation in connection with the exchange of copyrighted works.
d. If You Distribute, or Publicly Perform the Work or any Adaptations or Collections, You must, unless a request has been made pursuant to Section 4(a), keep intact all copyright notices for the Work and provide, reasonable to the medium or means You are utilizing: (i) the name of the Original Author (or pseudonym, if applicable) if supplied, and/or if the Original Author and/or Licensor designate another party or parties (e.g., a sponsor institute, publishing entity, journal) for attribution ("Attribution Parties") in Licensor's copyright notice, terms of service or by other reasonable means, the name of such party or parties; (ii) the title of the Work if supplied; (iii) to the extent reasonably practicable, the URI, if any, that Licensor specifies to be associated with the Work, unless such URI does not refer to the copyright notice or licensing information for the Work; and, (iv) consistent with Section 3(b), in the case of an Adaptation, a credit identifying the use of the Work in the Adaptation (e.g., "French translation of the Work by Original Author," or "Screenplay based on original Work by Original Author"). The credit required by this Section 4(d) may be implemented in any reasonable manner; provided, however, that in the case of a Adaptation or Collection, at a minimum such credit will appear, if a credit for all contributing authors of the Adaptation or Collection appears, then as part of these credits and in a manner at least as prominent as the credits for the other contributing authors. For the avoidance of doubt, You may only use the credit required by this Section for the purpose of attribution in the manner set out above and, by exercising Your rights under this License, You may not implicitly or explicitly assert or imply any connection with, sponsorship or endorsement by the Original Author, Licensor and/or Attribution Parties, as appropriate, of You or Your use of the Work, without the separate, express prior written permission of the Original Author, Licensor and/or Attribution Parties.
e. For the avoidance of doubt:

    i. Non-waivable Compulsory License Schemes. In those jurisdictions in which the right to collect royalties through any statutory or compulsory licensing scheme cannot be waived, the Licensor reserves the exclusive right to collect such royalties for any exercise by You of the rights granted under this License;
    ii. Waivable Compulsory License Schemes. In those jurisdictions in which the right to collect royalties through any statutory or compulsory licensing scheme can be waived, the Licensor reserves the exclusive right to collect such royalties for any exercise by You of the rights granted under this License if Your exercise of such rights is for a purpose or use which is otherwise than noncommercial as permitted under Section 4(c) and otherwise waives the right to collect royalties through any statutory or compulsory

8. Miscellaneous

a. Each time You Distribute or Publicly Perform the Work or a Collection, the Licensor offers to the recipient a license to the Work on the same terms and conditions as the license granted to You under this License.
b. Each time You Distribute or Publicly Perform an Adaptation, Licensor offers to the recipient a license to the original Work on the same terms and conditions as the license granted to You under this License.
c. If any provision of this License is invalid or unenforceable under applicable law, it shall not affect the validity or enforceability of the remainder of the terms of this License, and without further action by the parties to this agreement, such provision shall be reformed to the minimum extent necessary to make such provision valid and enforceable.
d. No term or provision of this License shall be deemed waived and no breach consented to unless such waiver or consent shall be in writing and signed by the party to be charged with such waiver or consent.
e. This License constitutes the entire agreement between the parties with respect to the Work licensed here. There are no understandings, agreements or representations with respect to the Work not specified here. Licensor shall not be bound by any additional provisions that may appear in any communication from You. This License may not be modified without the mutual written agreement of the Licensor and You.
f. The rights granted under, and the subject matter referenced, in this License were drafted utilizing the terminology of the Berne Convention for the Protection of Literary and Artistic Works (as amended on September 28, 1979), the Rome Convention of 1961, the WIPO Copyright Treaty of 1996, the WIPO Performances and Phonograms Treaty of 1996 and the Universal Copyright Convention (as revised on July 24, 1971). These rights and subject matter take effect in the relevant jurisdiction in which the License terms are sought to be enforced according to the corresponding provisions of the implementation of those treaty provisions in the applicable national law. If the standard suite of rights granted under applicable copyright law includes additional rights not granted under this License, such additional rights are deemed to be included in the License; this License is not intended to restrict the license of any rights under applicable law.

Creative Commons Notice

Creative Commons is not a party to this License, and makes no warranty whatsoever in connection with the Work. Creative Commons will not be liable to You or any party on any legal theory for any damages whatsoever, including without limitation any general, special, incidental or consequential damages arising in connection to this license. Notwithstanding the foregoing two (2) sentences, if Creative Commons has expressly identified itself as the Licensor hereunder, it shall have all rights and obligations of Licensor.

Except for the limited purpose of indicating to the public that the Work is licensed under the CCPL, Creative Commons does not authorize the use by either party of the trademark "Creative Commons" or any related trademark or logo of Creative Commons without the prior written consent of Creative Commons. Any permitted use will be in compliance with Creative Commons' then-current trademark usage guidelines, as may be published on its website or otherwise made available upon request from time to time. For the avoidance of doubt, this trademark restriction does not form part of this License.

Creative Commons may be contacted at https://creativecommons.org/.

3-Clause (Modified) BSD License

Copyright <YEAR> <COPYRIGHT HOLDER>

Redistribution and use in source and binary forms, with or without modification, are permitted provided that the following conditions are met:

1. Redistributions of source code must retain the above copyright notice, this list of conditions and the following disclaimer.

2. Redistributions in binary form must reproduce the above copyright notice, this list of conditions and the following disclaimer in the documentation and/or other materials provided with the distribution.

3. Neither the name of the copyright holder nor the names of its contributors may be used to endorse or promote products derived from this software without specific prior written permission.

THIS SOFTWARE IS PROVIDED BY THE COPYRIGHT HOLDERS AND CONTRIBUTORS "AS IS" AND ANY EXPRESS OR IMPLIED WARRANTIES, INCLUDING, BUT NOT LIMITED TO, THE IMPLIED WARRANTIES OF MERCHANTABILITY AND FITNESS FOR A PARTICULAR PURPOSE ARE DISCLAIMED. IN NO EVENT SHALL THE COPYRIGHT HOLDER OR CONTRIBUTORS BE LIABLE FOR ANY DIRECT, INDIRECT, INCIDENTAL, SPECIAL, EXEMPLARY, OR CONSEQUENTIAL DAMAGES (INCLUDING, BUT NOT LIMITED TO, PROCUREMENT OF SUBSTITUTE GOODS OR SERVICES; LOSS OF USE, DATA, OR PROFITS; OR BUSINESS INTERRUPTION) HOWEVER CAUSED AND ON ANY THEORY OF LIABILITY, WHETHER IN CONTRACT, STRICT LIABILITY, OR TORT (INCLUDING NEGLIGENCE OR OTHERWISE) ARISING IN ANY WAY OUT OF THE USE OF THIS SOFTWARE, EVEN IF ADVISED OF THE POSSIBILITY OF SUCH DAMAGE.

www.ingramcontent.com/pod-product-compliance
Lightning Source LLC
LaVergne TN
LVHW052248200926
848481LV00002B/310